This book is the first comprehensive account of homoeroticism in Renaissance drama. Mario DiGangi analyses the relation between homoeroticism and social power in a wide range of literary and historical texts from the 1580s to the 1620s, drawing on the insights of materialist, feminist, and queer theory. Each chapter focuses on the homoerotics of a major dramatic genre (Ovidian comedy, satiric comedy, tragedy, and tragicomedy) and studies the ideologies and institutions it characteristically explores. DiGangi examines distinctions between orderly and disorderly forms of homoerotic practice in both canonical and unfamiliar texts. In these readings, the various proliferating forms of homoeroticism are identified in relation to sodomy, against which there were cultural and legal prohibitions in the period. DiGangi's study illuminates, through a diverse range of plays, the centrality of homoerotic practices to household, court, and city life in early modern England.

Cambridge Studies in Renaissance Literature and Culture 21

The homoerotics of early modern drama

Cambridge Studies in Renaissance Literature and Culture

General editor
STEPHEN ORGEL
Jackson Eli Reynolds Professor of Humanities, Stanford University

Editorial board
Anne Barton, *University of Cambridge*
Jonathan Dollimore, *University of Sussex*
Marjorie Garber, *Harvard University*
Jonathan Goldberg, *Duke University*
Nancy Vickers, *University of Southern California*

Since the 1970s there has been a broad and vital reinterpretation of the nature of literary texts, a move away from formalism to a sense of literature as an aspect of social, economic, political, and cultural history. While the earliest New Historicist work was criticised for a narrow and anecdotal view of history, it also served as an important stimulus for poststructuralist, feminist, Marxist, and psychoanalytical work, which in turn has increasingly informed and redirected it. Recent writing on the nature of representation, the historical construction of gender and of the concept of identity itself, on theatre as a political and economic phenomenon and on the ideologies of art generally, reveals the breadth of the field. Cambridge Studies in Renaissance Literature and Culture is designed to offer historically oriented studies of Renaissance literature and theatre which make use of the insights afforded by theoretical perspectives. The view of history envisioned is above all a view of our own history, a reading of the Renaissance for and from our own time.

Recent titles include

Knowledge, discovery, and imagination in early modern Europe: the rise of aesthetic rationalism
TIMOTHY J. REISS, New York University

The project of prose in early modern Europe and the New World
edited by ELIZABETH FOWLER, Yale University, and ROLAND GREENE, University of Oregon

The marketplace of print: pamphlets and the public sphere in early modern England
ALEXANDRA HALASZ, Dartmouth College

Courtly letters in the age of Henry VIII: literary culture and the arts of deceit
SETH LERER, Stanford University

The culture of slander in early modern England
M. LINDSAY KAPLAN, Georgetown University

A complete list of books in the series is given at the end of the volume

The homoerotics of early modern drama

Mario DiGangi

Assistant Professor
Department of English
Indiana University

CAMBRIDGE
UNIVERSITY PRESS

PUBLISHED BY THE PRESS SYNDICATE OF THE UNIVERSITY OF CAMBRIDGE
The Pitt Building, Trumpington Street, Cambridge CB2 1RP United Kingdom

CAMBRIDGE UNIVERSITY PRESS
The Edinburgh Building, Cambridge CB2 2RU, United Kingdom
40 West 20th Street, New York, NY 10011–4211, USA
10 Stamford Road, Oakleigh, Melbourne 3166, Australia

First published 1997

Printed in the United Kingdom at the University Press, Cambridge

Typeset in Times 10/12 pt

A catalogue record for this book is available from the British Library

Library of Congress cataloguing in publication data
DiGangi, Mario
The homoerotics of early modern drama / Mario DiGangi.
    p.   cm. – (Cambridge Studies in Renaissance Literature and Culture: 21)
Based on the author's thesis (Ph.D., Columbia University).
Includes bibliographical references and index.
ISBN 0 521 58341 1 (hardback). ISBN 0 521 58701 8 (paperback).
1. English drama – Early modern and Elizabethan, 1500–1600 – History
and criticism.   2. English drama – 17th century – History and criticism.
3. Homosexuality and literature – England – History.   4. Politics and
literature – England – History.   5. Literature and society – England – History.
6. Eroticism in literature.   7. Sodomy in literature.   8. Renaissance – England.
9. Order in literature.   10. Sex in literature.
1. Title.   11. Series.
PB658.H58D54   1997
822'.309353 – dc21   96 37398   CIP

ISBN 0 521 58341 1 hardback
ISBN 0 521 58701 8 paperback

CE

Contents

Preface

For all its importance as a legal and ideological category used to define and police sexual behavior in the Renaissance, "sodomy" fails to describe a variety of same-sex relations that were central to the social organization and literary culture of early modern England. This book provides a sustained demonstration of why this should be so, and offers the concept of "homoeroticism" as an alternative foundation for the literary and historical analysis of early modern sexuality.

Lesbian and gay scholarship has shown that in the early modern period "sodomy" was neither a neutral description of a sexual act nor a synonym for homoerotic relations generally, but a political category deployed to stigmatize and control a multitude of social disorders. "Sodomy" identified the apparent violation of dominant religious, gender, economic, or social codes in conjunction with sexual transgressions often but not exclusively involving homoerotic intimacy. While recent scholarship has superbly exposed the ideological contradictions and political operations of sodomy discourses, it has not fully explored the implications of these findings for the study of other forms of Renaissance homoeroticism. The complex interplay between sodomitical and nonsodomitical forms of homoeroticism deserves a more detailed and nuanced account than it has heretofore received. In the interests of advancing a materialist understanding of early modern sexuality and society, this book will examine the full range of sodomitical and nonsodomitical homoerotic relations represented in English drama from about 1590 to 1620.

This examination begins from the position that an historical analysis of early modern sexuality must distinguish between socially "orderly" and socially "disorderly" forms of male homoeroticism. The difficulty of this task becomes immediately apparent. "Orderly" homoerotic practices cannot always be clearly identified and distinguished from "disorderly" ones. The distinction between "orderly" and "disorderly" homoerotic practices does not line up neatly with regard to distinctions of status, gender, age, or sexual behavior. It is not the case, for instance, that sex between men of unequal status was always tolerated, whereas sex between gentleman friends was always forbidden: nor were certain bodily acts (e.g., kissing) generally approved of, whereas others (e.g., anal intercourse) were universally proscribed. Rather, erotic relations in early modern England were evaluated according to their perceived consonance or dissonance with dominant social ideologies, and these evaluations were inevitably, and demonstrably, partial, limited, contradictory. Because the political significance of male relations therefore depended on the contingencies of interpretation, the definitional boundaries of "orderly" and "disorderly" homoeroticism were open to negotiation, manipulation, and contestation – in short, to local struggles for social and ideological power.

In a deconstructive analysis, the fundamental instability of these categories would be referred to the permeable structure of binary concepts: the "orderly" is always already constituted and internally divided by its nominally excluded and abjected other. Without question, the antiessentialist and antihierarchical implications of deconstruction have been useful for self-consciously political modes of criticism, including my own. However, since my interests lie in exploring the historical determinants of social and erotic categories, I examine the complicity between "orderly" and "disorderly" sexualities as an effect of the competing ideologies through which erotic practices, like other social practices, were organized, regulated, and transformed in early modern England. My methods for reading sexuality in Renaissance drama therefore derive from materialist feminist, cultural materialist, and queer theoretical paradigms. Apart from illuminating individual plays, I hope that this methodology will confirm that sodomy is not the paradigmatic example or master category of Renaissance homoeroticism, but one among many social and ideological determinants that make up the intricate network of same-sex relations in early modern England.

This book was originally written as a dissertation in the Department of English at Columbia University. My interest in Renaissance homoeroticism was initially encouraged by John Michael Archer, Margaret Ferguson, and Anne Lake Prescott. As a dissertation student, I was privileged to work with Jean Howard, David Kastan, and Jim Shapiro, whose teaching and scholarship have greatly shaped my own. I would also like to acknowledge the contributions of my peers in the Renaissance Dissertation Seminar and in the Lesbian and Gay Studies Group at Columbia, especially fellow organizers Sarah Chinn, Julia Giordano, Patrick Horrigan, and Liz Weisan.

The dissertation was completed under the sponsorship of a Judith

Lipsey Fellowship, a Whiting Fellowship, and a Mellon Foundation Fellowship for Summer Research. With the help of the latter I spent a productive month at the Folger Shakespeare Library, thanks to the library's expert staff and congenial patrons. The book was completed at Indiana University with the aid of a Summer Faculty Research Grant.

Several people have read the manuscript in whole or part and have given important direction and encouragement at various stages. They include David Armitage, Gregory Bredbeck, Mark Thornton Burnett, Julia Giordano, Jonathan Goldberg, Kim Hall, Martha Howell, Tom Ledcke, Curtis Perry, Nick Radel, Alan Sinfield, Bruce Smith, Valerie Traub, and an anonymous reader at Cambridge University Press. Gary Schmidgall generously provided me with a complete set of Beaumont and Fletcher plays. Stephen Orgel provided guidance and support from the very beginning; Josie Dixon ushered the book into its final stages.

Parts of this book have been published in other forms. Some of the discussion of Renaissance scholarship in chapter 1 first appeared in a review essay for *Textual Practice* ("Reading Homoeroticism in Early Modern England: Imagination, Interpretations, Circulations," *Textual Practice* 7 [Winter 1993]: 483–97) and in a review of Jonathan Goldberg's *Sodometries* in *Shakespeare Bulletin* 11 (Fall 1993): 45–46. Shorter versions of chapter 2 and of chapter 3 were published in *Shakespeare Quarterly* ("Queering the Shakespearean Family," *SQ* 47 [Fall 1996]) and in *English Literary Renaissance* ("Asses and Wits: the Homoerotics of Mastery in Satiric Comedy," *ELR* 25 [Spring 1995], 179–208), respectively. For permission to reprint I am grateful to Routledge, Lafayette College, the Folger Shakespeare Library, and the University of Massachusetts Press.

I want also to acknowledge the contribution of organizers, chair-people, copresenters, and audience members at meetings of the Modern Language Association (especially Richard Rambuss, Stephen Orgel, and Sara Deats); the Shakespeare Association of America (especially Greg Bredbeck, Dympna Callaghan, Nick Radel, and Jean Howard); the International Shakespeare Association (especially Bruce Smith, Fran Dolan, and Mark Thornton Burnett); the Wesleyan University Renaissance Studies Seminar (especially the late Gary Spear); and the fifth annual Lesbian and Gay Studies Conference (especially Valerie Traub and Alan Bray).

Finally, I want to thank my parents and brother for their unwavering confidence and support.

1 Introduction

Homosexuality/homoeroticism

Examining the homoerotics of early modern drama offers the chance to grapple with relatively neglected issues and texts in Renaissance scholarship. Paradoxically, whatever innovation I have to contribute to Renaissance studies is based on a commonplace in lesbian and gay studies: "homosexuality" is a modern concept that cannot be applied, without a great deal of historical distortion, to the early modern period. Presented with admirable economy and clarity in Alan Bray's groundbreaking book *Homosexuality in Renaissance England* (1982), this key thesis has received intense scrutiny from historians and cultural critics alike. While some scholars have produced nuanced qualifications and elaborations of Bray's findings, others have responded with more anxiety to the implication that there were "no homosexuals" in the Renaissance. The increasing volume and complexity of the debate over the past five years makes this an appropriate time to take account of the current state of lesbian and gay scholarship on early modern England. At the risk of retracing some familiar territory, then, I want first to map out some important critical positions and offer, from my own vantage point, an assessment of their value to an historical analysis of early modern culture. Establishing the current parameters of the field will also establish a genealogy and a context for my subsequent engagement with the particular issues informing the homoerotics of early modern drama.

Like Bray and his followers, I start from the premise that early modern homoeroticism cannot be defined as a minority sexual practice or a discrete erotic identity. The homophobic ideology that would eventually proscribe the eroticization of male "homosocial" bonds had not yet developed in sixteenth- and early seventeenth-century England.[1] Before the emergence of male–male sexuality as an identifiable practice or condition of deviation from "normal" gender identities, object choices, or sexual roles – and the concomitant naming of those deviant people and practices – homoerotic practices were "normal" aspects of even the most socially conventional relationships.[2] The "homosocial" and the "homoerotic," therefore, overlapped to a greater extent, and with less attendant anxiety, in the early modern period than would later be possible under a modern regime of sexuality.

We can maintain a sense of the characteristic pervasiveness of homoeroticism in early modern society by reserving the terms "homosexuality" and "the homosexual" for the specific concepts of sexual orientation and a sexual actor that developed in the medical, psychological, and sexological discourses of nineteenth-century Europe. The understanding of "homosexuality" as a historical product of these discourses receives its most powerful and provocative expression in David Halperin's influential essay "One Hundred Years of Homosexuality." At the core of Halperin's argument is the notion of orientation as the distinctive feature of modern sexological thought:

Before the scientific construction of "sexuality" as a supposedly positive, distinct, and constitutive feature of individual human beings – an autonomous system with the physiological and psychological economy of the human organism – certain kinds of sexual *acts* could be individually evaluated and categorized, and so could certain sexual tastes or inclinations, but there was no conceptual apparatus available for identifying a person's fixed and determinate sexual *orientation*, much less for assessing and classifying it.[3]

Despite the clarity of Halperin's explication, however, it is important to remember that modern concepts like "homosexuality" and "inversion" hazily emerged out of a complex political and ideological matrix. They were and they continue to be manipulated and redefined according to particular agendas.

The notorious case of Oscar Wilde effectively illustrates how the discourses of homosexuality actively construct what they purport merely to describe. In *Talk on the Wilde Side*, Ed Cohen argues that "homosexuality" emerged in Victorian England as the result of "a new, secular, criminal injunction against sexual relations between men, now labeled 'acts of gross indecency with another male person.'" According to Cohen, the convergence of middle-class legal, moral, and epistemological efforts to dictate normative masculinity produced Oscar Wilde as a "paradigmatic sexual figure": the male homosexual.[4] Eve Kosofsky Sedgwick has argued, however, that Wilde's erotic practices are accurately described neither by "homosexuality" nor by "inversion," the dominant paradigms available to him and through which he continues to be understood by literary critics today. Whereas "homosexuality" implies a fundamental similarity between sexual partners, she observes, Wilde's desires were "structured intensely by the crossing of definitional lines" around social class. "Inversion" alludes to the doctrine of gender transitivity (a woman's soul in a man's body); yet Wilde "does not seem very much to have seen or described either himself or those he loved in terms of inversion."[5] If the Victorian construction of Wilde as an abnormal sexual type served turn-of-the-century moral and legal ends, reasons Sedgwick, the postmodern construction of Wilde as a protopostmodern advocate of inversion likewise serves "many modern analytic, diagnostic, and (hence) even deconstructive needs."[6] Through the symbolically central figure of Wilde, Cohen and Sedgwick provide valuable insight into the political complexity of locating historically – synchronically *and* diachronically – the meanings of "homosexuality."[7]

The equally daunting challenge of situating "homosexuality" in relation to the early modern period has been skillfully negotiated by several critics, perhaps most effectively by Jonathan Goldberg and Valerie Traub. Although they are careful to historicize sexual categories, Goldberg and Traub observe certain links between early modern and modern forms of erotic definition and practice. On this count, both take issue with Foucault, or rather with literal interpretations of Foucault that would draw too sharp a boundary between historical periods. Attempting to bridge early modern and modern meanings for sexual desire, Traub writes:

Taken literally, Foucault implies that because neither sexuality nor its subsets (homosexuality, heterosexuality) were available in the early modern discursive field, no correlation exists between early modern erotic practices and modern significations. I would argue, however, that despite the absence of a specific discourse of sexuality, within early modern culture there circulated significations that, however incommensurate, can be usefully brought in tension with modern meanings.[8]

Similarly diverging from a literal Foucauldian scheme, Goldberg refers to "sexuality" in the Renaissance while simultaneously "recognizing that strictly speaking such a locution is preposterous." Goldberg establishes historical continuity by proposing that Renaissance erotic relations "provide the sites upon which later sexual orders and later sexual identities could batten."[9] Moreover, his exposure of the homophobic mobilizations of "sodomy" in contemporary American society brings into relief the incoherence of both modern and early modern sexual definitions. Following Traub and Goldberg, I will use "sexuality" to refer to the social organization of erotic meanings and practices in the Renaissance, but will use "homosexual" only in the most mechanical, banal, sense: to refer to sexual acts between people of the same sex. This usage of "homosexual" avoids oddly euphemistic locutions like "homoerotic sex." Because the phrase "homosexual desire" seems to ground erotic desire in a core sexual identity, I reject it in favor of "homoerotic desire," which to my mind signifies only a relation and not a causality (a desire that is ontologically "homosexual" or that emanates from a "homosexual" orientation).[10]

Despite the nuanced efforts of critics like Traub and Goldberg to plot the continuities between early modern and modern forms of sexual meaning, the historicist claims of what is generally called "social constructionism" are still controversial enough as to merit further clarification here.[11] The social constructionist argument goes something like this. Concepts like "homosexual" or "gay" imply a shared trait of desire or behavior that defines a class of people despite differences of status, class, race, or gender. Even to say "I am gay" requires inter-locking notions of sexual identity (*gay* is a minority political classifica-tion), sexual orientation (*am* implies an ontology), and sexual subjectivity (psychological self-definition by the speaking *I*). Discrete discourses of (homo)sexual identity, sexual orientation, or the rhetorical stance taken in relation to such an identity or orientation ("outness") did not exist in the Renaissance. Whatever patterns we might detect among them, Renaissance homoerotic relations were not subsumed under a term like "homosexual" or "gay" that prioritized same-sex object choice. Nor is the Renaissance term "sodomite" equivalent to "homosexual": when it referred to male–male sex, "sodomite" meant more than "a man who has sex with another man." The label also meant that this particular man was treasonous, monstrous, heretical, and so on, and that he shared these defining traits with other deviants who may or may not have participated in same-sex relations. Given these linguistic and social conditions, it is impossible to discuss homoerotic relations meaningfully outside of the social contexts that give them shape and language. As Halperin argues,

To the extent that histories of "sexuality" succeed in concentrating their focus on *sexuality*, to just that extent they are doomed to fail as *histories* . . . unless they also include as an integral part of their proper enterprise the task of demon-strating the historicity, conditions of emergence, modes of construction, and ideological contingencies of the very categories of analysis that undergird their own practice.[12]

For the historicist purposes of this book, placing sexual practices within their historical and ideological contexts – in one sense, giving the social an analytical priority over the sexual – requires precision concerning the various forms and meanings of homoerotic practices.

None of this is meant to deny that people in early modern England experienced erotic desire for people of the same sex. It *is* to deny that such desires were thought to be ontologically different from other desires and hence constitutionally determining of certain behaviors. Renaissance knowledges did not posit a genetic basis for same-sex desire, nor did they distinguish this desire, as a biological essence or psychological core, from the social forms through which it was expressed and given meaning. This can be illustrated in the Renaissance understanding of the relation between sexual and gender "inversion." As Alan Sinfield has argued, in the twentieth century "the homosexual" has been commonly associated with the "leisured, effeminate, aesthetic dandy," a stereotype derived from Oscar Wilde.[13] By contrast, Renaissance discourses define "effeminacy" as the "womanish" sensuality that might cause a man to indulge an excessive desire for women or boys. In the twentieth century, that is, homosexuality is sometimes understood to cause male effeminacy; in the sixteenth century, male effeminacy was understood to cause heteroerotic or homoerotic disorder. According to early modern logic, disorderly homosexual behavior becomes visible in tandem with, or as an effect of, other socially disorderly behaviors.[14]

To make this claim, it is not necessary to reject the possibility that sexual desires are in part biologically or genetically determined. Yet it is necessary to admit that the representational strategies of biological or genetic discourses limit and shape what can be understood about anatomical sex or sexuality at any particular historical moment, including our own. Thomas Laqueur's *Making Sex* argues that eighteenth-century epistemological and political developments led to the development of "sex," the concept of "two stable, incommensurable, opposite sexes" that differentiate (and dictate) the "political, economic, and cultural lives of men and women."[15] Far from providing an objective, purely scientific account of sexual difference based on new empirical data, the very language of biology was already laden with cultural and political assumptions about gender. No matter how "natural" the phenomena being described may appear to be – and what can be more natural than "the body" and its functions? – the discourses used to identify, describe, and evaluate them are always historically situated, hence politically charged. As Judith Butler cogently argues, while the "materiality" of the body is not reducible to discursive constructions (the body is not totally "constructed" or determined by language), it is nevertheless intelligible only through and as signifying practices, which are in themselves material practices (historically contingent and produced).[16] No diagnostic paradigm or discourse can give unmediated access to the essential "truth" or universal "reality" of homosexuality, if only because the claims for this "truth" and "reality" must themselves be linguistically constructed. Whatever claims modern science might make for homosexuality as a "materiality" pertaining to the body, they will still tell us nothing about the materiality of sexual practices and discourses – how bodies were used and understood – in early modern England.

Sodomy/homoeroticism

Having counterposed modern against early modern constructions of same-sex desire, I want now to narrow my focus to the various modalities of same-sex desire within the early modern period. If there are no "homosexuals" and no "homosexuality" in the Renaissance, then one cannot talk of pervasive "homophobia," the fear of homosexual people or of same-sex eroticism *tout court*. How, then, can the injunctions against certain kinds of homoerotic behavior be understood? If we need to speak of a culturally pervasive "phobia," then it would be more precise to coin a term like "sodomophobia." In *Sodometries*, Jonathan Goldberg demonstrates that the Renaissance category of "sodomy" was deployed to stigmatize people who were perceived to threaten dominant conceptions not only of sexuality, but of gender, class, religion, or race. "Sodomy" is not a politically neutral term: it always signifies social disorder of a frightening magnitude, and as such occupies one end of the spectrum of practices signified by the neutral term "homoeroticism." Unlike "sodomy," concepts like "homoerotic" and "heteroerotic" use-fully distinguish same-sex from different-sex relations, yet do not indicate in themselves – and may even elide – the status configurations or the political significance of such practices. Jean Howard observes that, in the early modern period, social status might be of equal or greater conse-quence in the establishment of sexual relations than similarity or difference of anatomical sex: an adult man might sexually enjoy a social subordinate of either sex.[17] As I will use the terms, "sodomy" is always politically freighted, whereas "homoerotic" is politically neutral and merely descriptive. For any particular instance, then, it becomes neces-sary to demonstrate exactly how a homoerotic relation is positioned with respect to ideas of social order.

By defining "sodomy" as a category that can include certain homo-erotic practices but hardly exhausts all homoerotic possibilities, I build upon previous work that has attempted to distinguish and describe nonsodomical forms of Renaissance homoeroticism. Different critics have defined these alternative homoeroticisms in different ways, and I would like to give a brief account of how my own project resembles and departs from previous studies. Alan Bray's *Homosexuality in Renaissance England* first demonstrated the coexistence of sodomitical and nonsodo-mitical homosexual acts in Renaissance society. Bray argues that a modern male "homosexual" role emerged only in the late seventeenth century, with the growth of a subculture of molly houses.[18] In the Renaissance, by contrast, orderly, commonplace, and even institutionalized homosexual behavior was rarely recognized as the metaphysically demonized sin of "sodomy," and thus rarely persecuted: "So long as homosexuality was expressed through established social institutions, in normal times the courts were not concerned with it; and generally this meant patriarchal institutions – the household, the educational system, homosexual prostitution and the like."[19] Bray attributes the widespread acceptance of hierarchical homosexual relations not to tolerance but to an epistemological inability to interpret such behavior according to the legal, religious, satiric, and nationalistic discourses that excoriated the disorderly "sodomite."

Bray's identification of the contradictory nature of Renaissance homoeroticism has provided a rich impetus for further projects. Both Jonathan Goldberg's *Sodometries* and Gregory Bredbeck's *Sodomy and Interpretation* emerge from and modify Bray's findings. Goldberg and Bredbeck focus primarily on sodomy, generally omitting any extended analysis of more orderly forms of homoeroticism. Goldberg argues that erotic desire in the Renaissance was limited neither by mandatory heterosexual object choice nor by the strict conceptual division between two distinct genders. Because erotic desires could more fluidly traverse identity categories, authorized homoerotic relations – male friendship, patronage, and pedagogy – were rhetorically and socially distinguished, albeit incompletely, from sodomitical relations. For instance, Goldberg shows that male colonizers used accusations of sodomy to justify their violence against native Americans, whom they viewed as monstrous practitioners of cannibalism, human sacrifice, cross-dressing, and body piercing. Yet the manifold ideological confusions of "sodomy" also prevented the colonizers from experiencing their own forms of male homosocial bonding as completely distinct from those forms of male–male intimacy they despised. For Goldberg, the definitional incoherence of "sodomy" in Renaissance society marks certain homoerotic relations for condemnation, while allowing other relations – or the same relations in different contexts – to flourish: "when brotherhood or shared beds replace sodomy, the act has not changed, but only what it is called."[20]

In *Sodomy and Interpretation*, Bredbeck similarly traces how social and political power works through the discourses of sodomy. Like Bray, Bredbeck acknowledges the impact of legal and moral stigmatizations of sodomy. Unlike Bray, he stresses the ideological contradictions and limitations of these discourses, their failure to signify comprehensively when confronted with alternative meanings for homoerotic desire. He explains the value of taking a deconstructive approach to official or "high" discourses:

Renaissance configurations of homoeroticism are uniquely able to expose the historical and social rifts typically concealed in higher discourses, for the language of sodomy throughout the entire Renaissance was a dynamic and fluid field that specifically took as its task defining the unacceptable; hence, the language of sodomy functions both as a demarcation between high and low and as a specification of a point where low transgresses high.[21]

As this account implies, Bredbeck is mostly concerned not with the material practices of homoeroticism but with interpretive and linguistic practices. The book opens: "Sodomy in the Renaissance was both done and written; perhaps it was written more interestingly than it was done."[22] For instance, Bredbeck argues that since homoeroticism always signifies in relation to other social discourses, the strategic representation of homoeroticism within or against these discourses could undermine their ideological pretensions to order and totality. A textual *representation* of homoeroticism might therefore produce a "sodomitical" or subversive rhetorical effect (where low transgresses high), even if the kind of homoeroticism *represented* in the text would not in and of itself be labeled "sodomitical" by official definitions. Thus Bredbeck calls the speaker of Shakespeare's *Sonnets* a "sodomite" not because he wants to imply that the speaker's expression of homoerotic desire would fall under the legal definition of sodomy, but because he wants to argue that the construction of "the sodomite" in legal texts provided the condition for alternative linguistic and social constructions of "the sodomite," just one of which appears in Shakespeare's text.[23] For Bredbeck, then, social conflict occurs most interestingly at the level not of material practice – the struggle between those who uphold and those who transgress socially orthodox homoerotic relations – but of textual practice – the contradiction between orthodox and subversive representations of homoerotic or sodomitical desire.

Whereas Bredbeck attributes a subversive force to strategically positioned representations of homoeroticism, Bruce Smith's *Homosexual Desire in Shakespeare's England* attributes a subversive force to imaginative expressions of homoerotic desire. In a broad examination of cultural texts, Smith discovers a contradiction between the stigmatized sodomy of legal and religious discourse and the positively valued homoeroticism found in poetic discourse and in normative, even institutionalized, male social relations. Smith finds diverse manifestations of homosexual desire, not a monolithic "sodomy," within six cultural "myths" of Renaissance England, ranging from the most universal, public, licit, and traditional –

male homosocial bonding – to the most particular, private, illicit, and new – the invention of a homosexual subjectivity in Shakespeare's *Sonnets* (1609).[24]

Like Smith, Valerie Traub acknowledges the diversity of homoerotic meanings in English Renaissance culture, although she distinguishes more precisely between the roles played by gender and sexual ideologies in the evaluation of homoerotic relationships. "Not only did legal, moral, religious, and literary discourses understand and evaluate homoeroticism differently," she observes, "but within each discourse there existed contradictory positions."[25] Hence the male homoerotic desire depicted in literary discourses is not equivalent to the "sodomy" condemned in legal discourse, a point she illustrates by arguing that the "masculine" homoerotic relation between Antonio and Sebastian in Shakespeare's *Twelfth Night* (1601) approaches "sodomy" only when it threatens to interfere with the reproductive sexuality that undergirds the patriarchal social structure. In "The (In)Significance of 'Lesbian' Desire in Early Modern England," Traub shows that female homoeroticism, which received even less official scrutiny than male homoeroticism, was not stigmatized as disorderly unless the women involved violated feminine gender roles or the imperatives of reproductive sexuality. Female homoeroticism was "insignificant" in early modern England to the degree that it failed to signify politically or to impact visibly upon dominant social structures.

While the insights of these critics have informed my own understanding of early modern homoeroticism, I find it necessary more fully to demonstrate several points: the pervasiveness of nonsodomitical or nonsubversive homoerotic relations in early modern England; the diversity of homoerotic relations as they are represented in a range of literary and nonliterary texts; the implication of homoerotic relations within social, economic, and ideological power structures. To my mind, the studies I have summarized exhibit three tendencies – in different degrees and combinations – which have prevented the above goals from being more fully realized:

(1) an emphasis on sodomy, as opposed to a detailed textual analysis of homoeroticism

(2) a reliance on psychoanalytic and deconstructive, as opposed to more rigorously materialist, methods

(3) a focus on largely familiar texts, especially by Shakespeare, as opposed to a less author-centered and more generically diverse consideration of cultural patterns.

I want to consider in some detail below, although not in the schematic way implied by the above enumerations, by what means my project displaces the centrality of sodomy and of Shakespeare to the study of Renaissance sexuality.

Sodomy/orderly homoeroticism

Alan Bray's important essay "Homosexuality and the Signs of Male Friendship in Elizabethan England" examines the ideological slippage between two seemingly antithetical social categories: the debased category of sodomy and the exalted category of male friendship. At first glance, Bray appears to define friendship as a homoerotic relation, yet a closer look reveals that his construction of friendship avoids the erotic. He explains that since "homosexuality" – not *sodomy* – was "regarded with a readily expressed horror" in Renaissance England, the intimacy between "masculine friends" was "in stark contrast to the forbidden intimacy of homosexuality."[26] Yet homosexual acts were not generally forbidden or regarded with horror in Renaissance England, as Bray's own book has shown.[27] In this essay, Bray effectively conflates "homosexuality" with "sodomy," implicitly reduces both to the commission of sexual acts, and then cordons off these proscribed sexual acts from the nonsexual intimacy appropriate for "friends." Thus it is only the presence or absence of an unspecified sexual act – anal intercourse, presumably – that will determine whether a male relationship promotes social disorder (sodomy) or social order (friendship). While granting that "[h]omosexual relationships did indeed occur within social contexts which an Elizabethan would have called friendship," Bray nevertheless does not consider the *homoerotics* of Elizabethan male friendship discourse.[28]

In what sense is the discourse of male friendship "homoerotic?" What, to reformulate the impasse in Bray's essay, is the difference between the expression of erotic desire and the performance of sexual acts? To answer this, we need only acknowledge the homoerotic possibilities within the language of friendship, possibilities clearly envisioned in an early seventeenth-century pastoral poem about Apollo and Hyacinth. Published in 1607, this unknown Ovidian poem by Lewes Machin relates how the sun god "did dote upon this lovely youth."[29] Once Apollo and Hyacinth are strolling hand in hand, things soon heat up:

> But *Phebus* heart did pant and leape with joy,
> When he beheld that sweete delicious boy.
> His eyes did sparkle, love his heart flamde fire,
> To see this sweete boy smile, is his desire.
> Then with an ardent gripe his hand he crusht,
> and then he kist him, and the boy then blusht,

That blushing coulour, so became his face
That *Phebus* kist againe, and thought it grace
To touch his lips, such pleasure *Phebus* felt,
That in an amarous deaw his heart did melt.   (sigs. E5v–E6r)

It is not entirely clear what sexual acts Apollo and Hyacinth perform: the poem speaks of dalliance, "toying," "play," "sport," embracing, and hours spent "in delight." On two occasions, however, their relationship is significantly defined. Hyacinth names their bond when he sententiously declares that the "parting of true friends all paines excell" (sig. E6r); Apollo finds the pleasures of women dull compared to those provided by his "male paramore" (sig. E6v). An erotic relation between an adult god and a mortal boy makes them at once "friends" and "paramours," blending what traditionally are designations for male–male and male–female relationships. In this poem, the language of friendship comprehends not only the expression of erotic desire but the performance of certain sexual acts. Even though the love of Apollo and Hyacinth ultimately results in the boy's accidental death, this tragic outcome cannot be taken as a sweeping condemnation of a sexualized male friendship. Interpreting Apollo's grief as an etiologic myth of the sun's withdrawal during the winter months, Machin gives this homoerotic friendship an enduring cosmic significance.

The mere existence of a homoerotic discourse of friendship reveals nothing conclusive about actual male sexual activity in early modern England. But considering the crucial social and epistemological division between sodomy and orderly homoeroticism, and the intensity of desire expressed in Machin's poem, it is impossible to be sure that sexual acts did *not* take place between friends who shared beds or other intimacies.[30] Furthermore, as the poem indicates, we cannot always be entirely confident that we know which bodily acts count as "sexual." When is kissing an expression of sexual desire, of affection, or of a social bond? Under what circumstances might our ability even to distinguish these realms be frustrated? In a patriarchal culture, is intercourse always more "sexual" than kissing? Is it more *erotic*? Might nonpenetrative eroticism, such as kissing between women or "sport" between men, subvert patriarchal sexuality? These questions cannot be answered outside of particular contexts, and even then with reservations. In any case, the indeterminacy of the "sexual" should make us skeptical of approaches that deem homosexual "acts" more subjectively and socially meaningful than homoerotic desires or discourses, and that require "evidence" of sexual acts – what would this entail for nonprocreative sex? – before granting the possibility that erotic desires existed.

At the same time, it is important neither to totalize nor to homogenize homoerotic possibilities in the period. Just because the discourse of male friendship allowed a place for homoerotic desire does not mean that all friendships were necessarily homoerotic. Discourses establish conditions of possibility for social relations and subjective meanings; yet the actual form any social practice takes is overdetermined by competing discourses, ideologies, and institutions, as well as by the various subjective positions taken in relation to them. Early modern representations of male intimacy reveal a multiplicity of possible social configurations, erotic investments, and sexual acts: this multiplicity cannot be reduced to a uniform system of behavior. And to insist that "everything" is homoerotic would be to universalize homoeroticism out of meaningful existence. We need to resist idealizing Renaissance homoeroticism by way of nostalgic disidentification – as a once universally available freedom we have lost – or by way of activist identification – as the disruptive practice of a minority who fought back against repression. It is pointless to claim that all male friendships in early modern England were homoerotic, let alone actively sexual. It is nevertheless the case that early modern gender ideology integrated orderly homoeroticism into friendship more seamlessly than modern ideological formations, which more crisply distinguish homoeroticism from friendship, sexual desire from social desire.[31]

If orderly homoeroticism is so prevalent as a possible component of male relations in early modern society, then why does sodomy exert such a powerful explanatory force in recent assessments of Renaissance "homosexuality?" The kind of extensive, detailed analysis that Renaissance scholars have devoted to the category of sodomy has yet to be applied to homoerotic relations generally. With few exceptions, what detailed work has been done on homoeroticism mostly concerns Shakespeare's plays and poems.[32] The attention given to Shakespeare may have the unfortunate consequence of establishing his depictions of homoeroticism as culturally "representative," even though such a claim must remain speculative, if not presumptuous, in the absence of equally thorough studies of his predecessors, contemporaries, and successors. On the other hand, such attention may render Shakespeare exceptional in the realm of homoerotic love, as in so much else. Bruce Smith argues that Shakespeare's articulation of a "private" or subjective homosexual desire in the *Sonnets* represents a radical divergence from cultural norms. Although Smith describes early modern English society as ideologically located somewhere between "homophobia" and "homophilia," he tends to dilute the force of this contradiction by attributing homophobia to legal and religious writings and homophilia to poetic writings, foremost among them being Shakespeare's *Sonnets*.[33]

As a result of this strategy, I think, Smith's crucial project to delineate a place for positive Renaissance homoeroticism does not forcefully enough displace the dominance of "sodomy" in discussions of Renaissance homosexuality. The dominance of "sodomy" as a critical paradigm explains the skewed perspective on homoeroticism in Leah Marcus's recent overview of Renaissance scholarship. Marcus articulates a characteristically modern notion of homosexuality as the always-already deviant in the very process of acknowledging that sexuality was organized differently in the Renaissance. Citing scholarship by Smith and Stephen Orgel on *homoeroticism*, not sodomy, Marcus writes that "the early modern era had vastly different, usually less rigid, ways of defining sexual deviance than our society does."[34] This formulation reproduces an assumption that Smith himself disputes: homoerotic practices in the Renaissance were not always considered "sexual deviance," but could be aspects of the most "straight" social relations.[35]

The tendency to collapse male homoeroticism into deviance may be a consequence of a similar operation in American sexual ideology. Not only political reactionaries promote deliberately pathologizing, judgmental, or fear-inducing representations of gay men as leather-clad freaks, bizarre cross-dressers, child molesters, or psychopathic serial murderers.[36] In an ideological climate of such extreme images of homosexuality, it is not surprising that Jeffrey Dahmer (a killer of gay men) merges in some minds with the fictional Jame Gumb (a freakish cross-dressing killer of women in the popular 1991 film *The Silence of the Lambs*), and that both men, despite psychopathic sexualities that hardly conform to liberal sexual identity categories, are readily understood as "gay."[37] Monstrous images of gay men are as memorable as they are pervasive. Alan Sinfield has observed that even the most celebratory representations of queer sexuality have been appropriated for homophobic agendas: "the prevailing order is hostile to same-sex passion, and will dirty up any image that we produce."[38] Homophobic appropriations of queer imagery operate under the premise that "we all know" what sodomy looks like – and it isn't pretty. Similarly, the Renaissance category of sodomy derived its stigmatizing power from threateningly exotic significations: the sodomite was devil, heretic, New World savage, cannibal, Turk, African, papist, Italian – these categories overlap – or a beastly defiler of boys, whores, and goats. By contrast, there is a relative paucity of specific imagery and language associated with orderly homoerotic desire in early modern England. The specificity, strangeness, and variety of sodomitical images doubtless contributes to our continued fascination with them.

Nevertheless, I want to argue the importance of dislodging the hegemonic status of sodomy as an explanatory theory and imaginary

referent for early modern homoeroticism. We might attribute the slip in
Marcus's text to an unconscious tendency to read early modern homoeroticism through modern categories of "gay" deviance or subversion.
Yet a more overt political agenda motivates certain accounts of early
modern homoeroticism as sodomitical. For some gay critics, these
accounts can provide a history of the Western persecution of "homosexuals." This history is then used to bolster a modern civil rights
discourse that defines homosexuals as an oppressed minority deserving
protection. Louis Crompton's 1978 article on gay history cites the 1533
English buggery law (which, he misleadingly claims, made "gay love a
felony") as one moment in a larger history of "gay genocide" from
Leviticus to Hitler.[39] Crompton concludes this grim survey by citing the
transhistorical "dilemma of the homosexual": many homosexual survi-
vors of Hitler's genocidal policies have remained as silent as "the men of
the sixth or eighteenth centuries" who suffered under the murderous
regimes of "religion" and "morality."[40]

Crompton's promotion of a transhistorical narrative of homosexual
oppression cannot be attributed merely to an early, "essentialist"
moment in gay historical scholarship that has since passed. A particularly
tortuous example of the desire to find an oppressed minority of homosexuals in Renaissance England appears in Joseph Cady's 1993 essay
"Renaissance Awareness and Language for Heterosexuality: 'Love' and
'Feminine Love.'" Cady claims that "the Renaissance not only had an
awareness and language for heterosexuality but held so strongly to other-
sex attraction as the norm of sexuality" that universal erotic terms such
as "love" usually referred by default only to heterosexual configurations.[41] Positing in this article and in a companion article the existence of
discrete languages of heterosexuality and homosexuality ("masculine
love"), Cady reinforces a traditional view of Renaissance sexual repres-
siveness.[42] This bleak picture is based not like that of older criticism on
the proscriptions of sodomy laws, which, as he rightly notes, were not
limited to homosexual acts but on the notion of a culturally oppressed
minority of homosexuals.[43] Discounting the work of diverse historians
and literary critics – Foucault, Bray, Goldberg, Weeks, Greenberg,
Halperin, Orgel, and Sedgwick – whom he lumps together and carica-
tures as "new inventionists," Cady concludes that his own examination
of erotic terms in a handful of literary texts reveals "a sexually con-
stricting and hazardous Renaissance whose official sexual boundaries
resembled the most repressive that still exist today."[44] Extolling the
virtues of traditional philology and close reading, Cady charges the new
inventionists with bad (read: poststructuralist) scholarship.

He also charges them with bad (read: anti-identity) politics. Not only will their theories have a "repressive effect" on gay studies by stifling inquiry into periods in which homosexuality supposedly "did not exist," but their denial of a long history of homosexual identity might "undermine gay people's relatively recent gains in positive self-understanding, openness of expression, and social freedom."[45] These very charges reveal the problematic assumptions driving Cady's own insistence on a history of homosexual oppression. Cady believes that homosexuals achieve liberation by overcoming "repression" and negative "self-understanding," yet this liberation requires, first, identifying with a legacy of homosexual repression throughout Western Christian history. Although the citation of a history of persecution has a certain purchase for gay politics within the liberal state, such claims also entail the paradoxical liability of appealing to victim status to demand rights, and of constructing a transhistorical identity to demand particular rights at a particular historical moment.

More problematically, the idea that homosexuals have been a historically repressed minority often results from a homophobic association between homosexuality and the abject, whether in the guise of criminality, sin, shame, death, or disease. In this regard, it is disturbing that many critics consider Marlowe's *Edward II* (1592) the *locus classicus* of homosexuality in Renaissance drama, since regardless of the sympathy an audience might feel for Edward, his demise seems to confirm a modern ideology of doomed homosexual desire. E. M. Forster explains that the happy ending of his 1914 novel *Maurice* "made the book more difficult to publish . . . If it ended unhappily, with a lad dangling from a noose or with a suicide pact, all would be well."[46] Fictional representations of homosexual desire are more acceptable when the participants end up dead, a point powerfully made by Vito Russo's classic study of homosexuality in Hollywood cinema, *The Celluloid Closet*. In an appendix called "Necrologies" Russo lists forty-three films, mostly from the 1960s and 1970s, in which "overt, active or predatory gays . . . were killed off," whereas the "repressed, tormented types usually committed suicide."[47] For all the theoretical and historical knowledge critics bring to bear on *Edward II*, they may still find in Marlowe's king the stereotypical "overt homosexual" who must be killed off. To straight and gay readers alike, especially in the age of AIDS, a homoerotic relationship ending in loss or death may seem "realistic," whereas for a heteroerotic relationship to end in tragedy (as in *Othello*) seems disturbingly "wrong."

Inasmuch as it is a manifestation of heterosexist thinking, then, the belief that homoerotic practices were repressed or persecuted in early modern England can inadvertently serve to reinforce homophobia, despite the antihomophobic intentions of a critic like Joseph Cady. The

most brutal recent reminder of the homophobic use to which a purport-
edly transparent "history" of homosexual repression can be put is the
1986 Supreme Court *Bowers* v. *Hardwick* case. In their ruling, the
majority justices denied the right of gay men to engage in private
consensual sex because "homosexuality," defined ahistorically and trans-
historically by the act of "sodomy," had always been legally proscribed
in Western societies, as witnessed by the first English sodomy statute in
1533.[48] Despite Cady's reassurances, therefore, to promote the blanket
construction of homosexuality as marginalized and of homosexuals as
oppressed throughout history does not necessarily combat homophobia.
In *Bowers* v. *Hardwick*, it reinforced it.

Sodomy/disorderly heteroeroticism

Immersion in modern sexual ideology makes a sodomitical account of
homoerotic desire sound familiar, even natural, to many scholars of
Renaissance history and literature. We can denaturalize the association
of homoerotic desire with social transgression by imagining a similarly
negative account of *heteroerotic* desire, which might sound something
like the following. In early modern England, heterosexuality was considered a shameful and dangerous practice; it was therefore socially and
legally proscribed. Laws and local customs punished those people who
engaged in premarital sex, had illegitimate children, or committed
adultery. Insults like "whore," "cuckold," and "bastard" reveal the
opprobrium attached to heterosexual acts. In sonnet sequences and
tragedies, heterosexual relations are often represented as anguished,
violent, or politically disastrous affairs, structured around male misogyny
and possessiveness, female rebelliousness and duplicity, and an overall
impasse of communication between the sexes. The prevalence of cuck-
oldry jokes in comedies suggests that husbands were unable to satisfy or
control their sexually promiscuous wives. Indeed, a variety of discourses
held that women were problematic sexual partners for men, and that men
were compromised, diminished, or endangered by their passion for
women. In the aggregate, these sources indicate that heterosexual
relations were highly stigmatized, often led to deviant behavior (including
"unnatural," nonprocreative, and nonmarital sexual acts, destructive
jealousy, and even murder), and hence had to be carefully monitored and
circumscribed.

Now, the illogic of this narrative should be obvious. It extrapolates
particular, and discursively contingent, instances of disorderly male–
female sexuality into the norm or truth of a monolithic system of
"heterosexuality," ignoring contrary evidence of heterosexual relations

that were orderly, supportive, or loving. But the dominant critical view of early modern homoeroticism likewise ignores evidence of orderly, normative male–male sexuality. Whereas early modern terms for disorderly sexuality in general ("sodomy," "incest," "adultery") and for orderly male–female relations in particular ("marriage," "love") seem intelligible to modern readers, those terms that could designate orderly homoeroticism, like "friendship," have largely lost their homoerotic valence in dominant usage, or, like "love," have never been thought to refer to specifically erotic desire in the first place. There seems to be no problem accepting the fact that some heterosexual practices are stigmatized, such as adultery and incest, whereas others are promoted, such as reproductive marital sex and companionate love. The problem is that while we have lost the ability, in the intervening centuries, to recognize the signs of orderly Renaissance homoerotic relations, we have at the same time inherited a modern ideology that posits heterosexuality as the norm – as constitutive of "order" itself in the realm of erotic relations.

Even though heteroerotic sexuality was not always orderly and homoerotic sexuality was not always disorderly in early modern England, it is nevertheless true that dominant ideologies and institutions did strenuously regulate certain kinds of sexual conduct between men. I do not mean to imply, therefore, a simple equivalence between disorderly homoerotic and disorderly heteroerotic behaviors. Same-sex practices that violated the institutions of marriage, patrilineage, and reproductive sexuality were highly transgressive, and, unlike mere heteroerotic adultery, could be punished with death. For example, John Fletcher's *The Honest Man's Fortune* (1613) alludes to the official death penalty for sodomy. Towards the end of the play, Laverdine, a foolish courtier, woos an unwilling page, Veramour, whom he suspects to be a woman in disguise. When Veramour falsely "admits" that he is indeed a woman, Laverdine expresses relief: "a woman? how happy am I! now we may lawfully come together without fear of hanging."[49] Laverdine fears being punished as a sodomite because he intends to *marry* Veramour: his desire not only violates the reproductive and social functions of marriage, but, given the boy's reluctance, might be considered a species of rape. The fear of being hanged for "sodomy" could police certain male relations. On the other hand, homoerotic relations between gentlemen and pages are not necessarily sodomitical. In the same play, the page Veramour loves his master Montague so completely and so jealously that a serving-woman teasingly accuses him of being a woman in disguise, although Montague himself questions neither the sex nor the devotion of his page. Fletcher's allusion to hanging therefore evokes the specific legal category of "sodomy" – an assault against reproduction and marriage – not a general proscription against men (or men and boys) who "come together."

"Sodomy," of course, was also traditionally linked with politically dangerous behaviors such as treason in ways that other categories of erotic disorder were not. As evidence for the proscription of homosexuality in early modern England, it is often remarked that even King James, a "homosexual" himself, condemned sodomy as a "horrible crime" in his *Basilicon Doron*.[50] Christopher Marlowe, on the other hand, is reported to have quipped that "all they that love not Tobacco & Boies were fooles."[51] The "love" of boys, when it is translated into the *Basilicon Doron*'s official discourse of political order, becomes the crime of "sodomy"; likewise, the love of tobacco becomes in King James's *Counterblaste to Tobacco*, an "effeminate" and "vile and stinking" custom imitated from "beastly" Indians.[52] James condemns the disorderly economic, social, and gender effects of tobacco in terms borrowed from the older discourse of sodomy: smoking is an outgrowth of "sinnefull and shamefull lust."[53] Although what two men do in bed – have sex and a smoke – might have negligible social consequences, "sodomitical" behaviors inevitably come under the scrutiny of the king, the guarantor of social order. Whatever his erotic tastes, it would be astonishing had the king *not* condemned sodomy.

It is significant that *Basilicon Doron* names incest along with sodomy as one of the crimes a king should never forgive. "Sodomy" signifies "male–male sex" in its totality no more than "incest" signifies "male–female sex" in its totality. One early modern definition of "adultery" illustrates how evaluations of sexual morality might be founded in a distinction between orderly and disorderly behaviors more so than between heteroerotic and homoerotic behaviors. In *The Foundation of Christian Religion* (1616), William Perkins writes that "to commit adultery, signifieth as much, as to doe any thing, what way soever, whereby the chastitie of our selves, or our neighbors may be stained."[54] He goes on to provide "adulterous" instances of heterosexual, autosexual, and homosexual lust. Just as adultery is not the only manifestation of heteroeroticism, sodomy is not the only manifestation of homoeroticism: both terms name a variety of socially disorderly sexual behaviors, and sometimes they name the same behaviors.[55] As the work of Gregory Bredbeck and Jonathan Goldberg has so admirably demonstrated, "sodomy" becomes a rich field for historical inquiry precisely because of its incoherences and contradictions, within both homoerotic and heteroerotic contexts. No more intrinsically orderly or disorderly than heteroerotic relations, homoerotic relations could sustain one ideology (the

master–servant hierarchy) while challenging another (companionate marriage). The point, then, is to identify as precisely as possible the social
and ideological contexts in which different kinds of erotic practice
accrued meaning.

The limitations of sodomy

Not only are there contradictions between those ideologies that promoted homoerotic relations and those that proscribed them; "sodomy
itself was an unstable, internally contradictory category."[56] By pointing
to symptomatic contradictions, I want briefly to demonstrate the limitations of legal and religious prohibitions against sodomy. Bruce Smith has
usefully analyzed the transformation of the legal definitions of sodomy
throughout sixteenth- and seventeenth-century England. He notes the
political origin of the first buggery statute: "making sodomy a felony
seems to have been a convenient way for Henry VIII to get rid of one
category of political enemies, priests who were loyal to Rome, and thus
consolidate his personal power."[57] Sodomy was created as a legal
category to serve as a weapon against Catholic priests, who had
traditionally been associated with homosexual practices. According to
Smith, subsequent laws in the reigns of Edward VI and Elizabeth I
moved away from a conception of sodomy as religious heresy, focusing
instead on its threat to the family. The seventeenth-century jurist Edward
Coke considered sodomy a personal crime: a species of rape, usually
committed by an adult man on a young boy. Smith concludes that the
English sodomy laws did not criminalize all homosexual acts (e.g.,
mutual masturbation); nor did they criminalize homosexual desire or
sexual relations generally between adult men.

Smith's diachronic analysis of the legal definition of sodomy in the
Renaissance provides a valuable lesson. By showing how the official
definition of sodomy changed according to broad cultural shifts and the
political agendas of different monarchs, Smith reveals that the basis for
these laws is arbitrary and ideological, not logical and natural. It is also
possible to demonstrate, deconstructively, why it is a mistake to interpret
the existence of sodomy laws as denoting a widespread cultural proscription of homoeroticism. The sodomy law does not merely name an act or
person that has an independent, objective, existence in the world; rather,
it discursively produces and reproduces the disorderly category of
sodomy. Judith Butler describes this as the "performative" quality of a
discourse to construct what it names by reproducing its own textually
grounded authority:

When the law functions as ordinance or sanction, it operates as an imperative that brings into being that which it legally enjoins and protects. The performative speaking of the law, an "utterance" that is most often within legal discourse inscribed in a book of laws, works only by reworking a set of already operative conventions. And these conventions are grounded in no other legitimating authority than the echo-chain of their own reinvocation.[58]

That the law "produces" homosexual anal intercourse as sodomy does not mean that all discourses understand homosexual anal intercourse as sodomy or understand sodomy as homosexual anal intercourse. In sum, homosexual anal intercourse is not "really" sodomy: there is no singular or "real" definition of what sodomy is. Having named what kinds and degrees of actions constitute sexual disorder, the law can be evoked to punish them. But since the English statute was so rarely and selectively evoked to name and punish male homosexual activity as "sodomy," its effectiveness and reach in so defining homoerotic relations and desires must have been limited.

Renaissance legal discourse does not even mention homoerotic desire; religious discourse does, yet not always under the banner of sodomy. Traditional exegesis and iconography permitted homoerotic interpretations of certain figures, most notably David (when paired with Jonathan), St. Sebastian and the disciple John (both of whom are paired with Jesus). These traditions were well known to Renaissance English writers. Raymond-Jean Frontain sees the homoerotic treatment of David in poems by Cowley and Drayton as a poetic strategy for praising male beauty while "avoiding the negative social codal identification of sodomy or pederasty." In this context, Frontain records King James's citation of scriptural authority to justify his love for the Duke of Buckingham: "Christ had his John and I have my Steenie."[59] Like David, St. Sebastian is often depicted as a beautiful, androgynous young man. In Italian Renaissance paintings, this saint who sacrificed himself for the love of Christ is commonly portrayed as a naked Apollonian figure suggestively penetrated by arrows.[60] Moreover, the frequent Renaissance linking of St. Sebastian and St. Antonio as patrons of the sexually diseased may explain the prevalence of homoerotic Sebastian–Antonio pairs in the English drama.[61] Christ himself becomes the focus of homoerotic passion for seventeenth-century English poets, who construct what Richard Rambuss calls a "devotional homoerotics" around the image of their savior's naked and pierced body.[62]

Such homoerotic readings of David, St. Sebastian, St. John, and Jesus do not constitute representations of sodomy, although they are available to sodomitical reinscription, as in Marlowe's supposed claim that Christ used John "as the sinners of Sodoma."[63] Perhaps more surprising than

Marlowe's inversion of official religious imagery is the example of a
religious text that explicitly condemns Sodom's vices while acknowledging its pleasures. The text is *Lot's Wife*, a sermon by Robert
Wilkinson published in 1607, the same year as Lewes Machin's homoerotic pastoral poem discussed above. Wilkinson intends to teach the
citizens of London twelve lessons based on the destruction of Sodom and
Gomorrah, whose citizens paid so "sweetly" for their "pride, idlenes, and
fulnes of bread."[64] The anomalous use of "sweetly" to describe destruction by fire and brimstone is explained by Wilkinson's account of the
manifold pleasures in which Sodom's citizens indulged. Lot's wife looks
back at the city, for which disobedience she is turned into a pillar of salt,
because she cannot bear to depart

from her house where shee had dwelt, from her gardens, and from her pleasures,
from sweet aire, greene pastures, and pleasant waters, yea from a paradise, (*For
as was the garden of the Lord, even so was Sodom before it was destroyed, Gen.* 13)
from thence came this wofull woman, and as if she thither would againe, thither
she lookes . . . (pp. 22–23, sigs. D3v–D4r)

Wilkinson provides an astonishingly pastoral view of the wicked city that
he is exhorting Londoners to reject. Moreover, he represents Lot's wife's
farewell to Sodom as a lover's valediction:

And must I leave thee, Sodom, and part for ever from thee? then once againe let
me looke upon thee, since I must looke no more, yea let me die with thee, since
thou must live no more; for where was ever Paradise if not in thee! or what wil
heaven be when thou art gone! O thou the light of mine eies, and delight of my
soule, whom heaven it selfe doth but match in happinesse, overmatching only in
eternity; What a life it was to live in thee! If we wished for wealth, we wallowed in
it; if for honor, it waited on us; and when we would bee merrie, Plentie, ease, and
peace sang melodie to it. (p. 23, sig. D4r)

How are we to understand this loving appreciation of Sodom, and
Wilkinson's recording of it? Gregory Bredbeck observes that sixteenth-
century translations and glosses of the Sodom passages in Genesis and
Judges "tend to figure the incidents as examples of general debauchery
and sin," not of a specifically defined male homoerotic lust.[65] Bredbeck
renders the gap between the biblical city and the sexual crime named
after it with the diacritical mark "Sodom/y." The gap between the city
and the sin appears as well in Wilkinson's interpretation of Sodom.
Although the sermon offers the punishment of Lot's wife as a warning
against pursuing the wrong kinds of desire, it represents no "sodomy"
within "Sodom."

The sermon not only fails to condemn sodomitical lust, it produces
only an ambiguous condemnation of erotic desire. Lot's wife certainly

represents base worldly desires: she is a disobedient, outspoken woman who turns back to the forbidden city instead of following the husband from whom she receives her social identity. Dying alongside her beloved city, she adulterously rewrites her identity as the wife of Sodom rather than of Lot. Yet her desire for Sodom has less to do with sexual license than with a yearning for happiness, wealth, honor, and peace. From her perspective, the idleness and pride for which the city is destroyed sound more like civic virtues to be embraced than sins to be eschewed. However unintentionally, the sermon appears to dissociate the annihilation of Sodom from the practice of forbidden desires. Lot's wife may transgress in desiring Sodom, but she is not destroyed in the same manner or for the same reasons as the city and its citizens.

What does Wilkinson's representation of a woman's desire for Sodom say about the disorderly male–male desire that his audience at Paul's would have associated with the legal and political category of "sodomy?" On the one hand, Wilkinson does not explicitly name "sodomy" or disorderly male lust as one of the *sins* justifying Sodom's destruction; on the other hand, he does portray Sodom as the locus of *desire* for a peaceful and bountiful life. One of the sermon's ideological effects, therefore, may be the separation of homoerotic desire from sodom/y. This sermon stands as a good illustration of the ways in which sodomy, despite its cultural force as a prohibitive category, might be traversed by contradictory discourses of homoerotic desire. Alan Bray has argued that religious discourse rendered sodomy so hellish and alien that no one would associate commonplace homosexual behavior with it. My point is rather different: official religious discourse itself – even a discourse about Sodom – might not even associate the devilish sin of sodomy with the expression of homoerotic desire.

An outspoken, erotically rebellious woman, Lot's wife inadvertently calls our attention to the contradictory representations of desire and prohibition in Wilkinson's text. In John Marston's contemporary play *The Dutch Courtesan* (1604), another outspoken woman, Crispinella, deliberately calls attention to a similar contradiction. Defending the naturalness of sexual desire, Crispinella seems to glance towards Sodom: "I love no prohibited things, and yet I would have nothing prohibited by policy, but by virtue; for as in the fashion of time those books that are call'd in are most in sale and request, so in nature those actions that are most prohibited are most desired."[66] Unlike Lot's wife, Crispinella loves no prohibited things. Nevertheless, she implies that official policies against sexuality are not only unwise but unnatural. As her marketplace analogy indicates, such policies may draw attention to the social effects of the prohibition itself rather than to the "naturally" transparent wickedness of the thing prohibited, perhaps thus demystifying the political motives of the prohibition. Ironically, Marston implies, prohibitions may produce the desire for behaviors that they discursively produce *as* undesirable.

The homoerotics of early modern drama

Marston's insight about the relation between erotic desire and social prohibition brings me back to the drama, and to non-Shakespearean drama in particular. The field of early modern drama comprises an extremely diverse range of texts, representing multiple, sometimes contradictory, forms of homoeroticism.[67] In what follows, I hope to avoid some of the limitations of studies based largely on Shakespeare's texts by considering representations of homoeroticism and sodomy in a wider range of plays, poetry, and historical texts from the 1580s through the 1620s. Each chapter focuses on the homoerotics of a particular dramatic genre and of an ideology or institution characteristically explored by that genre. In these readings, sodomy plays a specific function as a kind of limit category by which to identify and assess nonsodomitical forms of homoeroticism. That is, under certain circumstances, a culturally pervasive form of homoeroticism (for instance, between masters and servants) might become intelligible, from a certain vantage point, as sodomitical deviance. The fact that sodomy becomes visible only in certain situations and under charged political circumstances reveals the importance of looking for signs of nonsodomitical homoeroticism. This dynamic also raises certain questions. What representational strategies differentiate orderly homoerotic relations from sodomy? Can we also distinguish less disorderly forms of homoeroticism from the extreme disorder of "sodomy?" At what point in an intimate relation between men can the attribution of sodomy be made? What is the relation between erotic desire, sexual practice, and social power? How do competing, incoherent, ideologies allow homoerotic relations to proliferate, despite cultural and legal prohibitions against sodomy?

Chapter 2, "The Homoerotics of Marriage in Ovidian Comedy," critiques the heterosexism of modern definitions of the "family" and the ahistoricism of projecting a modern notion of the heterosexual nuclear family back onto the Renaissance household. In the Renaissance household, both homoerotic and heteroerotic desires found expression. The possibility that a husband might sexually desire other males instead of his wife is acknowledged in several late sixteenth-century texts that draw upon a common Ovidian discourse of erotic conflict and metamorphosis. The myths of Ganymede, Hylas, and Orpheus provide Renaissance writers with a common vocabulary for alluding to this conflict between male homoerotic desire and chaste marital (hetero)sexuality. Through their linkage of misogyny, male homoeroticism, and sodomy, I will argue, these myths comprise a crucial subtext for the sexual politics of Shakespeare's *As You Like It* (1599) and *Twelfth Night*, as well as Spenser's *The Faerie Queene* (1596). As the inclusion of Spenser suggests, one of the assumptions of this study is that dramatic literature can be isolated neither from its social contexts nor from the other literary and nonliterary discourses that also comprise those contexts. My goal throughout has been to integrate close analysis of plays with theoretical and historical analysis of early modern homoerotic relations more generally.

Chapter 3, "The Homoerotics of Mastery in Satiric Comedy," turns to satire and urban homoerotic environments in the plays of Jonson, Chapman, and Middleton. In these plays, characters attempt to achieve their erotic and social ambitions through what I call the "homoerotics of mastery." This term acknowledges the pervasive homoerotic dynamics of satiric plots in which men master other men; it more specifically points to the homoerotic potentiality within the master–servant bond. Early seventeenth-century satiric comedies reveal that the homoerotics of a relationship between master and servant can work either to solidify or to subvert the authority of the master, thus sodomitically challenging social order.

Chapter 4, "The Homoerotics of Favoritism in Tragedy," examines the representation of the court favorite in Elizabethan and Jacobean tragedies of state. The favorite's physical proximity to his monarch's body at once upholds and potentially undermines sovereign power. Marlowe's *The Massacre at Paris* (1593) and *Edward II* initially locate "sodomitical" disorder in the relation between disruptive favorites and the king; however, the plays finally shift the source of political disorder to rebellious nobility, who more gravely threaten monarchical authority. Shakespeare's *Richard II* (1595) and Jonson's *Sejanus* (1603) insistently figure royal favorites as sodomitical parasites, yet in *Sejanus* the sovereign nevertheless remains in power. Jonson shows that sodomy, when embodied in the sovereign, can actually become a source of political power. In Chapman's four tragedies about the Renaissance French court (*Bussy D'Ambois* [1604], *The Conspiracy and Tragedy of Byron* [1608], *The Revenge of Bussy D'Ambois* [1610]), erotic conflict is produced from the rivalry between patrons for the devotion of a single favorite. Developing an explicitly erotic language to describe patron–favorite relations, Chapman's plays are crucial in demonstrating the existence of a nonsodomitical homoerotic discourse about the early modern court.

Chapter 5, "The Homoerotics of Masculinity in Tragicomedy," examines militarism and male gender identity in the plays of John Fletcher and his collaborators. These tragicomedies participate in the frequently articulated anxiety about male effeminacy and male heteroerotic desire in Jacobean England. Three plays in particular – *The Nice Valour* (1615–16), *The Humorous Lieutenant* (1619), and *The Mad Lover* (1617) – reveal the disorderly effects of male heteroerotic desire by linking it to effeminate or sodomitical behavior, and by contrasting disorderly male lovers with masculine soldiers who renounce disruptive passions. In each of these plays a male character forgoes women, redirecting his social and erotic energies back into orderly – and potentially homoerotic – military relations. The representation of disorderly homoeroticism in these plays therefore stigmatizes not male homoerotic desire in particular, but the "effeminacy" of men who act like women or desire women. Having shown the incompatibility of masculinity and heteroerotic desire in these plays, I turn to Fletcher's *The Island Princess* (1619–21), a tragicomedy that successfully incorporates heteroerotic desire into the imperatives of male sexual and military domination. Because colonialist ideology valorizes the "masculine" European conquest of a "feminine" Indian nation, male honor and heteroerotic desire reinforce each other in *The Island Princess* in a way not possible in the other tragicomedies.

For each chapter, the relation mapped between a dramatic genre and a particular ideological conflict or social practice is meant to be fluid and supple. I have not attempted to establish an absolute or exclusive correlation between dramatic conventions and social relations; rather, my purpose has been to examine how and why a particular social institution is represented through the discursive strategies of a particular dramatic form. For instance, my focus in chapter 2 is not meant to imply that playwrights inevitably draw upon Ovidian mythology to express the conflict between male homoeroticism and marital (hetero)sexuality. *The Merchant of Venice* (1596), which deeply explores this conflict, is not a particularly "Ovidian" play. Nevertheless, Ovidian mythology provided a vocabulary and a set of conventions through which Renaissance writers could and did explore this contemporary social issue. Likewise, homoerotic bonds between masters and servants appear in plays other than the satiric comedies discussed in chapter 3. Pages, for instance, are the subjects and objects of homoerotic affection in many plays not even mentioned in that chapter: Fletcher's *The Honest Man's Fortune*, discussed above, provides only one example. Nevertheless, there is a particular correlation between satiric discourse and the representation of sexually disorderly masters and servants, and such conjunctions of form and ideology have determined my organizational categories and selection of texts throughout.

I have yet to explain the place of female homoeroticism in *The Homoerotics of Early Modern Drama*. My analysis focuses on the ways in which homoerotic relations shaped dominant, hence predominantly male, social and political practices in early modern England. The overall emphasis I give to male–male relations is itself suggested by the gender-separatist character of early modern homoeroticism. As Eve Sedgwick has shown, a dominant strand of modern homosexual definition implies the existence of a separate minority of people who share the essential trait of same-sex desire, despite intercategorical differences in gender, race, class, or age, and intracategorical differences in erotic tastes and practices.[68] Modern sexual ideology subsumes gender difference under the gender-neutral (albeit often implicitly male) category "homosexuality," which is defined against the gender-neutral category "heterosexuality." In the Renaissance, on the contrary, same-sex desire was not a trait that brought men and women together as a distinct minority; same-sex desire cemented normative bonds *between* men (e.g., through court patronage) and *between* women (e.g., through premarital friendship). To render this dynamic according to Sedgwick's theoretical scheme, Renaissance homoeroticism was separatist in regard to gender and universalizing in regard to sexual possibilities within genders and between genders.[69] A girl who shared a bed with her friend was not in the same category of erotic experience as a boy who shared a bed with his master.

Neither was this girl in the same legal or social category as her male counterpart. Legal definitions of "sodomy" in England do not mention female homoeroticism, because female sexuality in general was disciplined by "an already well-established set of precepts, practices, and discursive conventions at both the elite and popular levels," as Margaret Hunt has observed.[70] The thoroughly patriarchal culture of early modern England defined a woman according to her marital status as a maid, wife, or widow – that is, in relation to men, usually a father or husband. Since political, domestic, cultural, and economic power were largely in male hands, and since homoerotic practices were generally dispersed throughout the culture rather than being marginalized, conditions were prime for the eroticization of male–male relations. It is not surprising, then, that male homoerotic relations are more frequently depicted than female homoerotic relations in early modern literary texts.

Despite the presence of a woman on the English throne, playwrights exploring the sexual aspects of political power in the 1580s and 1590s tend to depict not female homoerotic relations but erotic relations between male monarchs and male favorites (*Edward II*), between male warriors (*Tamburlaine* [1587], *Campaspe* [1584]), and, occasionally, between female rulers and their male companions (*Henry VI* [1590], *Dido*

[1586]). There are significant exceptions. The courtly plays of John Lyly at once celebrate the political integrity of Elizabeth's virginity and register its threat as female homoeroticism: hence the lovesick queen Sapho of *Sapho and Phao* (1584) and the allegory of England as the unconquerable island of Lesbos (ruled, however, by a *king*) in *Midas* (1589). The few Shakespearean and non-Shakespearean plays that provide sustained representations of female homoeroticism have begun to receive careful attention from critics such as Valerie Traub, Philippa Berry, and Theodora Jankowski; these plays will repay further analysis from diverse critical perspectives.[71] Whenever possible, I have tried to advance our knowledge of early modern female homoeroticism by bringing certain unfamiliar texts to light and by juxtaposing the different social effects of female and male homoerotic desires. I hope that future work on gender and sexuality in Renaissance drama will provide a more balanced analysis of male and female homoeroticism, or at least a more extended consideration of the effects of male homoerotic relations on women.[72]

It is also to be hoped that additional evidence of female homoeroticism will appear as other neglected texts are read or reread through a lesbian/gay critical practice. My own reading of less familiar city comedies and tragicomedies has turned up unexpected instances of female homoeroticism. More often, however, I have been struck by the explicit, often pervasive, yet mostly unnoted male homoeroticism of *familiar* non-Shakespearean plays. If the few plays that represent female homoeroticism are as yet unknown or underread, the many plays that represent male homoeroticism are already central to the canon of Tudor–Stuart drama. These plays are commonly taught in university courses and are readily available in anthologies and single volume editions such as the Revels and New Mermaids. As in the case of George Chapman, these plays may comprise a significant portion of an author's corpus, or, in the case of satiric comedy, of an entire genre.

Not only is homoeroticism central to works that are already canonical, but noncanonical works look much more important and interesting when read through a methodology that synthesizes sexuality, gender, and power. For this reason, I avoid giving individual readings of some important texts whose homoerotic aspects are generally acknowledged – Shakespeare's *Sonnets*, *Troilus and Cressida* (1602), *A Midsummer Night's Dream* (1595), and *The Merchant of Venice*; Middleton and Dekker's *The Roaring Girl* (1611); Lyly's *Gallathea* (1585) – in favor of an approach based on mapping ideological and dramatic structures common to a range of texts. I do not ignore these more familiar texts because they contradict my arguments; on the contrary, I hope they will be used to corroborate, modify, or challenge the paradigms I have developed using texts whose homoerotics have gone largely unexplored. At this stage in the development of theoretical and historical knowledges about early modern homoeroticism I prefer to bring a new text into the dialogue rather than take a position on a perennially debated play like *The Merchant of Venice*.

Aside from these methodological considerations, a polemical and strategic purpose has determined my choice of texts: the decentering of Shakespeare. Francis Barker has argued that bourgeois criticism values the rich language of Shakespeare's plays over the corporal displays found in other Jacobean plays. Barker finds the consequent indictment of non-Shakespearean playwrights for "sensationalism" a particularly modern moral and aesthetic judgment that elides "the theatricality of this theatre."[73] What contributes to the theatricality of the Renaissance theater, I believe, is the persistent visual and verbal presence of male bodies – not only at the level of theatrical practice (as is often remarked in discussions of transvestite players) but also at the level of dramatic representation, as a glance at the plays of Jonson, Chapman, or Fletcher immediately reveals. The display of male bodies on the Renaissance stage, if sometimes sensationalistic, is often undeniably sensual. We ignore the homoerotic sensuality of the drama at the cost of misjudging the centrality of homoeroticism to the ideological and social practices of early modern England. Aside from contributing to emerging knowledges about Renaissance sexuality, then, I hope that *The Homoerotics of Early Modern Drama* will renew interest in non-Shakespearean plays that are infrequently read – and rarely read queerly.

2   The homoerotics of marriage in Ovidian comedy

Queering the family

Is there anything queer about the family in early modern England? Until the mid 1980s, scholarship on early modern marriage and domestic life proceeded as if homoerotic desire were largely irrelevant to its concerns. A significant example of this tendency is Lawrence Stone's influential *The Family, Sex and Marriage in England 1500–1800*, which, despite its monumental scope, has very little to say about the relation of homosexuality to the family, sex, or marriage throughout 300 years of English history.[1] As gay, lesbian, feminist, and queer scholarship has demonstrated with increasing subtlety and cumulative force, however, to ignore the place of same-sex desire or nonreproductive sexuality in early modern domestic life is not to provide an historically accurate portrait of Renaissance social structures. It is to project back onto the Renaissance particularly modern biases and ideologies, especially the notion that there are two distinct sexualities, heterosexuality and homosexuality, and that only the former has anything to do with the constitution and production of families.[2]

Given the centrality of Shakespeare to Renaissance studies and his dominant reputation as the dramatist of romantic married love, queer scholarship on the family in early modern England faces a double task. One, it must insist on the homoerotic dimensions of courtship, marriage, and domestic experience inside the Shakespearean canon. Two, it must also look outside the canon to less familiar, even obscure texts that depict the homoerotic dimensions of these institutions and experiences more explicitly, or, at least, differently from Shakespeare's. As I plan to demonstrate in subsequent readings of the plays of Jonson, Chapman, Middleton, and Fletcher, Shakespeare simply does not exhaust the possibilities for representing the homoerotic practices of his society. For instance, Shakespeare's contemporaries often present a fuller picture of the early modern household and the same-sex relations enabled by its particular functioning and composition.[3] Perhaps Shakespeare's status as the most familiar Renaissance playwright depends in part on his status as the most familial: the one who seemingly celebrates the affective heterosexual couple that we "recognize" as the source, both biologically and historically, of the modern family. Indeed, Lynda Boose's essay "The Family in Shakespeare Studies; or – Studies in the Family of Shakespeareans; or – The Politics of Politics" exerts much of its rhetorical power precisely by reinscribing a familiar, naturalized notion of the family even as it critiques familiar/familial gender politics. Boose, writing in 1987, observes that scholarship *on* the family is repeating the power dynamics *of* the family: feminists write about female subjectivity, gender, and the domestic, while male new historicists write about male subjectivity, power, and the state, effectively marginalizing their female colleagues. While Boose rightly insists that the patriarchal nuclear family is an historical and ideological construction, her essay reconstructs this family as a trope, as the "natural" way to describe the political relations between male and female Shakespeare scholars and their metaphorically male and female methodologies.[4]

In order to understand the significance of homoeroticism to representations of early modern English domestic life, I want to begin by examining the institution and ideology of marriage. The relation between late sixteenth-century romantic comedy and marital ideology has been a major theme of feminist Shakespeare scholarship. A prominent example, Catherine Belsey's "Disrupting Sexual Difference," argues that an older dynastic ideology of marriage and an emergent affective ideology of marriage were coming into explicit contradiction in late sixteenth-century English society. Belsey's reading of *As You Like It* (1599) aims to show that these contradictions suspended or blurred the difference between male and female, masculine and feminine, briefly establishing men and women as equals in romantic love. With a slightly different emphasis, Mary Beth Rose, in *The Expense of Spirit: Love and Sexuality in English Renaissance Drama*, finds a similar conflict between "two dominant forms of sexual discourse": an older, "dualistic sensibility" in which women and eros are either idealized or degraded; and a newer, Protestant idealization of holy matrimony. Among the texts adduced as evidence for the "gradual shift" from the former discourse to the latter during the period, Rose cites Puritan marriage tracts and harmonious Elizabethan comedies.[5]

However, neither critic discusses "sexuality" other than as it occurs between women and men. The "sexual difference" of Belsey's title turns out to mean gender difference; the "love and sexuality" of Rose's subtitle is misleadingly inclusive, since the analysis itself concerns only "heterosexual love and marriage."[6] Despite this, we might note that the emergent ideology of affective marriage clashed not only with the dynastic marital ideology described by Belsey or with the dualistic sexual ideology described by Rose, but with a gender ideology that encouraged men to form intimate friendships (which could accommodate homoerotic desire, as Bruce Smith argues) and that regarded women as the moral and intellectual inferiors of men.[7] Moreover, female sexuality was commonly understood in the period to be inherently uncontrollable and dangerous to men.[8] From the perspective of misogynist ideologies, the pleasures of male homoerotic companionship might appear equivalent or even superior to those of heteroerotic companionship. According to the ideal of chaste and affectionate marriage, however, a husband's homo-erotic interests are likely to be interpreted as disorderly, especially when the perspective of a neglected wife is taken into account. The transition from male adolescence to adulthood could therefore precipitate a contra-diction between an emergent ideology of affective companionate mar-riage and a traditional ideology that considered men to be the only fully satisfying companions for men.

Recognition of and response to this possible marital crisis appears in several late sixteenth-century texts that draw upon a common source: Ovidian myths in which male homoerotic desire actively disrupts marital (hetero)sexuality. Ovidian myths inform the sexual politics of many comedies from this period, including *A Midsummer Night's Dream* (1595), *As You Like It*, *Cynthia's Revels* (1600), *The Maid's Metamorphosis* (1600), *Twelfth Night* (1601), and *Narcissus* (January 1603).[9] In what follows, however, I will focus on Renaissance reinscriptions of three related myths – those of Ganymede, Hylas, and Orpheus – and on the significance of these myths to the representation of erotic desire and marriage in three major texts: Spenser's *The Faerie Queene* (1596), and two Shakespearean comedies, *Twelfth Night* and *As You Like It*. Although Spenser's epic might seem out of place in a study of the drama, a significantly theatrical episode in *The Faerie Queene*, the Masque of Cupid, becomes the site of conflict around the homoerotics of marriage. Spenser's allegory provides a useful starting point for mapping the ideological contradictions between orderly and disorderly homoeroticism in the queer familial structures of late sixteenth-century England.

Male homoeroticism and the disruption of marriage

Ganymede and Hylas: the homoerotics of 'Fancy'

As has long been recognized, the Masque of Cupid in book 3 of *The Faerie Queene* is an allegory of the disorderly love that prevents Amoret

and Scudamour from properly consummating their marriage. Critics
have had more trouble explaining what kind of sexual disorder the
masque represents, and why it is led by Fancy:

> The first was *Fancy*, like a lovely boy,
>   Of rare aspect, and beautie without peare;
>   Matchable either to that ympe of *Troy*,
>   Whom *Jove* did love, and chose his cup to beare,
>   Or that same daintie lad, which was so deare
>   To great *Alcides*, that when as he dyde,
>   He wailed womanlike with many a teare,
>   And every wood, and every valley wyde
> He fild with *Hylas* name; the Nymphes eke *Hylas* cryde.
>
> His garment neither was of silke nor say,
>   But painted plumes, in goodly order dight,
>   Like as the sunburnt *Indians* do aray
>   Their tawney bodies, in their proudest plight:
>   As those same plumes, so seemd he vaine and light,
>   That by his gate might easily appeare;
>   For still he far'd as dauncing in delight,
>   And in his hand a windy fan did beare,
> That in the idle aire he mov'd still here and there.[10]

Iconographically and narratively, this is an odd moment. What is Fancy
doing in this masque? What is his allegorical relation to Amoret and
Scudamour? And why is he associated with beautiful boys loved by men?

Spenser's Fancy has been largely ignored and never satisfactorily
explained by commentators, despite his primacy in the masque. Leonard
Barkan finds the masque "an allegorical pageant displaying the psychological conditions of unhealthy love," specifically "Petrarchan love," yet
he does not explain why Fancy represents the love of boys. James W.
Broaddus argues that "the masque itself is an allegory of the corruption
of sexuality by a life of ease, idleness and luxury most clearly indicated
by the first couple," Fancy and Desire, the former of which is "tainted"
with homoeroticism. While Broaddus attempts to explain the significance
of Fancy, he says nothing more of the relation of homoeroticism to
idleness, nor of the connection between Fancy and Scudamour. Harry
Berger Jr.'s claim that Fancy is a "homosexual object" fails to account
for the significance of homoeroticism to the masque. More careful with
terminology, Simon Shepherd places Fancy within the context of idealized male homoeroticism in *The Faerie Queene*, yet in doing so overlooks
the negative connotations Fancy imparts to Scudamour's behavior.[11]

In my own reading, Fancy personifies both a female and a male fancy:
Amoret's idle imagination (her "fancy" or fantasy), and Scudamour's
idle lust (his homoerotic "fancy"). Taken in conjunction, the wife's and

the husband's fancy reveal Spenser's Fancy to be an allegory of the marital crisis initiated by male homoerotic desire.[12] Through Fancy, that is, Spenser represents the potential of male homoerotic desire to disrupt marital chastity. However, the Masque of Cupid's representation of male homoeroticism as a disorderly desire must be recognized as partial and contested, inasmuch as it contradicts the positive valuation of male homoeroticism and the negative valuation of heteroerotic desire found elsewhere in *The Faerie Queene*, as well as in Renaissance versions of the Ganymede and Orpheus myths and in Shakespeare's *Twelfth Night*.

To understand the role of Amoret in the Masque of Cupid, it is necessary to understand Fancy as an iconographic representation of a disorderly psychological process. According to Renaissance psychological theory, the fantasy is the "notoriously fragile" faculty through which images of the sensual world are collected in the brain and represented as in a mirror to the understanding, which then directs the will.[13] In book 2, Spenser represents the faulty workings of the idle imagination through Phantastes. Although Phantastes's "working wit" is "never idle," it paradoxically produces "idle thoughts and fantasies" (2.9.49, 51). Fancy, "vaine and light," is likewise always in motion, and his symbolic attribute, which puns on his name, is a "windy fan . . . That in the idle aire he mou'd still here and there" (3.12.8).

Idleness and its correlates – vanity, lightness, change – all symbolized in the fan, gender the fantasy as feminine. Hence "dames" are prominent among those in whose "idle fantasies doe flit" the "[i]nfinite shapes of things" (2.9.50). Along these lines, one might usefully compare Spenser's Phantastes to Jonson's Phantaste, a court lady who appears in the play *Cynthia's Revels*. Initiating a game in which participants must declare their greatest wish, Phantaste decides – with characteristic indecision – that she has two fantasies: to be able to change her shape into "all manner of creatures," and to be the richest and most beautiful woman in the kingdom for a year.[14] Given the cultural association between women and idleness, it is hardly surprising that as many "maladies" appear in the Masque of Cupid "as there be phantasies / In wavering wemens wit" (3.12.26).

Fancy's association with women's wit corroborates the theory that Amoret's fantasy is responsible for generating the images that torment her in the Masque of Cupid.[15] As we learn later in book 4, Amoret's fragile psychic state affects her imagination. Amoret fears a sexual assault not only from Britomart, whom she believes to be a man, but from Arthur, though "cause of feare sure had she none at all" (4.9.19). Despite seeing no evidence of Arthur's sexual desire, Amoret's fancy projects the image of what would happen "[i]n case his burning lust should breake into excesse" (4.9.18). Her worry is understandable, of course, given the sexual violation she has just suffered at the hands of Busirane. If her prior fear of Busirane evokes the imaginary scenario of being raped by Arthur, then what prior fear generated the nightmarish Busirane in the first place?

Fancy may personify Amoret's fearful, wavering mind; yet Fancy, Phantastes, and other idle figures in *The Faerie Queene* (such as Idleness in book 1 and Pleasure's Porter in book 2) are not in fact women but effeminate males. James Broaddus's opinion, that the Masque of Cupid represents "an evil which Busyrane attempts unsuccessfully to impose" upon Amoret, allows one to see the sequence as the projection of a male as well as a female psyche.[16] Spenser's depiction of Fancy as an effeminate and effeminizing boy implicates Scudamour, Busirane's allegorical substitute, as the subject of disorderly homoerotic fancy. Through Fancy's association with the myths of Ganymede, Hylas, and Orpheus, Scudamour is tainted, more precisely, with an effeminizing and misogynist homoerotic lust that threatens the marital chastity Spenser promotes in book 3. Early modern sexual ideology does not construct homoerotic and heteroerotic desires as mutually exclusive or incompatible. Nor is disorderly homoeroticism the only kind of "false love" unbridled in the House of Busirane. Nevertheless, since male homoerotic desire could disrupt marital chastity, it must be acknowledged as one of the "thousand monstrous formes" that sexuality takes in the masque (3.11.51). Amoret's fears of Scudamour are evoked by the disorderly homoerotic desire that threatens to disrupt the chastity of their marriage.

The Masque of Cupid premieres at the couple's bridal feast, an event marred by disorderly theatrical reveling. The spectacle of Fancy "dauncing in delight" among "wanton Bardes, and Rhymers impudent" clearly signifies the debilitating effeminacy associated with theatrical revels in the Renaissance (3.12.5, 8).[17] "[H]eedless and ill hedded," the drunken wedding guests fail to suppress the masque that serves Busirane's "sinfull lust" (4.1.3–4). Scudamour fails to recognize the danger of Busirane's masque because of his own complicity in "sinfull lust," the disorderly homoeroticism Spenser evokes by comparing Fancy to Ganymede. Within the House of Busirane, Ganymede first appears in the tapestry room devoted to the gods' pageants of lust. The tapestry depicts Jove's eagle abducting the lovely shepherd boy as his frightened companions gaze up in wonder. Ganymede is the only mythological figure carried over from the still pageantry of the tapestry room into the live pageantry of the masque. Moreover, Fancy is the only figure in the masque who is aligned with a mythological figure at all. Spenser's unique use of the

Ganymede myth provides a key for interpreting the sexual disorder of the entire masque.

Many critics have found Jupiter's desire for Ganymede of signal importance in describing the particular age- and status-inflected structure of male homoeroticism in early modern England. But the myth also exists in an extended version as a familial drama involving Jupiter's wife Juno and their daughter Hebe, who is Juno's favorite and the royal cupbearer. According to Thomas Cooper's influential classical dictionary, when Hebe one day "chaunsed to fall, and disclosed further of hir neather partes, then comliness woulde have to be shewen, Jupiter, to the great displeasure of his wyfe Juno, removed her from that office, and appointed Ganymedes to serve hym at his cuppe."[18] What is the meaning of Hebe's downfall? Does the uncomeliness of her fault reside in the public disclosure of "neather partes" or in the fact that specifically female "neather partes" have been disclosed? The latter explanation is suggested by Marlowe's treatment of the myth in *Dido, Queen of Carthage* (1586), where Jupiter has no qualms about risking the public display of Ganymede's nether parts. The play opens with Jupiter "dandling Ganymede upon his knee" and "playing" wantonly with him.[19] When Juno later expresses her "hate of Trojan Ganymede, / That was advanced by my Hebe's shame" (3.2.42–43), she reinforces the sense that it is the display of "shameful" female parts (the "pudendum") that provokes Jupiter's ire.[20] Jupiter not only rejects Hebe but openly declares his love for Ganymede, "say Juno what she will," and bestows on his favorite the necklace that "Juno ware upon her marriage-day" (1.1.2, 43).[21] The little familial drama of this myth reveals a great deal of anxiety about female sexuality.

It is, therefore, significant that in comparing Fancy to Ganymede, Spenser alludes not to the initial abduction of the boy but to the later, more discordant, development in which Jupiter chooses Ganymede as his cupbearer. Jupiter's love for Ganymede constitutes a single homoerotic affair among numerous heteroerotic affairs that angered Juno. Yet because Jupiter replaces his female servant with a male servant and his wife with a boy, the story of Ganymede uniquely links the offense of a husband's marital infidelity with his rejection of women. According to James Saslow's sociological account of the Ganymede myth in the Renaissance,

Jupiter's preferment of Ganymede over Hebe and Juno's consequent jealous resentment were often interpreted as a parable of two closely connected social phenomena: the subordinate status or worth of women and the potentially disruptive effect of a man's homosexual infidelities on the relations between husband and wife.[22]

While Saslow bases his interpretation mostly on visual and literary
sources from sixteenth-century Italy, Spenser and his English contemporaries also understood the Ganymede myth as a parable about male
debasement of female sexuality and sexual conflict between husbands
and wives.

The rejection of women and devaluation of female sexuality are
recurring themes in Renaissance versions of the Ganymede myth. In
John Lyly's *Gallathea* (1585), the virgin rejected as a sacrifice because
she is "not the fairest" is appropriately named "Hebe." In John
Mason's play *The Turk* (1607), the courtier Bordello cites Jupiter's
substitution of Ganymede for Hebe as a precedent for his renunciation
of all women:

> BORDELLO. Pantofle.
> PANTOFLE. At your pleasure sir?
> BORD. Thou hast bene at my pleasure indeed *Pantofle*, I
> will retreate into the country, hate this amourous, Court
> and betake my selfe to obscurity: I tel thee boye I wil
> returne by this *Circyan* Isle without transformation since
> *Hebe* hath discovered her secrets I will turne *Jupiter*, hate
> the whole sexe of women, and onely embrace thee my *Ganimede*.
> PANT. Sfoot sir you are as passionate for the
> disloyalty of your Sempstresse, as some needy knight would
> be for the losse of some rich magnificos widdow: doe you not
> see how the supporters of the Court, the Lady of the labby
> gape after your good parts like so many grigges after fresh
> water, and can you withhold the dew of your moyster element?
> BORD. I tel thee should the Lady *Julia* when she was
> alive have profered me her cheeke to kisse, I would not have
> bowed to that painted image for her whole Dukedome: *Mercury*
> had no good aspect in the horoscope of my nativity: women
> and lotium are recipiocall, their savour is noysome.

Betrayed by a woman who "discovered her secrets" like Hebe, Bordello
transforms himself into a Jupiter who will have sexual relations only with
his Ganymede, or page. In Marlowe's *Edward II* (1592), after Queen
Isabella has been sexually rejected by her husband she finds in the myth a
model for her own grief: "Like frantic Juno will I fill the earth / With
ghastly murmur of my sighs and cries; / For never doted Jove on
Ganymed / So much as he on cursed Gaveston." The court favorite in
Marston's *The Malcontent* (1603) is similarly blamed for precipitating a
conjugal rupture: "Duke's Ganymede, Juno's jealous of thy long stock-
ings."[23] Marston had already used the myth in his verse satire *The
Scourge of Villainy* (1598) to signify female animosity towards the spread
of pederasty in England: "Marry, the jealous queen of air doth frown, /

That Ganymede is up, and Hebe down." Thomas Heywood explains that his depiction of Jupiter's same-sex adultery in *Pleasant Dialogues and Dramas* (1637) actually condemns "base sordid lust in man." In one rather unpleasant dialogue, Juno complains, "Since this yong Trojan Swain to heav'n thou hast brought, / O *Jupiter*, thou set'st thy Wife at nought." She elaborates, "I wish in my place you had that Lad wedded, / With whom you ofter than with me have bedded / Since his arrive." Making an antithetical point about marital relations, Robert Greene illustrates proper wifely submission by observing that, when Juno hoped to placate her angry husband, she called upon her rival Ganymede to serve him nectar.[24]

As these examples indicate, Renaissance writers readily alluded to this familiar myth to convey the disruptions in male–female sexual relations and marital harmony caused by male homoerotic desire. If the allusion to Ganymede in Spenser's Masque of Cupid evokes an effeminate boy who might attract an adult man's fancy, the allusion to Hercules (Alcides) conversely evokes the image of the effeminate pederast. Although Renaissance writers generally present Hercules as a paragon of heroic masculinity, his maleness is compromised on those notorious occasions when he lusts after women and boys, notably Omphale and Hylas. According to Thomas Cooper, Hercules won Hylas in a battle and made him his page, whom "ever after he favoured and loved as his owne." When the boy accidentally drowned, Hercules scoured the land, "seekyng and criyng" for "his derlynge Hylas."[25] In Spenser's version, "He wailed womanlike with many a teare, / And euery wood, and euery valley wyde / He fild with *Hylas* name" (3.12.7). Hercules's unmanly outburst reveals an excessive and disruptive desire for the "daintie lad, which was so deare" to him. Scudamour's indulgent behavior outside the House of Busirane likewise reveals the detrimental effects of idle lust. Having willfully abandoned his armor and shield, Scudamour is discovered "all wallowed / Upon the grassy ground," groaning and whining about his impotence to save Amoret (3.11.7).[26]

Scudamour's lust manifests itself not only as effeminate debilitation, but also, paradoxically, as hypermasculine aggression. This aggression is personified by the giant Ollyphant, whom Britomart spies as he chases a young man "with hideous / And hatefull outrage" (3.11.3). Spenser underscores the suspicion that Ollyphant's outrageous pursuit of this man constitutes a sin "[g]ainst natures law" (3.7.49) by adducing the parallel example of Ollyphant's twin sister, who lusts after an unwilling knight. Ollyphant's elephantine girth symbolizes the enormity of the lust he directs in "beastly use" behind the boy:

> For as the sister did in feminine
> And filthy lust exceede all woman kinde,
> So he surpassed his sex masculine,
> In beastly use that I did euer find;
> Whom when as *Britomart* beheld behind
> The fearefull boy so greedily pursew,
> She was emmoued in her noble mind,
> T'employ her puissaunce to his reskew . . .   (3.11.4)

Chasing Ollyphant, Britomart discovers Scudamour. For Berger, "that Scudamour materializes in place of the giant suggests a symbolic equivalence and transference."[27] The symbolic equivalence is further signaled by the similarity between Ollyphant's "greed[y]" pursuit of the boy and Scudamour's "greedy will" to repossess Amoret, a will inflated by "envious desire," "threatfull pride," and "huge impatience" (3.11.26–27).[28] At once effeminizing and hypermasculinizing, homoerotic Fancy renders Scudamour impotent to achieve orderly sexual fulfillment with his wife. Britomart's discovery of Scudamour in place of the unnatural Ollyphant pushes the subsequent personification of Scudamour's disorderly homoerotic Fancy into the symbolic register of sodomy. Although Spenser never names "sodomy," he introduces it in canto 11, via the beastly Ollyphant, as a framing concept through which the reader might interpret the Masque of Cupid that follows in canto 12.

The obstruction of marital (hetero)sexuality by male homoerotic desire in *The Faerie Queene* illuminates the similar crisis of male heteroerotic desire in Shakespeare's *Twelfth Night*, which I would like to consider before returning to *The Faerie Queene*. Although *Twelfth Night* opens with Orsino expressing his love for Olivia, the play contrasts Orsino's narcissistic passion and insufficient respect for Olivia with Antonio's insurmountable devotion to Sebastian.[29] Orsino's protean fancy, which overwhelms and diminishes the object of his desire, does not bode well for his future wife:

> O spirit of love, how quick and fresh art thou,
> That, notwithstanding thy capacity
> Receiveth as the sea, nought enters there,
> Of what validity and pitch soe'er,
> But falls into abatement and low price,
> Even in a minute! So full of shapes is fancy,
> That it alone is high fantastical.[30]

Not only are his desires fickle and superficial, Orsino considers women less valuable once they have lost their virginity, as he informs Cesario:

> let still the woman take
> An elder than herself; so wears she to him,

So sways she level in her husband's heart:
For boy, however we do praise ourselves,
Our fancies are more giddy and unfirm,
More longing, wavering, sooner lost and won
Than women's are.
VIO.   I think it well my lord.
ORS. Then let thy love be younger than thyself,
Or thy affection cannot hold the bent:
For women are as roses, whose fair flower
Being once display'd, doth fall that very hour.   (2.4.29–39)

Orsino teaches Cesario that men are more inconstant and fantastical than women. To compensate for this deficiency in male heteroerotic desire, he advocates an age differential, the woman's greater youth leveling out the man's lesser affection.

Orsino's language of swaying the level and holding the bent recalls the notorious crux that has been the subject of much recent theoretical speculation on the nature of homo- and heterosexual desire in the play and in early modern England. I am referring, of course, to Sebastian's explanation to Olivia of her "mistaken" desire for Cesario/Viola:

So comes it, lady, you have been mistook.
But nature to her bias drew in that.
You would have been contracted to a maid;
Nor are you therein, by my life, deceiv'd:
You are betroth'd both to a maid and man.   (5.1.257–61)

Most commentators read this enigmatic "bias" as a metaphor from bowling, where bias describes the curved course drawn by the ball on the path towards its goal. For Stephen Greenblatt and Thomas Laqueur, the bias describes the indirect course taken by natural *heterosexual* desire. Joseph Pequigney, conversely, reads the bias as a description of the lesbian or *homosexual* desire that naturally deviates from heterosexual desire.[31] To my mind, this passage should not be read as Shakespeare's totalizing commentary on the naturalness of either "heterosexuality" or "homosexuality," which did not exist as conceptual categories during the period. The passage does, however, describe the three modalities of erotic desire that apply to the experiences of its speaker (Sebastian) and its addressee (Olivia): a woman's desire for a woman, a woman's desire for a man, and a man's desire for a man. Revealing nothing conclusive about the naturalness of any one kind of desire, the passage instead reveals more about the play's exploration of the fourth modality of erotic desire, experienced, I want to argue, by none of its characters: a man's desire for a woman.

The radical ambiguity of this passage depends on the indeterminacy of the phrase "drew in that." The two different ways of coupling the preposition – drew *in that* or *drew in* that – yield two different readings of sexual desire. If nature to her bias drew *in that*, then Olivia's mistake in loving Viola was only natural. On the other hand, if nature to her bias *drew in* that, then nature restricted or contained Olivia's mistaken desire for a woman, allowing her to fall in love with the male "Cesario" and to marry Sebastian. In the former reading, Nature, a female figure, draws Olivia to another woman according to her bias or tendency to love someone of her own sex.[32] Joseph Pequigney writes of the homoerotically inclined Nature in *Sonnet* 20: "The fact that she initially made the youth female does not prevent Nature from falling in love, and, once in love, she cannot doom her unfinished creature to the 'deprived' state of womanhood but must add the perfecting touch that will transform 'her' into 'him.'"[33] Pequigney finds Olivia's love for Viola no less natural: "this homoerotic swerving or lesbian deviation from the heterosexual straight and narrow cannot be considered unnatural since it is effected by nature herself."[34] Like the Nature of the sonnet, Olivia dotes on Viola/Cesario, a woman/eunuch who lacks "a little thing" (3.4.307), only eventually to betroth Sebastian (a Viola/Cesario "pricked out" with that thing). When read in the context of Shakespeare's play, a sixteenth-century emblem titled "Mary thy lyke" might undermine the opposite-sex configuration of marriage by likewise suggesting the naturalness of same-sex love: "Like will to like, and that I like, / that like should mary like."[35] In *Twelfth Night*, a maid (Olivia) would have been contracted to her like, another maid (Viola) with an anagrammatically like name. And Olivia is indeed contracted to her like, both maid and man: a *maid* (virgin) who is a *man* of comparable birth (Sebastian) who looks just like the *man* (Cesario) and *maid* (Viola) that she first liked. Hasn't nature's "homoerotic" bias drawn Olivia to like and to marry her like?

In the second possible reading of the passage, Sebastian declares that nature's bias *drew in* Olivia's mistaken love for a woman so that she could rightly love a man (Cesario or Sebastian). Olivia's mistaken desire for Viola, instead of drawing her to be "contracted" to a maid, is itself naturally shrunken or contracted.[36] Justifying the naturalness of Olivia's attraction to a man, Sebastian follows in a long misogynist tradition clearly articulated by Lord Gaspar in Castiglione's *Book of the Courtier* (tr. 1561). Gaspar explains that men lose sexual interest in women because, according to Aristotle, male bodies are more perfect than female bodies:

a greate Philosopher in certein Problemes of his saith: Whens commeth it that naturally the woman alwaies loveth the man, that hath bine the first to receive of her, amorous pleasures? And contrariwise the man hateth the woman that hath bine the first to coople in that wise with him? and addinge therto the cause, affirmeth it to be this: For that in this act, the woman receyveth of the man perfection, and the man of the woman imperfection: and therfore everie man naturallye loveth the thinge that maketh him perfect, and hateth that maketh him unperfect.[37]

According to this logic, Nature's bias would draw both women and men to love men, who are more perfect or equally perfect in nature. This is why the Nature of *Sonnet* 20, having fallen in love with the woman she created, makes her a male, hence perfect. Even a defender of women in the *Courtier* implicitly corroborates Gaspar's argument about the insufficiency of male heteroerotic desire when he claims that "it is to be seene in all Histories, that alwaies (in a maner) wives love their husbandes better then they their wives."[38] In *Twelfth Night*, Sebastian patronizingly explains to Olivia that she (like himself) naturally loves a man.

Of the three modes of erotic desire potentially raised by Sebastian's speech to Olivia – female-to-female, female-to-male, male-to-male – it is impossible positively to determine if one is *the* natural, if one is *more* natural, or if all are *equally* natural. On this, the passage allows us to conclude, as Gregory Bredbeck concludes of the radical indeterminacy of *Sonnet* 20, only that "nature does not dictate *one* course of desire."[39] What the crux line does dictate within the context of *Twelfth Night*, I think, is that a man's desire for a woman may be the least "natural" or most problematic course of all. The objects of erotic desire in the play are men: Viola desires Orsino; Sebastian and Antonio desire each other. Cesario detects the shallowness of Orsino's "will," or sexual desire, for Olivia: "We men may say more, swear more, but indeed / Our shows are more than will: for still we prove / Much in our vows, but little in our love" (2.4.117–19).[40] Sebastian does not evince any erotic interest in Olivia; he marries her when swept away by a "flood of fortune" (4.3.11), words that recall Orsino's initial description of fancy as a devouring and fickle sea. By contrast, Sebastian expresses ardent passion when reunited with his friend: "O my dear Antonio / How have the hours racked and tortured me, / Since I have lost thee!" (5.1.216–18).

Perhaps Viola is the only woman in *Twelfth Night* who is an object of erotic desire. Yet it would appear that both Olivia and Orsino are attracted to "Cesario" as an effeminate young man, a pretty but subservient youth whom these domineering aristocrats would find an appropriate partner. Moreover, the play explicitly calls into question Orsino's love for Viola *qua* Viola. Orsino renders his marriage proposal to Viola in the contractual terms of service between master and page: "And since you call'd me master for so long, / Here is my hand; you shall from this time be / Your master's mistress" (5.1.323–25). More disturbingly, his declaration of affection for his wife, which closes the play proper, evokes what he had earlier described as his "giddy and unfirm" fancy:

> Cesario, come;
> For so you shall be while you are a man;
> But when in other habits you are seen,
> Orsino's mistress, and his fancy's queen.   (5.1.384–87)

Instead of saying, as we might expect, that Cesario's change of attire will transform him into *Viola*, Orsino's mistress, Orsino's sustained address to "Cesario" implies that he fancies seeing his page, "a man," in a woman's habit. That is, he imagines not *Viola* in her female clothes but a transvestite *Cesario*.

At this moment of comic closure, Cesario is transformed not into Viola but Ganymede: the effeminate page, the transvestite boy player, the master–mistress as his "master's mistress" (5.1.324).[41] Unlike Valerie Traub, who detects in these closing lines Orsino's anxiety about desiring *Cesario*, I detect in them his anxiety about desiring *Viola*.[42] We never actually see Cesario properly transformed into and established as Orsino's wife. Viola might succeed at swaying level in her husband's heart to the extent that she resembles the young boy he once found so attractive. But Orsino's final promise that Viola will become his "fancy's queen" – a powerful woman like Olivia, no longer a submissive boy like Cesario – might well signal the end of his erotic desire.

For Orsino as well as Scudamour, therefore, homoerotic fancy and the devaluation of women interfere in the achievement of sexually orderly marriage. Their desire for effeminate boys conforms to a pederastic model that Spenser's Masque of Cupid associates with disorderly homoeroticism. However, it is important to recognize that male homoerotic desire in *The Faerie Queene* also takes the alternative form of androphilia, or orderly love between men. In book 3, the Legend of Chastity, the Hercules–Hylas myth illustrates disorderly homoeroticism (the antithesis of the book's virtue); in book 4, the Legend of Friendship, it illustrates orderly homoeroticism (the exemplar of the book's virtue). Whereas in book 3 Hylas is presented as the object of Hercules's pederastic lust, the Ganymede to his Jove, in book 4 Hylas is presented as the coeval friend of Hercules, the Damon to his Pythias. Approaching the Temple of Venus, from which he will abduct Amoret, Scudamour encounters two groups of lovers, the first comprising a "thousand payres of lovers" who

> together by themselves did sport
> Their spotlesse pleasures, and sweet loves content.

> But farre away from these, another sort
> Of lovers lincked in true harts consent;
> Which loved not as these, for like intent,
> But on chast virtue grounded their desire,
> Farre from all fraud, or fayned blandishment;
> Which in their spirits kindling zealous fire,
> Brave thoughts and noble deedes did evermore aspire.   (4.10.26)

This second "sort" of lovers are adult men: Hercules and Hylas top the list of six exemplary male couples "tyde / In bands of friendship" whose "loves decayed never" (4.10.27). What distinguishes the love of the first group from that of the male friends? In what "intent" of love do they differ? Against the usual reading of this passage I would argue that Spenser does not distinguish here between physical heterosexual love and nonphysical male friendship, since for him "chastity" implies not sexual abstinence but devotion to a single sexual partner.[43] Spenser instead distinguishes the orderliness and durability of male friendship from the potential "fraud" or "fayned blandishment" of the other lovers. Hence the first lovers are defined by their endless discourse – "Ne ever ought but of their true loves talkt" (4.10.25) – whereas the friends are defined by the brave thoughts and noble deeds eternally inspired by love. Scudamour responds enviously to his vision of an ideal friendship in which men, "possessing" their love's desire, achieve spiritual and physical consummation with each other: "I thought there was none other heaven then this; / And gan their endlesse happinesse envye, / That being free from feare and gealosye, / Might frankely there their loves desire possesse" (4.10.28). While orderly homoeroticism seems natural, honest, and easy to possess, Scudamour's attainment of Amoret is a chore: she must be possessed by force.

That Spenser interprets the "same" myth of Hercules and Hylas antithetically in different contexts illustrates how Renaissance authors used classical mythology for particular ideological agendas. In early modern England there was no singular, authoritative text of "Ovid," let alone a single, authoritative interpretation of Ovidian myths. Any myth, through whatever hermeneutic it was understood, could be accommodated to an ideology of social order or disorder. Thus, we are always wrong to argue that mythical pairs like Damon and Pythias or Hercules and Hylas "were" or "were not" either "homosexual" or "just friends." To certain writers, even Jupiter's desire for Ganymede could be interpreted as nonsexual or spiritual. The seventeenth-century mythographer Alexander Ross called Christ "the true Ganimedes."[44] To a sensibility like Marlowe's, on the other hand, even Christ and St. John could be read as sodomites.[45] The perspective and the agenda of writer and reader will determine whether the affection of such mythical male pairs is understood as sexual or spiritual, disorderly or orderly. None of these figures, that is, can be accurately evaluated outside of a specific rhetorical and political context.

In book 4 of *The Faerie Queene*, the Hercules–Hylas myth takes one of its contexts from a didactic passage that debates the relative merits of different desires: "affection unto kindred," "raging fire of love to woman kind," and "zeale of friends combynd with virtues meet" (4.9.1). Spenser determines that "faithfull friendship" is the best relationship, since "love of soule doth love of bodie passe" (4.9.2). This implicit denial of male homoerotic lust accords with the gloss to "January" in *The Shepherd's Calendar* (1579), which claims that "pederastice," or the "chast virtue" through which one man loves another man's soul, is "much to be praeferred before gynerastice, that is the love which enflameth men with lust toward woman kind."[46] The gloss clearly distinguishes virtuous pederastice from the sin of sodomy. Nevertheless, Jonathan Goldberg has argued that the denunciation of sodomy in the gloss denies neither Hobbinol's nonsodomitical desire for Colin nor the homoerotic structures of Elizabethan patronage which their relationship reflects.[47]

In both *The Faerie Queene* and *The Shepherd's Calendar*, Spenser appears to draw a primary distinction between *disorderly male lust* and *orderly male love*. In these terms, male friendship (pederastice) must be superior to male lust for women (gynerastice). Likewise, chaste marriage must be superior to sodomy. The real question is whether male friendship is preferable to marriage.

Orpheus: homoeroticism and the rejection of women

Aside from Ganymede and Hylas, the mythological character who most directly links male homoeroticism with the obstruction of marital (hetero)sexuality is Orpheus. The Masque of Cupid may associate Scudamour with Jupiter and Hercules, but he identifies himself with Orpheus in the Temple of Venus episode of book 4. Having captured Amoret from the Temple, Scudamour once again confronts the giant Danger, who had earlier blocked his access:

> No lesse did *Daunger* threaten me with dread,
> When as he saw me, maugre all his powre,
> That glorious spoyle of beautie with me lead,
> Then *Cerberus*, when *Orpheus* did recover
> His Leman from the Stygian Princes boure.   (4.10.58)

Thomas Cain observes that in comparing himself to Orpheus, Scudamour ironically not only "draws attention to the next stage of his own story," that is, the loss of his wife to Busirane, but stains himself with the disorderly lust signified by Orpheus' loss of Eurydice in medieval interpretations of the myth.[48] In Golding's rendering of Ovid, Orpheus, following the bitter loss of Eurydice, "did utterly eschew / The woman-kynd . . . / He also taught the *Thracian* folke a stewes of Males too make / And of the flowring pryme of boayes the pleasure for too take."[49] It is fitting that Scudamour identifies with Orpheus, for the "Danger" that obstructs his access to Amoret represents the danger of his disorderly homoerotic desire. Disdaining to "creepe betweene his legs," Scudamour assaults the loathsome giant "with manhood stout" (4.10.19), and upon defeating him "did backeward looke": "And loe his hindparts, whereof heed I tooke, / Much more deformed fearefull ugly were, / Then all his former parts did earst appeare" (4.10.20). When Scudamour looks back at Danger's hindparts, he sees deformity, or sodomy. In the courtly love tradition, Danger is a stock figure who personifies the mistress's disdain of the male lover. Spenser's Danger suggests an alternative reading: one of the dangers obstructing successful heteroerotic union is the homo-erotic lust that a man must forcefully subdue. Orpheus experiences homoerotic desire as a *result* of losing his wife. Scudamour confronts such desire *before* winning his wife, only to lose her because he fails to recognize this "Daunger" when it reappears in Busirane's disorderly wedding masque (3.12.11). Seeing the dangers of homoerotic lust only by looking backwards, that is, sodomitically, Scudamour is unable to "prevent [them] with vigilant foresight" from resurfacing later on (4.10.20). As if to emphasize Scudamour's sodomitical inversion through narrative form, Spenser places the Danger episode after the chronologi-cally later Busirane episode.[50]

Spenser's allusion to Orpheus is merely one example of the way this myth was deployed in early modern England to evoke the complex ideological connection between male homoerotic desire, misogyny, and sodomy. Because of the diversity of its classical sources and medieval explications, the Orpheus myth was subject to radically divergent inter-pretations by Renaissance writers. The traditional understanding of Orpheus as a great poet, orator, and musician runs throughout the period.[51] Another tradition stresses the erotic aspects of his story, although earlier sixteenth-century treatments tend not to be explicit about Orpheus' misogyny and homoeroticism.[52] Thomas Cooper's dic-tionary entry of 1565 explains that Orpheus was murdered by women because "for the sorow of his wyfe Eurydice, he did not onely himself refuse the love of many women, and lyved a sole lyfe, but also disswaded other from the company of women."[53] Cooper's Orpheus apparently rejects not just women but love and companionship altogether. In the 1590s, the flourishing of erotic satires and mythological narratives brings Orpheus' misogyny and homoeroticism more directly to the fore.[54] A discussion of female imperfection in John Dickenson's *Shepherd's Complaint* (1596) leads to a misreading (or deliberate alteration) of the myth in which Eurydice, not Orpheus, looks back to Hades:

Euridice, which living could not bee accused of inconstancie, was after death blemished with unkindnesse, because forgetting the covenant of her returne from hell, she fondly looked backe. The silver-tongued Thracian, whom Apollo had endued with a double gift of musicke and poetrie, beeing mooved with this, hated and with hatefull disgrace disparadged the woorth of that sexe which before hee had honoured by his matchlesse Art.[55]

Although Dickenson's Orpheus rejects women entirely, he does not consequently turn to boys.

Orpheus' misogyny does produce homoerotic consequences in two verse treatments of the myth from the mid 1590s. Discontented husbands flock to Orpheus in R. B.'s *Orpheus His Journey to Hell* (1595):

> And in invective Ditties [Orpheus] daylie singes,
>   th'uncertain pleasure of unconstant Love:
> How manie woes a womans beautie bringes,
>   and into what extreames this joy doth shove
> Poore foolish men, that ere they be awarre
> Will rashlie overshoot themselves so farre.
>
> There gins he sing of secrete Loves deceites,
>   and womens fawning fickle companie.
> The outward golden shew of poysoned baytes,
>   that drawes so many men to miserie.
> And for an instance sets himselfe to shew,
> One that had suffred all this pleasing woe.
>
> Whose songs did sort unto such deepe effect,
>   as draw mens fancies from thir former wives:
> Womens vaine love beginning to neglect,
>   and in the fieldes with *Orpheus* spend their lives:
> With which sweet life they seem'd so well content,
> As made them curse the former time they spent.[56]

In itself, Orpheus' misogynist lore is nothing extraordinary: it derives from the standard Renaissance gender ideology that considered female sexuality to be inherently dangerous and uncontrollable. By drawing "mens fancies from thir former wives," Orpheus merely brings misogynist rhetoric to the logical, if extreme, conclusion of male separatism. In *Of Loves Complaint with the Legend of Orpheus and Eurydice* (1597), Orpheus' rejection of women produces a more overtly sexual consequence, the sinful practice of sodomy:

Now still he cryes to flye that weaker kinde,
And addeth base dishonour to their name,
And sayes that nature first hath them assign'd
As plagues to kindle mens destructions flame:
    whose heate once ruling in our inner parts,
    Doth never die, but with our dying harts.

But what, my chaster Muse doth blush to heare
The onely fault and sinne of this his youth,
It shames to tell unto anothers eare,
Sometimes it profits to conceale the truth;
    Better it were none knew the way to sinne,
    For knowing none, then none would enter in.

Hee in this path sette his defiled foote,
which leades unto the tree of sinne and shame,
Woe is his fruite, and wickednes his roote,
Both these he tasted, and to both he came;
    Such are the snares which craftie sinne doth lay,
    That justest men doe stumble in theyr way.

Now he doth teach the soule to sinne by Art,
And breake the Law which Nature had ordaind,
And from her auncient customs to depart,
which still ere this were kept untoucht, unstaind,
    Teaching to spoyle the flower of that kinde,
    Whose flower never yet could any find.[57]

Teaching "the soule to sinne by Art" and to break Nature's Law,
Orpheus' devilish inducements to sodomy are silenced only when the
slandered Thracian women tear him apart. For the writer of this poem,
who is courting a scornful mistress, Orpheus' monstrous rejection of
women deserves swift and violent retaliation.

It is not only in the plays and poems of early modern England that we
find male homoerotic desire or sodomy in conflict with marital
(hetero)sexuality. William Perkins's marriage manual *Christian Economy*
(1609) offers advice regarding the possibility of marital sodomy: "What if
either of the married folks commit fornication or any sin of the same
kind greater than fornication, as incest, sodomy, lying with beasts or
such like[?]" If Perkins deems marriage a "sovereign means to avoid
fornication and consequently to subdue and slake the burning lusts of
the flesh," then why does he worry that married folks might commit
sodomy?[58] In the *New Atlantis* (1627), Francis Bacon posits the simple
inadequacy of the marital bond to slake the unruly lusts of the flesh.
According to a citizen of Bensalem, the world's chastest nation, European men delay or forego marriage altogether since they "have at hand
a remedy more agreeable to their corrupt will," a seeming reference to

masturbation (alone or with other men?) or prostitution.[59] The passage goes on to condemn the resort to prostitutes by men who marry only for "alliance or portion or reputation, with some desire (almost indifferent) of issue":

> They hear you defend these things, as done to avoid greater evils, as advoutries [adulteries], deflowering of virgins, unnatural lust, and the like. But they say this is a preposterous wisdom, and they call it *Lot's offer*, who to save his guests from abusing, offered his daughters; nay, they say farther that there is little gained in this, for that the same vices and appetites do still remain and abound, unlawful lust being like a furnace, that if you stop the flames altogether, it will quench, but if you give it any vent, it will rage. As for masculine love, they have no touch of it, and yet there are not so faithful and inviolate friendships in the world again as are there. (443–44)

In short, a husband's "unlawful lust" for women might complement or even fuel his "unnatural lust" for men. That *heteroerotic* lust could be justified as a preventative to *homoerotic* lust is therefore a "preposterous" or sodomitical belief.

The logic of both Perkins's and Bacon's accounts of adultery is not the modern logic that heterosexuality and homosexuality are antithetical forms of desire, but that lust can and probably will take both heteroerotic and homoerotic forms. "Adultery," despite the modern inclination to read it straight, does not in early modern usage necessarily refer to male–female sexuality. Perkins writes in *The Foundation of Christian Religion* (1616): "To commit adultery, signifieth as much, as to doe any thing, what way soever, whereby the chastitie of our selves, or our neighbors may be stained." He furnishes examples of heteroerotic, autoerotic, and homoerotic lust.[60] In Bacon's chaste Bensalem, one finds neither courtesans nor "masculine love."[61] Yet the masculine love that Bacon places outside of his Utopia could be readily found inside his England. In his autobiography, Sir Simonds D'Ewes accuses Bacon himself of sodomy: he "desert[ed] the bed of his lady, which he accounted as the italians and turks do, a poor and mean pleasure in respect of the other."[62] Like most men in early modern England, Bacon married. It is impossible to say how many of these men, perhaps like him, found their erotic pleasures elsewhere, outside the marriage bed.

Nevertheless, we can begin to delineate the "elsewhere" in which such pleasures might have been pursued. There is evidence of male homoerotic activity in the geographically and socially accessible spaces of brothels, alehouses, taverns, and public theaters, the latter significantly located, as Steven Mullaney has demonstrated, in the unruly Liberties of London.[63] Paul Seaver records a Puritan artisan's belief that God destroyed London Bridge in 1633 as retaliation for the city's sins: "he had just heard of a group of married men in Southwark who had 'lived in the sin of buggery and were sworn brothers to it' some seven years, committing this sin on Sabbath morning at 'sermon time.' "[64] As Stephen Orgel observes in his commentary on this passage, sodomy comprehends not merely the "sin of buggery" but a range of social transgressions: "an affront to marriage, the sabbath, the church and the minister at his sermon." These married suburban men place their devotion to a sinful "brotherhood" above their marital and religious responsibilities.[65]

Other evidence of contemporary sexual practices may be found in popular ballads that admonish unthrifty husbands to avoid the lewd company of the alehouse. In one such ballad, "The Lamentation of a new-married man," a wife scolds her frequently absent husband:

> Quoth she, "You do not love me,
>   To leave me all alone;
> You must goe a gadding,
>   And I must bide at home,
> While you, among your minions,
>   Spend more than is your owne."
> *This life leads a married man.*[66]

Although the term "minion" in Renaissance usage can refer to either gender, it is often applied to men in homoerotic contexts, as in *Twelfth Night*, where Orsino calls his beloved Cesario Olivia's "minion" (5.1.123), or in Marlowe's *Edward II*, where it denotes the king's favorite, Gaveston.[67] Having transferred his love to his minions, the husband in this ballad may "spend" with other men what he should rightfully save for his wife – not only money but semen. In a similar ballad, "Robin and Kate; or, A bad husband converted by a good wife," Kate objects to her husband's visits to the alehouse: "Let not thy companions thus lewdly intice / Thy heart from thy Kate." Robin offers the dubious assurance that he seeks the company of men: "I seek not for wenches, but honest good fellowes: / A pipe of tobacco, a pot, or a jugg, / These are the sweet honies that I kisse and hugg."[68] Robin's sarcasm ("*These* are the sweet honies that I kisse"), even as it intends to deny one kind of erotic interest (in "wenches"), may nevertheless reveal another (in "fellows").

Of course, a husband could pursue male homoerotic desire closer to home. Abandoning his wife's bed, Bacon made "his servants his bed-fellows."[69] The following chapter will explore the representation of homoerotic relations between masters and servants as a function of the early modern ideologies of service and sexuality that structured the household. These ideologies structured relations between hosts and guests as well as masters and servants: in Thomas Heywood's *A Woman*

Killed with Kindness (1603), Wendoll's adultery with Anne Frankford is all the more heinous for his homoerotic relation to John Frankford, his patron and host: "I am to his body / As necessary as his digestion, / And equally do make him whole or sick."[70] Wendoll may depend on Frankford for money and lodging, but Frankford's bodily health depends upon Wendoll's physical proximity to him.

More research is required on the material conditions that facilitated homoerotic activity within marriage in early modern England. I have attempted to examine a wide range of sources for evidence of and attitudes about such activities: verse, prose, and dramatic treatments of the myths of Ganymede, Hylas, and Orpheus; Spenserian epic and Shakespearean comedy; Puritan diaries and marriage manuals; popular ballads and emblem books; philosophical texts from Erasmus to Bacon. Of course, none of these sources can tell us just how common it was for husbands in early modern England to seek homoerotic pleasure outside the marriage bed. Nor have I chosen to address the theoretically and historically distinct issue of female homoerotic desire within marriage. Here it suffices to observe that, for men at least, patriarchal privilege meant that marriage did not necessarily curtail homoerotic desire, especially since the constitution of the early modern household and the absence of a distinct ideology of heterosexuality allowed a wider range of (adulterous) sexual practices than an ahistorical notion of the family would admit.

Courtship, marriage, and the banishment of homoeroticism

Recognizing that male homoerotic desire was acknowledged in early modern England as a potentially dissonant force within marriage, we can understand the ideological motives of texts that attempt to displace, contain, or marginalize this threat to marital (hetero)sexuality. One such text is *As You Like It*. Although Shakespeare's play occupies a central place in recent scholarship on early modern gender and sexuality, prior discussions have not fully appreciated the significance of Ovidian mythology to its sexual politics. The crucial mythological subtext of *As You Like It* is the familiar story in which Jupiter replaces Hebe with Ganymede, thereby angering Juno and alienating her from the marriage bed. An analysis of this mythological subtext in the play brings into sharp relief the discordant aspects of Rosalind's enactment of Ganymede, by means of which female homoerotic desire (Celia's for Rosalind) and male homoerotic desire (Orlando's for Ganymede) are both finally rejected. The play's concluding marriages succeed to the extent that premarital female homoerotic desire and postmarital male homoerotic desire have been successfully banished.

Queer theory offers the strategy of examining the representation of mobile erotic relations instead of fixed erotic identities. Rather than considering Shakespeare's characters as the stable embodiments of mythological identities (e.g., that Rosalind "is" Ganymede), I will argue that certain characters occupy contingently the familial and erotic roles delineated by this mythological narrative. This approach to the play, inasmuch as it unmoors desire from identity, is indebted to the work of Valerie Traub. Her analysis distinguishes between gender and eroticism and severs erotic desire from erotic identity – both strategies of queer theory – and concludes that the polymorphous desire traversing *As You Like It* finally "prevents the stable reinstitution of heterosexuality, upon which the marriage plot depends."[71] Her emphasis here on the affirmative quality of the play's homoeroticism is later qualified in an indispensable essay, "The (In)Significance of 'Lesbian' Desire in Early Modern England," which argues that, because the plot of *As You Like It* moves towards heterosexual marriage and reproductivity, "an implicit power asymmetry" distinguishes the woman who enunciates and clings to homoerotic desire (Celia) from the woman who abandons it (Rosalind).[72] Traub's later reading, which still resists mapping erotic identity onto characters, moves closer to the position I take as my own – namely, that anxieties about homoeroticism in *As You Like It* are manifested and managed through the asymmetrical, shifting erotic roles taken by or imposed on characters.

The discordant connotations of the Ganymede myth should alert us to similar conflicts and anxieties that attend the comic marriage plot of *As You Like It*. Behind the disruption of familial bonds in Shakespeare's play lies the mythic disruption of Jupiter's family caused by his banishing Hebe and advancing Ganymede. Touchstone's claim to be exiled as was "Ovid . . . among the Goths" reminds us obliquely of the *Metamorphoses* as it pointedly recalls those forced into exile by the "most unnatural" behavior of Duke Frederick and Oliver (3.3.6; 4.3.122), the "tyrant Duke" and "tyrant brother" who destroy familial harmony (1.2.278). The poet William Barksted describes Jupiter's dismissal of Hebe as an act of destructive rage:

> With this he storm'd, that's Priests from altars flie
> streight banish'd *Heboe*, & the world did thinke
> To a second Chaos they should turned be,
>   the clouds for feare wept out th'immortal drinke.[73]

Like Hebe in Barksted's poem, Rosalind is "streight banish'd" by a capricious patriarch. But Celia willingly appropriates Hebe's role when she insists that, by banishing Rosalind, Duke Frederick has actually banished his own daughter. Shakespeare does not establish a firm correspondence between an Ovidian figure and a single character; rather, the Ovidian myth provides a repertory of possible erotic/familial roles which the characters draw on in different ways. Hence Rosalind not only exchanges the disgraceful position of banished Hebe for the more exalted position of adopted Ganymede, "Jove's own page" (1.3.120); she further adopts the fluid erotic (though not the angry paternal) agency of Jupiter. Just as Jupiter transfers his affections from the female sex (Hebe and Juno) to the male sex (Ganymede), so Rosalind has begun to transfer her affections from Celia to Orlando.

In the triangular structure that will develop in Arden, then, Rosalind plays both Ganymede and Jupiter. She plays Ganymede to Orlando's Jupiter – a "fair youth" wooed by a man (3.2.375); she plays Jupiter to Celia's Hebe/Juno – a "man" who turns from female to male companionship (1.3.112). It is no wonder that Celia, given the Hebe/Juno role, delays telling Rosalind of Orlando's arrival in Arden, impugns the sincerity of his love for her, and hesitates in saying the words of the mock marriage between them. At precisely the moment Rosalind confidently adopts "no worse a name" than Ganymede, Celia names her own worsened state as "Aliena" (1.3.120, 124). Whereas "Celia" suggests Hebe's divine birth and habitation, "Aliena" not only describes Celia's present alienation from her father's love, but also foreshadows her increasing alienation from Rosalind's love.

Rosalind's desire for Orlando relegates Celia's desire for her to a safely distanced past.[74] For Celia, this is an ideal past symbolized by Juno, the "*Lady of mariage, and governesse of child-birth*" by whom Roman women swore.[75] The wedding song that closes the play proclaims that "Wedding is great Juno's crown, / . . . blessed bond of board and bed" (5.4.140–41), and Celia figures her bond with Rosalind, in which they shared board and bed, as just such a marriage:

> We still have slept together,
> Rose at an instant, learn'd, play'd, eat together,
> And whereso're we went, like Juno's swans,
> Still we went coupled and inseparable.   (1.3.69–72)

Coupled like swans, Celia and Rosalind together serve under Juno, the patron goddess of female sexuality. Swans, however, were the birds not of Juno but of Venus. In the contemporary play *The Maid's Metamorphosis* (1600), Juno herself makes much of this distinction, bitterly complaining that rival Venus' "Doves and Swannes, and Sparrowes" are

prized above her own "starry Peacocks."[76] By assigning Venus' swans to
Juno, Shakespeare has Celia peacefully "couple" these often combative
goddesses of love and marriage, just as she couples herself to Rosalind.
Hence she reminds Rosalind that "thou and I am one" (1.3.93). Very
soon after Celia evokes their seemingly permanent union, however,
Rosalind takes on the role of Ganymede; during the time she plays this
role, Juno is never mentioned. Instead, allusions to Jupiter proliferate,
beginning with the first words Rosalind speaks as Ganymede: "O Jupiter,
how weary are my spirits!" (2.4.1). Ganymede swears twice by his master
and lover – "Jove! Jove!" (2.4.57), "O most gentle Jupiter" (3.2.152) – and
praises as "Jove's tree" the oak under which Orlando is found (3.2.232).
As the latter instance makes especially clear – not least to Celia –
Ganymede's evocations of Jupiter signal the shift in Rosalind's affections
from her childhood companion to the man she hopes to marry.

In conjunction with the substitution of Orlando for Celia (and of
Jupiter for Juno), a more purely symbolic or emblematic substitution
facilitates the courtship between Rosalind and Orlando. Even before
Rosalind impersonates a boy, a role that allows her to couch her
heteroerotic desire for Orlando as a homoerotic desire for Jupiter, the
sport of wrestling, an unmistakably masculine activity otherwise unavailable to her except as a spectator, offers her a language of desire. The
spectacle of vigorous male–male combat staged before Rosalind not only
occasions heteroerotic desire but becomes a central metaphor for it.
Witnessing Orlando's victory over Charles, Rosalind confesses that he
has "overthrown / More than your enemies"; he too feels "overthrown"
and "master[ed]" by "Charles or something weaker" (1.2.244–45,
249–50). Orlando is mastered not by Charles, of course, but by the
weaker young woman who must "wrestle" with her own new affections,
which "take the part of a better wrestler than [herself]" (1.3.20–21).
Orlando's attribution of his erotically induced confusion to *Charles*,
while comic, signals a transition from wrestling as a male–male sport
conducted in the court to wrestling as a figure for the male–female sport
pursued in the forest. In Arden, Celia confirms this transferal by
describing Orlando to Rosalind as the person "that tripped up the
wrestler's heels and your heart, both in an instant" (3.2.208–10).
Rosalind, in turn, recalls the wrestling match as an erotic as well as a
competitive event: "Looks he as freshly as he did the day he wrestled?"
(3.2.226–27). The subsequent exchanges between Ganymede and
Orlando constitute mental and emotional wrestling matches that substitute the friction of physical struggle between men with the friction of
linguistic struggle. In short, once Charles is "borne out" of the play
(1.2.209 sd), Ganymede emerges as Orlando's new wrestling partner.

That this substitution requires the complete physical and verbal incapaci-
tation of Charles illustrates emblematically the point made narratively by
the alienation of Celia and analogically by the discordant aspects of the
Ganymede myth: Rosalind and Orlando's movement towards marriage
implies strife and loss as well as concord and pleasure.

With her discovery of Orlando's presence in Arden comes Rosalind's
first intimation that her impersonation might involve loss or compromise.
Yet despite her initial dismay – "Alas the day! What shall I do with my
doublet and hose?" (3.2.215–16) – she soon realizes that the disguise
provides certain opportunities. Playing an "effeminate" (3.2.398) boy
who can plausibly impersonate Rosalind allows her to carry on a
flirtation with Orlando. At the same time, playing a "saucy lackey"
allows her to test his qualifications as a lover and husband, to ascertain
whether he will be like or unlike most men, who are "April when they
woo, December when they wed" (3.2.290–91; 4.1.139–40). Ganymede
initially questions the sincerity of Orlando's publicly declared passion:
"you are rather point-device in your accoutrements; as loving yourself
than seeming the lover of any other" (3.2.372–74). This skepticism about
Orlando's effusiveness is understandable, considering that the only time
Rosalind spoke to him in her own person, he neither thanked her for her
gift of a chain nor reciprocated her compliments. Her plan to "cure"
Orlando of his lovesickness seems actually designed to cure her own
doubts about his sincerity and constancy: "I would cure you, if you
would but call me Rosalind and come every day to my cote and woo me"
(3.2.414–15). The plan instates a daily regimen in which Ganymede elicits
and Orlando performs his love for Rosalind.

The problem, of course, is that it becomes extremely difficult under
these circumstances to ascertain the meaning or sincerity of Orlando's
performance. This is where the Ganymede role seems to work against
Rosalind, producing the very uncertainties about Orlando's desire that it
seems meant to resolve. For instance, when Orlando misses his appoint-
ment with Ganymede, Rosalind has trouble interpreting his failure: "But
why did he swear he would come this morning and comes not?"
(3.4.17–18). Has Orlando stood up Rosalind? Or has he merely stood up
Ganymede? Would he behave more reliably with the actual Rosalind?
How can she tell? Although the ambiguity of playing Ganymede-playing-
Rosalind thwarts Rosalind's ability to interpret Orlando's neglect, the
disguise does allow her safely to rebuff him for it. Ganymede's imperious
dismissal of Orlando is a bluff that the "real" Rosalind could hardly
afford to risk: "You a lover! And you serve me such another trick, never
come in my sight more" (4.1.37–39). Playing multiply gendered roles
enables Rosalind to test, observe, and correct the man she wants to

marry; yet at the same time it prevents her from determining whether or not he actually loves her.

To Rosalind's string of questions regarding Orlando's apparent neglect – "But have I not cause to weep?" "Do you think so?" "Not true in love?" (3.4.4, 20, 24) – Celia furnishes some rather discouraging answers. Repeatedly maintaining that Orlando is not in love, Celia observes that "the oath of a lover is no stronger than the word of a tapster. They are both the confirmer of false reckonings" (3.4.27–29). Celia's *non sequitur* – "He attends here in the forest on the Duke your father" (3.4.29–30) – associates Orlando's falseness to Rosalind with his loyalty to Duke Senior and reminds Rosalind that she is competing with her father for Orlando's time and devotion. Enticing Orlando from her father's side is no small task, given how lovingly Duke Senior welcomes Orlando into his all-male forest community (note how Rowland de *Boys*, the "name of the father" that unites Duke Senior and Orlando, contains a bilingual pun uniting *boys* and *bois* [woods]). The wifeless Duke takes no women to Arden. He is initially accompanied by "three or four loving lords," his "co-mates and brothers in exile," and joined later by "many young gentlemen" who "flock to him every day, and fleet the time carelessly as they did in the golden world" (1.1.100–1; 2.1.1; 1.1.117–19). For Charles, who reports the Duke's situation in the play's opening scene, Arden replicates the golden world of Robin Hood and his "merry men" (1.1.115). However, Arden recalls as well the all-male golden world of Orpheus as it is described in the contemporary poems discussed above.

The male communities of Duke Senior and Orpheus are linked by way of Ganymede, at the level of Ovidian allusion: Ganymede's story, so central to Shakespeare's play, is told in the *Metamorphoses* by Orpheus, who celebrates the "prettie boyes / That were the derlings of the Gods."[77] If we recall that in Ovid – and in certain of his Renaissance imitators – misogyny drives Orpheus towards male friends and lovers, we can understand how this myth's resonance with the male forest community of *As You Like It* contributes to Rosalind's uncertainty. Whom or what does Orlando really love: Rosalind? the idea of marrying Rosalind? the public pose of a Petrarchan lover? himself? Ganymede? Ganymede's impersonation of Rosalind? the company of other men? The myth becomes important in appreciating Rosalind's doubts about Orlando because, as R. B.'s poem *Orpheus His Journey to Hell* indicates, Orpheus' misogyny and homoeroticism do not always seem aberrant or reprehensible to Renaissance writers. R. B. sympathetically portrays Orpheus as the king of a homoerotic golden world tragically destroyed by female vengeance and vainglory. When Orpheus lures the local husbands to his retreat, the abandoned wives grieve for "their fading glorie" and plot revenge. Having put together their "busie head[s]," the women "flocke incontinent" to Orpheus,

> And finding him alone without his traine,
> Upon him fall they all with might and maine.
>
> And with confused weapons beat him downe,
>   quenching their angrie thirst with his warm blood:
> At whose untimely death though heavens frowne,
>   yet they defend their quarrell to be good,
> And for their massacre this reason render,
> He was an enemie unto their gender.[78]

Ambushing their defenseless foe, these violently self-righteous women seem merely to confirm Orpheus' tales of the misery that women inflict upon men.

R. B.'s polarity between a loving male community and an invasive, disorderly, female sexuality suggests the obstacle that the all-male golden world of Duke Senior's court presents to Rosalind in her attempt to assay the sincerity of Orlando's love. At least one contemporary of Shakespeare believed that classical idealizations of male love could actually have the Orphic effect of dissuading Englishmen from marriage. Translator Philemon Holland, reflecting upon Plutarch's dialogue "Of Love" remarks:

This Dialogue is more dangerous to be read by yoong men than any other Treatise of Plutarch, for that there be certeine glaunces heere and there against honest marriage, to upholde indirectly and underhand, the cursed and detestable filthinesse covertly couched under the name of the Love of yoong boyes.[79]

Holland worries that the misogynist promotion of male homoeroticism might well divert the sexual desires of impressionable young men away from wives and towards boys. Holland's fear is, I would suggest, Rosalind's own.

If Rosalind competes with her own father for Orlando's attention during their courtship, she also risks furthering the Orphic project of making a pretty young Ganymede seem erotically attractive to her future husband. My discussion of Scudamour and Orsino suggested the danger that a husband's desire for boys posed to orderly marital (hetero)sexuality. By making herself into Ganymede and Orlando into Jupiter, Rosalind seems to choose the one name that would most inescapably suggest or even promote her husband's disorderly pederastic desires.[80] If the Ganymede myth provided a vocabulary for articulating the early modern phenomenon of marital strife arising from male homoerotic desire, Ganymede himself had his early modern counterparts in the young male servants who populated the public and private worlds of Shakespeare's

London.[81] Homoerotic desire for a male subordinate informs the early modern institution of personal service for which the myth provided a recognized classical analogue. Orlando and Ganymede are therefore legible as a sexually involved gallant and page – a familiar couple in the "street, the ordinary, and stage" of late sixteenth-century London, if we are to believe the satires contemporary with *As You Like It*.[82] This kinship of Rosalind/Ganymede with the London ganymede or sexually available page is further suggested by Adam's curious disappearance from the play. Why should Adam suddenly vanish only after Orlando has encountered the "pretty youth" in the forest (3.2.328)? A possible explanation for the disappearance of old servingmen appears in Marston's play *Histrio-Mastix* (1599, exactly contemporary with *As You Like It*), in which faithful old retainers blame their former masters' sons for replacing them with erotically alluring "rascall boyes."[83]

Rosalind therefore needs to insure that by playing Ganymede (the enticing page) when she woos, she will not play Juno (the rejected wife) when she weds. That is, she needs to reassure herself that her husband will not one day replace her with an actual boy. Immediately following their mock marriage, Rosalind tests Orlando's reaction to the threat of being outwitted and cuckolded by his wife. Yet, I want to argue, she simultaneously tries to determine if Orlando will express a homoerotic desire for Ganymede, whom he has just "married," or if he will remain constant to the absent Rosalind whom Ganymede portrays. Ganymede first warns Orlando that Rosalind will "laugh like a hyen" when he wants to sleep (4.1.147–48). Why is the laughing hyena an analogue for the wife who disturbs her husband's peace in bed? According to medieval and Renaissance animal lore, the hyena experienced an annual sex change; for this reason, as John Boswell has shown, it was commonly viewed as the symbolic type of an adulterer or homosexual seducer.[84] This wonderful ability to transform itself earns the hyena a brief mention in Ovid's *Metamorphoses*: "interchaungeably it one whyle dooth remayne / A female, and another whyle becommeth male againe."[85] By comparing herself to the mocking, adulterous hyena, Rosalind can elicit Orlando's reaction to the possibility of being cuckolded. At the same time, mentioning the hermaphroditism and homosexual behavior commonly associated with the hyena could provoke Orlando into expressing his possible pleasure at finding a "hyena" in his bed. Like the hyena, Rosalind switches between female and male genders, between the forms of Rosalind and Ganymede: might Orlando be tempted to switch his wife for an actual "ganymede" – a page or household servant – in their marriage bed? Reassuringly, Orlando fails to respond with enthusiasm to the amorphous hyena as a figure for the possible homoerotic alternatives to marital (hetero)sexuality: "But will my Rosalind do so?" (4.1.149).

Approaching the problem of Orlando's potential homoeroticism from a different angle, Rosalind next raises the threat of adulterous sexuality outside the household. Ganymede warns Orlando that he might find his wife "going to your neighbour's bed." When Orlando wonders what she could say to excuse her infidelity, Ganymede quips, "Marry to say she came to seek you there" (4.1.160, 162). Tellingly, Rosalind fails to specify the sex of the neighbor who occupies the bed. She appears to be alerting Orlando that what he might do with another wife, she might do with another husband. Yet her ambiguous phrasing also recognizes the possibility that Orlando as well as she might be caught in bed with the same neighbor – the necessarily *male* neighbor with whom she threatens to cuckold him. Ganymede's wit conveys Rosalind's warning: if you commit adultery with the man nextdoor, she implies, you give me an occasion and an excuse to do the same. Rosalind fights sodomy with shrewishness.

Ironically, Ganymede's insistence on the jealousy, inconstancy, and shrewishness of wives risks promoting the very misogyny that, in the Orphic model, turns husbands away from wives to the company of men or boys. Ganymede claims to have once performed an essentially Orphic role by curing a lover's passion for a woman – the same role he offers to play for Orlando. By means of a stereotypically misogynist impersonation of this man's mistress, Ganymede supposedly converted the former lover of women into an Orpheus-figure himself, a recluse who lived in "a nook merely monastic" (3.2.408–9). Orlando does not know that this is Rosalind's fabrication; from his perspective both the substance and the ultimate rhetorical effect of Ganymede's misogynist satire – turning Orlando's lovesick predecessor into a gender separatist – may seem credible enough. As Celia complains to Rosalind, "You have simply misused our sex in your love-prate" (4.1.191–92). As long as Rosalind continues to misuse her sex by playing a misogynist Ganymede, she will never achieve the kind of clarity about Orlando's desires that she so desperately requires.

Whereas Rosalind struggles continuously and anxiously to direct the course of Orlando's desire, even anticipating his possible marital infidelities, the play rechannels Celia's homoerotic desire with far less subtlety. Rosalind's unbelievably hyperbolic account of Celia's attraction to Oliver suggests how ideologically motivated is the play's need to match her with a marriageable partner. Late in the play, Ganymede informs Orlando that Celia and Oliver have fallen instantly in love: "And in these degrees have they made a pair of stairs to marriage, which they will climb

incontinent, or else be incontinent before marriage. They are in the very
wrath of love, and they will together" (5.2.36–40). Attributing to Celia
and Oliver a sexual impropriety characteristic of rakish men and simple
women (e.g., Touchstone and Audrey), Rosalind represents Celia not as
her loving childhood companion or devoted "sister," but as a bride
impatient for the pleasures of the wedding night. By so describing Celia,
Rosalind not only marks the end of their homoerotic friendship, thereby
positioning both Celia and herself as marriageable women; she also
provides Orlando with a model of marriage based in vigorous heteroerotic desire.

Yet female homoeroticism has not been eliminated so much as
transferred onto Phebe, who falls in love with Rosalind/Ganymede as
immediately as Celia falls in love with Oliver. Phebe, of course, believes
that she has fallen in love with a boy named Ganymede. Nevertheless, as
Valerie Traub has convincingly argued, what Phebe finds alluring are the
particularly "feminine" features of Ganymede's physique.[86] Phebe's
desires for Rosalind/Ganymede are at once homoerotic and heteroerotic.
More to the point, her desires for this unavailable object are ridiculed
and ultimately rejected. It is through this rejection that the role of Hebe
formerly occupied by Aliena is transferred to Phebe, whose name
incorporates Hebe's own. Ganymede's initial admonishment of Phebe
contains the only mention of a mother in a play that continuously
returns to fathers: "Who might be your mother, / That you insult, exult,
and all at once, / Over the wretched? What though you have no beauty
. . . ?" (3.5.35–37). The implication that Phebe derives her inflated pride
from her mother recalls Hebe's status as the daughter of Juno, whose
bird was the conventionally proud peacock. In the medieval poem
"Ganymede and Hebe," Ganymede deflates Hebe's pride through a
gendered and racialized discourse of ugliness – "a vile old woman with
the hand of a Moor – / A shrew like this" – much as Rosalind/Ganymede
disparages Phebe's "inky brows," "black silk hair," "bugle eyeballs,"
and "Ethiop words" (3.5.46–47; 4.3.35).[87] Phebe is humiliated for her
folly in pursuing a "boy" who does not love women (Ganymede) and
who actually is a woman (Rosalind). Whereas female homoerotic desire
had once been a source of strength for Celia in her union with Rosalind,
it compromises Phebe's power to negotiate her own marriage. Barred
from wedding Rosalind, Phebe is required to accept Silvius: "You to his
love must accord, / Or have a woman to your lord" (5.4.132–33).

When she discards Ganymede, Rosalind is simultaneously released
from her promise to marry Phebe and enabled to marry Orlando.
Whereas Viola becomes a Ganymede at the end of *Twelfth Night*,
Ganymede is banished at the end of *As You Like It*. Banishing the boy

who disrupts Juno's marriage, Rosalind reenters with Hymen, the god of marriage, who presides over her reunion with Orlando as if divine intervention were necessary to guarantee the permanence of a marriage so precariously fashioned through homoerotic courtship. Significantly, when Juno's name returns for the second time in the play, the goddess is no longer linked with Venus as the patroness of women and protector of a female–female couple. She now appears as the goddess of marriage, linked with Hymen, who assures the fertility of male–female couples:

> Wedding is great Juno's crown,
> O blessed bond of board and bed.
> 'Tis Hymen peoples every town;
> High wedlock then be honoured.   (5.4.140–43)

The banishment of Ganymede and Jupiter from the play seems to signal the banishment of the male homoeroticism instrumental in Rosalind's courtship of Orlando but potentially disruptive to their marital harmony. Moreover, with the official sanction of Celia's desire for Oliver and the displacement of Hebe's role to the humiliated Phebe, youthful female homoeroticism no longer obstructs noble maidens' placement within the reproductive marital economy.

Hymen's marital "bands" are further secured by the epilogue, which disavows the homoerotic mobility that earlier served to orchestrate individual figures into marriageable couples (5.4.128). It seems impossible to fix the speaker of the epilogue as female or male, Rosalind or Ganymede, the "lady" of the play or the boy who played her. But while this fluidly gendered speaker disrupts what Catherine Belsey calls "sexual difference," he/she nevertheless conjures up a consistently heteroerotic model of sexual desire, directly addressing the audience as women who love men and men who love women:

> I charge you, O women, for the love you bear to men, to like as much of this play as please you. And I charge you, O men, for the love you bear to women – as I perceive by your simpering none of you hates them – that between you and the women the play may please.   (5.4.209–14)

Not even an appeal to the collapse of gender difference (and thus of the distinction between homoerotic and heteroerotic relations) produced by the boy actor/Rosalind/Ganymede can deny that these words not only clearly distinguish between actual men and women playgoers but direct them into heteroerotic exchanges. The epilogue presents male heteroerotic desire in particular as a completely transparent and universal phenomenon: "I perceive by your simpering none of you [men] hates them [women]." There is simply no acknowledgment that desire among these men and women might also circulate homoerotically. Queer theory, however, allows us to recognize the epilogue's conceptual division between gender identity (multiple and fluid, at least for the boy actor) and erotic desire (singular and fixed, at least among the playgoers).

A note of contingency is seemingly injected into heteroerotic fixity when the boy actor confesses to his male spectators, "If I were a woman, I would kiss as many of you as had beards that pleased me," for he at least acknowledges the possibility of erotic contact with these men (5.4.214–16). Moreover, we may assume that, at the Globe, the boy playing Rosalind/Ganymede would have been complemented by an adult actor (though one with "but a little beard" [3.2.208]) playing Orlando, thus replicating in the casting the homoerotic roles of the plot.[88] The epilogue's metadramatic self-reflexiveness might well remind the audience that when Rosalind played a boy, she was perhaps not adding a layer of disguise so much as stripping one away, revealing the homoerotic foundations underpinning the play's marital structure.

Yet despite the contemporary belief that boy players, also known as ganymedes, erotically delighted adult men both onstage and off-, this particular boy player in effect refuses, in the epilogue, to realize his homoerotic potentiality. He would have sexual contact with a man only "if" he were a woman, which he is not, even if he has just played one and even if boys are like women. The epilogue's *if* serves not like the earlier *if*s in the play to promote "erotic contingency" – the sense that anything goes – but to relegate it to what has gone before.[89] Those *if*s were instrumental in arranging the various couplings between the "appropriate" partners. Once the marriages have transpired onstage, the virtue of the epilogue's *if* is to suggest that homoerotic play has been left behind: in courtship, in adolescence, in Arden, in the theater itself. The epilogue thus redirects attention from Rosalind's erotic play with the conditional to the erotic conditions of playing Rosalind. The actor's homoerotic flirtation is playful precisely because he is figuring homoeroticism *as* play, as dramatic device. His playing the alluring ganymede for male spectators constitutes a "kind offer" designed to solicit their applause (5.4.219); Rosalind likewise plays Ganymede for Orlando to accomplish her immediate (erotic) designs. But the actor reminds these men that he really is neither woman nor ganymede offstage. Just as Orlando must leave Arden without Ganymede, so these male spectators are encouraged to relinquish to the theater (and to the Arden still represented there at play's end) the fantasy of kissing an attractive ganymede.

In short, the epilogue not only reveals the homoeroticism of the theater but attempts to establish the theatricality of homoeroticism. Having so openly staged male homoerotic courtship, the play discourages male spectators from identifying with the sodomitical marital role of Jupiter once offered to Orlando. Instead, male homoerotic desire is finally offered as a retrospective theatrical pleasure. This anxiety about appropriate marital sexuality and comic form explains the epilogue's tendentious promotion of heteroerotic bonds among its audience. Of course, what an actual audience makes of the gender/sexual ideology of the epilogue might exceed the text's explicit attempt to reassert hetero-erotic desire. Weren't there any ganymedes in the Globe audience, pages who had sexual relations primarily with men? Weren't there any Orlandos, whose simpering for women was indistinguishable from their simpering for boys? Could such a spectator, attuned to (or identified with) the kind of homoerotic desire represented in the play, assume that Orlando might indeed play adulterous Jupiter to Rosalind's rejected Juno?

If we recognize the possibility that female homoerotic desire could forestall marital courtship, or that male homoerotic desire could interfere with marital harmony, we can see that the homoerotic desires banished in *As You Like It* could have taken other courses. I hope to have demonstrated that the contradictions in early modern gender and sexual ideologies open the space for a critique of the "naturalness" of the marital (hetero)sexuality that appears to coalesce at the end of Shake-speare's romantic comedy. Indeed, the successful comic conclusion of *As You Like It*'s final configuration of male–female couples largely depends on our assent to an ideological imperative, the epilogue's "charge" that men love women, women love men, and that between men and women "the play may please." The epilogue intimates that the play will please to the extent that heteroerotic play pleases its audience. For queer readers, then, such (a) play may not please. I would like to believe that my efforts to queer the family in early modern England will prevent readers from responding with uncritical pleasure to the epilogue's heteroerotic inter-pellation, and will perhaps offer another kind of pleasure to certain readers. Such a queer perspective would mean no longer accepting as simply natural, psychologically inevitable, or blithely comedic – for our time or Shakespeare's – the play's displacement of male and female homoeroticism from the scene of marriage and the formation of the "family."

Finally, more is at stake in my analysis than a queer distrust of "the family" and familial metaphors – although such distrust is certainly justified by the ongoing political and legal assaults against gays and lesbians undertaken in the name of "family values" and the "traditional family." In *The Anti-social Family*, Michèle Barrett and Mary McIntosh argue from a socialist feminist perspective that familial ideology actually impairs other forms of communality and solidarity: "the stronger and more supportive families are expected to be, the weaker the other supportive institutions outside of them become."[90] As in Boose's essay on the "Family of Shakespeareans," recourse to familial language for describing social communities like academia not only erases the disjuncture Barrett and McIntosh find between "the family" and "the community" but perpetuates, however unintentionally, a conservative and naturalizing definition of the heterosexual nuclear family. As gay historian Jeffrey Weeks observes, the "family is potent as a trope even in the hands of those whose adherence to a traditional model is dubious. The language of the family pervades our thinking about private life."[91] To Weeks's insight, I would add that the language of the family also pervades – hence limits – our thinking about public life: not only the notion of professional life that we construct for ourselves as a community of Renaissance scholars but also the notion of domestic life that we construct for early modern England, a construction in which Shakespeare's comedies for the public theater enjoy such a familiar place.

The homoerotics of mastery

In the early years of the seventeenth century, playwrights were fond of constructing satiric plots in which a clever "wit" schemed to establish mastery over a foolish "ass." The mastery takes various forms – financial, erotic, social, or intellectual dominance – but the "wit" typically possesses what Theodore Leinwand describes as a glamorous self-confidence based on his high social status and ability to employ "exemplary ingenuity" against fools and gulls.[1] Obviously, the "wit" is named for the intellectual power that equips him to control himself and master others. Yet what remains to be explored is why the satiric wittiness that exposes the folly of the "ass" so frequently focuses on the ass – an overdetermined part of the body in which sexual, sadistic, and scatological activities converge.

Anality becomes the vehicle for satire in a surprising number of comedies. In *Satiromastix* (1602) Dekker scorns a rival playwright by having Asinus call Horace (that is, Jonson) a "ningle."[2] The anal economy of Dekker's play demotes Pithias, Damon's noble friend of legend, to "Pithyasse" (1.2.332). Jonson himself frequently uses anality as a mode of abuse and humiliation. In *The Case is Altered* (1598) Juniper brands Valentine his "Ingle," while miserly Jaques buries his gold under horse dung.[3] *The Alchemist* (1610) is a persistently anal play. "I fart at thee" (1.1.1), Subtle's opening scoff at Face, is only the first of many instances in which a character asserts dominance by evoking the lower body. Kastril likewise threatens Dame Pliant – "Asse, my suster, / Goe kusse him . . . / I'll thrust a pinne i' your buttocks else" (4.4.73–75) – and Dapper nearly suffocates in a privy. Although Jonson is particularly fond of anal tropes, they derive not from a psychological quirk unique to him but from the broader culture, as indicated by the presence of Bottom the ass in Shakespeare's *A Midsummer Night's Dream* (1595) or by the Glisters and Purges in Middleton's *The Family of Love* (1603).[4]

These plays might be illuminated by an examination of the ideological and dramatic use of scatological grotesque, much as Gail Kern Paster has discussed anal purging in *The Alchemist* and *A Midsummer Night's Dream*.[5] However, my primary interest is to remark how the ass becomes an especially potent signifier for the relation between social power and eroticism in early seventeenth-century comedy. Although "ass" and "arse" are not etymologically related, both Eric Partridge and Frankie Rubinstein observe that "ass" was available as a homonymic pun for "arse" in early modern England. Partridge cites several such bawdy Shakespearean uses of "ass"; Rubinstein explains that Shakespeare and his contemporaries "used 'ass' to pun on . . . the ass that bears a burden and the arse that bears or carries in intercourse."[6] "Ass" can signify at once the beast of burden and the bodily locus of disciplinary/sexual subordination: a convergence of servitude and eroticism that becomes particularly meaningful within the early modern discourse of male service.[7] Although historical and literary scholarship has begun to examine the homoerotic aspects of service in early modern England, dramatic representations of homoerotic relations between masters and servants remain largely unexplored, despite the importance of mastery to satiric plots. In a significant number of plays by Jonson, Chapman, and Middleton, characters attempt to achieve their erotic and social ambitions through what I am calling the *homoerotics of mastery*. This term conveys two kinds of power dynamics. Primarily, it points to the homoerotic potentiality within the master–servant power structure, a potentiality that may be activated to accomplish a witty scheme. More broadly, it recognizes the importance of homoerotic relations within satiric plots of mastery.

By focusing on the ass and the tropes of eroticism and submission that give it social meaning, I hope to accomplish two goals, one general and one specific. First, I want to demonstrate that a historicist analysis – of rhetorical strategies (satire, metatheatrical commentary, irony); of cultural discourses (concerning theatricality, social status, inversion); and of stage practices (lying down, embracing, kissing, role-playing, cross-dressing) – can reveal the centrality to this drama of the homoeroticism that has been invisible to dominant criticism for so long. Renaissance playwrights used terms like "preposterous" and "monstrous" – as well as fashioning preposterous situations and monstrous characters – to signify disorderly sexual practices that could not be represented on stage. We need to attend to the discourse of sexuality in these texts, especially since terms like "ingle" and "ganymede" reveal the power differentials common to the early modern organization of service and homoeroticism.

My more specific aim is to argue that early seventeenth-century drama manifests an anxious awareness that the homoerotic conventions and power structures informing relations of service could be manipulated not only for the master's profit, but for the servant's, either in collaboration with or at the expense of the master, thus challenging social order. I attribute this anxiety in part to the social and economic transformations in the institution of service during this period, and to resultant uncertainties about the shifting boundaries of power and propriety between master and servant. Briefly, personal service was gradually developing from a patronage system employing gentleman retainers into a modern wage system employing a more diverse population of nongentle servants, with a resultant decline in the perceived dignity and "familial" status of the servant.[8] At the same time that these transformations were destabilizing relations of service, cultural representations of homoeroticism were becoming more widespread and specific.[9] In particular, the satiric texts of the late 1590s did much to disseminate the disorderly terms and character types upon which Jonson, Chapman, and Middleton drew for their satiric comedies.

The satires of late sixteenth-century England depict sexual relationships based on lust, deceit, self-interest, or economic exchange, typically within an urban context.[10] Following the lead of verse satires, with their "affinity for sodomitical allusions," satiric comedies expose the sexual and social transgressions arising from the eroticized bonds of domination and dependency between masters and servants.[11] Jonson's *Every Man Out of His Humor* (1599), *Volpone* (1606), *Epicoene* (1609), and *The Alchemist* together delineate the social conditions under which orderly male hierarchical bonds might or might not be transformed into disorderly homoeroticism or "sodomy."

Although women are marginal to the concerns of *Every Man Out of His Humor* and *Volpone*, they contribute more fully to the complex dynamics between masters and servants in other plays. In Chapman's *The Gentleman Usher* (1602), a disorderly homoerotic friendship between a prince and a male household servant at once facilitates and threatens the prince's marriage to an aristocratic woman. Women are even more central to the homoerotic economies of Middleton's *Michaelmas Term* (1605) and *No Wit, No Help Like a Woman's* (1611). *Michaelmas Term* shows how a wife can disrupt a male homoerotics of mastery; the wife in *No Wit, No Help* goes further, fashioning her own female homoerotics of mastery. By dissociating female homoerotic mastery from "sodomitical" disorder, *No Wit, No Help* reveals the ideological process by which the threat of female homoerotic transgression could be neutralized in early modern England. By contrast, the sodomitical effects generated by male masters and servants in plays such as *Volpone* and *The Gentleman Usher* tend to linger and stick.

In the aggregate, Jonson, Chapman, and Middleton dramatize the problems confronting those who would retain mastery within and over a shifting social and economic institution. At what point does a master's affection for a servant diminish or undermine the master's power? How might the homoerotic affection that normally subordinates a servant work in other situations to empower the servant? When does homo-eroticism become sodomy?

Whipping asses: Jonson's homoerotics of mastery

In the literature and drama of the 1590s, male homoeroticism was a hot topic. Part of its appeal, no doubt, can be attributed to the novelty of the social, ideological, and linguistic developments responsible for the new ways of signifying male–male relations in the last decade of the sixteenth century. Steve Brown has found that the words "ganymede," "ingle," and "catamite" first appeared in English texts in 1591, 1592, and 1593 respectively.[12] Richard Barnfield's love poems to Ganymede appeared in 1594 and 1595; the verse satires of Guilpin, Middleton, and Marston attacked urban gallants and their prostitute ganymedes in 1598 and 1599.[13] When the Blackfriars Children resumed playing in 1600, Jonson had three of their "fine enghles" erotically banter in the induction to *Cynthia's Revels* (1600), his first play for the company. As for the public theaters, the Chamberlain's Men put Ganymede in their newly built Globe with *As You Like It* (1599). But Shakespeare's company played homoerotic parts in a different, less discussed, inaugural event of 1599, Jonson's first "Comicall Satyre" and first play at the Globe, *Every Man Out of His Humor*.

Perhaps because it was his first "Comicall Satyre," Jonson took some rather laborious steps to ensure that his audience and readers would understand the curious nature of *Every Man Out of His Humor*. The continuous onstage presence of a metadramatic chorus (Cordatus and Mitis) provides a running commentary on the justness of Jonson's plot and character developments. In the lengthy induction, the authorial Asper presents a model by which we can understand the punitive nature of the satirical action that drives the play:

> Well I will scourge those apes;
> And to these courteous eyes oppose a mirrour,
> As large as is the stage, whereon we act:
> Where they shall see the times deformitie
> Anatomiz'd in every nerve, and sinnew,
> With constant courage, and contempt of feare.   (ind., 117–22)

The passage makes several conventional moves: the familiar put-down "apes," the metadramatical image of holding the mirror up to nature, the metaphor of the satirist as a surgeon who "anatomiz[es]" the "times deformitie" in order to rid the social body of infectious matter. With characteristic Jonsonian anality, Asper threatens to give these apes "pills to purge" (ind., 175).

Despite the conventional nature of his threats, however, Asper reveals much about the particular concerns of the highly unconventional play that follows. Asper's reiterated desire to scourge fops to their bare sinews establishes the play's homosocial economy and ideology of masculinity. For Cordatus, aristocratic masculinity manifests itself in the "sinowie, and altogether un-affected graces" of the true courtier (2.6.157). At the other end of the social scale, common men like Shift can get the "name of manhood" by swaggering about and claiming to have fought in the Low Countries (4.5.28). Masculinity resides in the musculature of the gentleman's unpretentious breeding or of the soldier's physical valor. Men such as Asper, Macilente, and Carlo display their masculinity through the biting wit they direct to and against other men. Shift's exposure as an impostor is appropriately punctuated by Carlo's threat to rack his companions' "sinewes asunder" with slander if they fail to meet him for dinner (5.3.88). Jonson envisions satire as a fundamentally masculine mode, the public verbal lashing of every man who is out of a properly masculine humor.

If satire works to chastise unmanly men, it also serves to extol masculine men. The implied ideal society of much Jonsonian satire would be constituted not through orderly courtship and marriage rituals between men and women, but through the homosocial fellowship of aggressive male wits.[14] Jonson celebrates the intimate bonding of wits in *Every Man in His Humor*, *Epicoene*, *The Alchemist*, and *The Devil is an Ass* (1616), whose Eustace Manly renounces women altogether. Compared to Jonson's better-known homosocial comedies, *Every Man Out of His Humor* may suffer in critical appreciation because of its dearth of wits and preponderance of asses. It features no character named "Truewit," "Lovewit," or "Wittipol," whose ingenuity might attract our admiration or whose master scheme might unify the plot. Humor afflicts every man in the play, even those who are astute enough, like the envious Macilente or the scurrilous Carlo, to detect and purge the humors of others. While the more witty characters sometimes achieve mastery over the more foolish characters, then, no-one is exempt from being mastered in turn.

These men are put into their humors by homosocial emulation, camaraderie, and rivalry. In *Every Man in His Humor* Jonson defines "humor" as "a gentleman-like monster, bred, in the speciall gallantrie of our time, by affectation; and fed by folly" (3.4.20–22). The most foolish humors involve conspicuous self-fashioning, failed attempts to master the codes of courtly manners and attire. Fungoso, a law student, spends himself into debt trying to acquire the ever-shifting outfits modeled by Fastidious Briske. Both Briske, a "Neat, spruce, affecting Courtier" (36), and Sogliardo, an "essentiall Clowne" (78), hire male servants as a step to mastering social forms. Briske keeps a page, mimics courtly language and fashion, and falsely boasts of his popularity among great lords and ladies. In his desperation to become a gentleman, Sogliardo solicits advice on fashionable conduct, purchases a coat of arms, and employs a follower to teach him how to smoke. Each man keeps a male servant as a means of identifying, displaying, and promoting his social aspirations. In Jonson's satire, these servants serve a contrary purpose: the page signifies Briske's effeminacy and the follower exposes Sogliardo's baseness.[15]

Briske's effeminacy involves him with women, but not in the way of romantic comedy. The seventeenth-century biographer John Aubrey recorded the "ingeniose remarque of my Lady Hoskins, that B. J. [Ben Jonson] never writes of Love, or if he does, does it not naturally," and indeed Jonson himself calls attention to the fact that he is not writing a comedy of "natural" love.[16] Following a scene in which virtually all the male characters and no female characters appear, Mitis objects that *Every Man Out of His Humor* is too "neere, and familiarly allied to the time" (3.6.200–1); he prefers a traditional comedy of heteroerotic romance, "as of a duke to be in love with a countesse, and that countesse to bee in love with the dukes sonne, and the sonne to love the ladies waiting maid: some such crosse wooing, with a clowne to their servingman" (3.6.196–99). The two main female characters of Jonson's play serve instead to demonstrate the foolishness of "crosse wooing" when it involves a fop like Fastidious Briske. Scorning her doting citizen husband, Fallace unsuccessfully woos Briske, who in turn woos a court lady only as a means to display his courtly skills before other men.

In Jonson's play, then, eroticism circulates among men, most evidently in the relationship between Briske and his page. Any playgoer familiar with the graphic satires of Marston or Guilpin would have easily recognized Briske as the fop who has sex with his page and courts his mistress by the book. One "fine fellow" in Guilpin's satire "is at every play, and every night / Sups with his *Ingles*." This meticulously groomed gallant "smels of Musk, Civet, and Pomander, / . . . spends, and outspends many a pound a yeare, / . . . pertly jets, can caper, daunce, and sing, / Play with his Mistris fingers, her hand wring."[17] Similarly, Briske "sleepes with a muske-cat every night, and walkes all day hang'd in pomander chaines for penance: he ha's his skin tan'd in civet, to make his complexion strong, and the sweetnesse of his youth lasting in the sense of his sweet lady. A good emptie puffe" (2.1.97–101). Furthermore, contemporary satire features playgoing gallants who use pages for sexual service. Marston, for instance, rails against "male stews" and homosexual prostitution in London: "But ho! what Ganymede is that doth grace / The gallant's heels? One who for two days' space / Is closely hired."[18]

Although the sexual service provided by Briske's page may not be evident to us, it may well have been to Jonson's audience. Briske's page is named Cinedo, a word defined in John Florio's Italian dictionary of 1598 as "a bardarsh a buggring boy, a wanton boy, an ingle."[19] The term also appears in Marston's gibes against a "lewd Cinaedian" and a gallant who lusts after "fair Cinaedian boys."[20] Jonson's use of the Italian form "Cinedo" for the page's name further indicates the sexual disorder of the boy's services, since the English often claimed that sodomy came from Italy. Significantly, Briske apparently uses Cinedo not only as a sexual object but as a means of self-promotion, as when he directs Carlo's attention to his page's appearance: "How lik'st thou my boy, Carlo?" (2.1.4). Briske's desire for Cinedo seems inseparable from his desire to display the boy as a sign of his courtly status.

Whereas the sexual relationship between Briske and Cinedo clearly exposes Briske's courtly effeminacy, the sexual dynamics between Sogliardo and Shift are more complex. In early modern English texts, explicit expressions of male homoerotic desire overwhelmingly represent the object of desire as a youth or "boy," as in the notorious statement attributed to Marlowe that "all they that love not Tobacco & Boies were fooles."[21] Briske and Sogliardo love tobacco, but it is not clear that they share an equivalent love for boys. Upon learning that gentlemen typically keep pages, Sogliardo at first demurs: "Nay, my humour is not for boyes, Ile keepe men, and I keepe any" (1.2.143–44). However, after privately whispering with Cinedo, Sogliardo mysteriously announces that he is "resolute to keepe a page" (2.1.143). That Sogliardo "leapes from whispering with the boy" when interrupted may reveal that Cinedo has given him some inside knowledge about pages that he likes and wants to keep secret (2.1.143 sd).

Although Sogliardo does not, in fact, hire a page, through his relationship with Shift he imitates Briske's sexual mastery of Cinedo. Shift had offered his services in two posted advertisements, one addressed to "any young gentleman" who "is affected to entertaine the most gentlemanlike use of tabacco," the other addressed to "any lady, or gentlewoman . . . that is desirous to entertaine (to her private uses) a yong, straight, and upright gentleman . . . who can serve in the nature of a gentleman usher" (3.3.33–37, 48–53). Because Sogliardo "has subscrib'd" to both bills and "is most desirous to become [a] pupill" (3.6.133–34), he implicitly engages the sexual services Shift offers to any gentlewoman desiring the "private uses" of a "straight, and upright" usher. As I will discuss more fully with *The Gentleman Usher*, contemporary satire frequently claimed that gentleman ushers either pandered for or engaged in sexual activity with their masters and mistresses. Sogliardo reiterates the bawdy in-nuendo of the bill when he calls Shift "one that it pleases mee to *use* as my good friend, and companion" (4.5.3–4; my emphasis). As if to indicate the progression of his humor towards complete emulation of Briske, Sogliardo gives Shift a French crown, an echo of the "french crowne" mentioned in a previous scene between Briske and Cinedo (2.1.113). Since "French crown" punningly alludes to the baldness that accompanies the French pox, Jonson implies that both men are capable of giving their male followers a venereal disease. Disorderly sexuality between master and servant is marked not only by the commodification of the male body on the open market, but by the physical abuse and corruption of that body. Having imitated the social and sexual disorder of Briske, Sogliardo finally achieves his position as a "new-created gallant," with Shift "his villanous Ganimede" (4.3.81, 83).

Unlike Briske and Cinedo, Sogliardo and Shift define their own relationship not in terms of sexual or social service, but of friendship. Jonson represents Sogliardo and Shift as incapable of true friendship not because they have an eroticized relationship, but because they lack the social and moral virtue implied in the Renaissance concept of friendship to which they appeal. Homoeroticism does not vitiate friend-ship; social climbing and mercenary service, which can be expressed as a *disorderly* homoeroticism, do. The adoption by Sogliardo and Shift of the names of the famous Greek friends Orestes and Pylades is inap-propriate not because classical male friendship could be (and was) interpreted erotically by Renaissance readers and writers.[22] It is inap-propriate because Sogliardo and Shift can imitate the physical intimacy of the Greek friends, but not their virtuous comportment or high rank. Under mild ridicule from Carlo and Macilente, Sogliardo and Shift abandon these names and adopt the proffered alternatives, *Countenance* and *Resolution*, which signify an orderly patronage relationship between a gentleman and his retainer. Personified nicknames were a courtly affectation; their adoption by a low-class mercenary and a clownish upstart is clearly grotesque.[23]

In *Every Man Out of His Humor*, male friendship between equals is vitiated not only by class difference and mercenary self-interest, but because the extremes of courtly effeminacy and urban hypermasculinity impart a disorderly gender style to male homoerotic bonds. In a reading of the *Discoveries*, Ronald Huebert remarks that Jonson's concept of properly masculine behavior eschews the extremes of foppishness and boorishness: "Like effeminate language, the rough and broken style is an affectation, though at the opposite end of the scale."[24] Briske speaks an inappropriately feminine (i.e., florid, conceited) courtly language; Carlo speaks an inappropriately masculine (i.e., vulgar, harsh) satiric language. Briske's plea for attention may be cloying: "Nay, Carlo, I am not happy i' thy love, I see: pr'y thee suffer me to enjoy thy company a little (sweet *mischiefe*) by this aire, I shall envy this gentlemans place in thy affections, if you be thus private" (2.1.104–7); yet his petulance hardly conveys the extreme sensuality of Carlo's praise for Macilente: "Dam'me, I could eat his flesh now: divine sweet villaine! . . . pure, honest, good *devill*, I love thee above the love of women: I could e'en melt in admiration of thee now!" (4.4.98–99, 116–18). Carlo's images of edible and dissolvable flesh impart to his love "above the love of women" an eroticism far more tangible than any found in Briske's courtly formulas. When Carlo further muses that he could love Macilente "next heaven, above honour, wealth, rich fare, apparell, wenches, all the delights of the belly, and the groine, whatever" (5.4.30–32), he is clearly not celebrating pure friendship, which he finds "a vaine idle thing, only venerable among fooles" (4.3.111–12). At once a "violent rayler, and an incomprehensible *Epicure*" (ind., 357–58), Carlo epitomizes the satirist who practices the sensual vices he attacks. A contemporary poem, *The Whipping of the Satyre* (1601), chastises such disorderly satirists through the discourse of sodom/y: "For if this Land be Sodomiz'd with sinne, / It's not your lots to be at Lots therein."[25]

Yet Carlo's disorderly desire for a fellow satirist seems not so much the antithesis to but an exaggeration or vulgarization of the male fellowships that permeate Jonson's comedies. At the opening of *Every Man in His Humor*, we learn that Edward Knowell is almost "growne the idolater" of his clever friend Wellbred (1.2.68). The play ends with noteworthy symmetry, by punishing a poetaster, Matthew, and by exalting a wit, the servant Brainworm. Justice Clement initiates Matthew's disgrace by quoting some verses about a scatologically inclined Saturn; conversely, he celebrates Brainworm's accomplishments in explicitly homoerotic terms. As the pairs of male–female lovers leave the stage, Clement announces, "Here is my mistris. Brayne-worme! to whom all my addresses of courtship shall have their reference" (5.5.86–88). Moreover, with their parodies of and personal attacks on other poets, Jonson's early comedies display his own fraught relationships with his male peers. James Shapiro reminds us that "the drama of this period witnessed both a fellowship of poets and a Poets' War."[26]

As for male homosocial dynamics in Jonson's later comedies, George Rowe has argued that, beginning with *Volpone*, competition between wits replaces the more typical competition in satire between wit and gull. Hence the goal of comic intrigue becomes "supremacy, the creation of a new hierarchical relationship out of an apparent democracy of equals, the elevation of one wit above the others."[27] Although he elucidates the dynamics of male competition among the three gallants in *Epicoene*, Rowe does not acknowledge the particularly homoerotic dynamics of Dauphine's mastery over other men. By duping Morose into sodomitical marriage with a boy, Dauphine forces him to relinquish his estate, humiliates the fops who boast of their sexual prowess with Epicoene, and makes silent women of the actual epicoenes, the collegiate women with their threatening "*hermaphroditicall* authoritie" (1.1.80). As Truewit concedes, Dauphine has also "lurch'd [his] friends of the better halfe of the garland" (5.4.224–25). Dauphine triumphs because he has employed his epicoene boy in a scheme of true wit and not merely for sexual pleasure, as the idle Clerimont is assumed to employ his "engle at home" (1.1.25).

Whether or not he has sexually enjoyed the "epicoene" boy, Dauphine achieves his goals without being compromised by or suspected of sodomy. On the other hand, I hope to demonstrate that even though Morose has clearly *not* had sex with Epicoene, his marriage to the boy is sodomitical. Jonathan Goldberg has argued that "sodomy" is a term "incapable of exact definition," a term that might name any sexual act "that does not promote the aim of married procreative sex."[28] In its most common Renaissance usage, however, "sodomy" labels acts of social deviance that can be associated with, attributed to, or represented by disorderly intimacy between men. The perception of "sodomy" can occur without the visual evidence of sex between men. As Goldberg has shown, when confronted by the cross-dressed and pierced bodies of male Indians, European explorers labeled them "sodomites."[29] Whether or not sexual activity occurs between men does not determine the presence or absence of the label "sodomy" so much as the social context in which male intimacy occurs. The normative, socially orderly nature of much early modern homoeroticism explains why the laws that did narrowly define sodomy in terms of specific sexual acts were so rarely and selectively deployed. For instance, Simonds D'Ewes wrote that Francis Bacon's habit of keeping a servant for "his catamite and bedfellow . . . was the more to be admired, because men generally after his fall began to discourse of that his unnatural crime which he had practised many years."[30] Bacon's continuous homosexual activity with a servant became the subject of discourse – was identified as disorderly sodomy – only after *he* had been identified as a disorderly subject. In Goldberg's useful formulation, if

> sodomy named sexual acts only in particularly stigmatizing contexts, there is no reason not to believe that such acts went on all the time, unrecognized as sodomy, called, among other things, friendship or patronage, and facilitated by the beds shared, for instance, by servants or students.[31]

Before Bacon was stigmatized as a disorderly subject, his "sodomy" was simply the *status quo* of mastery.

The Renaissance epistemology of sodomy explains the different fates of Dauphine and Morose in *Epicoene*. Morose, his authority and household completely overturned, confesses a humiliating sexual disorder: "Utterly un-abled in nature, by reason of *frigidity*, to performe the duties, or any the least office of a husband" (5.4.46–47). Morose may be lying about his impotence, yet his public confession of *sexual* disorder confirms and tersely represents his many violations of *social* order: his unnatural humors and his mistreatment of his nephew, servants, and wife. Epicoene's presence thus brings into the arena of sexuality – as unnatural frigidity, or, after her unmasking as a boy, unnatural sodomy – the disorder Morose has promoted throughout the play. A sodomitical effect has been created in the absence of homosexual sex. Even though Morose *has not* had sex with Epicoene, his disorderly marriage to the transvestite boy marks him as a sodomite. Conversely, homosexual sex does not guarantee a sodomitical effect. Even if Dauphine *has* had sex with Epicoene, he is not marked as a sodomite. Sexual or not, Dauphine's relationship with Epicoene is orderly because of its economic outcome – reestablishing his proper inheritance – and its maintenance of social hierarchy – Epicoene's faithful subordination to Dauphine. Unlike a hired servant, who might transfer his loyalty to whatever patron offered the greatest opportunity for financial or social advancement, Epicoene, a gentleman's son, would have little reason to betray Dauphine. No mercenary Shift for him, Dauphine has chosen his young companion wisely and it pays off in his intellectual, social, and financial mastery over all the wits and asses of the play.

Dauphine's mastery hinges upon his ability to separate potential homoeroticism (his own) from a sodomy (Morose's) associated with theatrical cross-dressing.[32] In *Volpone*, by contrast, Jonson stages a theatrical homoeroticism that becomes inseparable from sodomy. A homoerotic cooperation in theatrical role-playing allows Volpone and Mosca to overmaster the foolish legacy hunters. Yet Volpone's loss of authority over Mosca reveals that a master's erotic desire for his servant might have contradictory effects, not only confirming the servant's subordinate status but enabling the servant to disrupt that status. Mosca is both an *eroticized* and a *disorderly* servant. Before discussing his eroticism, I first want to situate his disorderliness within the general context of household service in early modern England.

In a study of domestic rebellion in the drama, Frances Dolan finds Shakespeare's Caliban representative of domestic servants in general, who, difficult to locate within the early modern social order, could have been seen as "monstrous in their conflation of categories." Thomas Moisan, discussing servants in *The Taming of the Shrew* and *The Merchant of Venice*, agrees that "the social identity of the servingman in particular seems often to have eluded neat taxonomies." He argues that Grumio's contention with Petruchio "gives comic expression to contemporary stresses inhering in the servant's occupational role as employee and in his quasi-mythic identity as surrogate family member and extension of his master."[33] Servants did not form a distinct economic or social class. They were a geographically and socially mobile population, often employed during a transitional period of life (from adolescence to adulthood), during which they were sexually mature but often instructed to remain celibate; and they were usually temporary, although intimate and instrumental members of a household.[34] To explain the rise of vagrancy in the period, A. L. Beier argues that "[l]iving in was an unstable as well as declining prospect"; he finds in conduct books and statutory regulations "considerable evidence that breakdowns occurred" in relations between masters and servants.[35] Whereas Beier discusses the bleak employment prospects of poor servants and laborers, Dolan argues that the unstable conditions of service could threaten a master's sense of safety and authority: "Dependent yet depended upon, familiar yet not wholly known or controlled, a class yet not one, servants blurred boundaries and confused categories."[36] Not only did they blur boundaries, they did so within one's own home.

The systemic instability of household service receives physical expression in Volpone's three servants – a dwarf, a eunuch, and an hermaphrodite – who are at once monstrous boundary-blurrers and "knowne delicates" committed to pleasing their master (3.3.5). But it is Mosca who receives Volpone's kisses, embraces, and ecstatic praises. Following their victories over the gulls, Volpone warmly cries, "Excellent, Mosca! / Come hither, let me kisse thee" (1.3.78–79), and gushes, "I cannot hold; good rascall, let me kisse thee" (1.4.137).[37] Volpone's evident delight in Mosca explains why he dallies with a servant instead of continuing the patriarchal line by securing a wife and legitimate heir. *Volpone* fully stages the exclusive homoerotic "marriage" between a patron and his follower that *Twelfth Night* only shadows in Antonio's exclusive desire for Sebastian, who finally marries Olivia.[38] That Mosca's role in this relationship seems so unstable further adds to the disorder of Volpone's household. Although Mosca appears to be not a wage-earning servant hired by the year but an established "parasite" in Volpone's household, at least for the three years during which Volpone has been baiting the legacy hunters, his identification as "fly" implies the capacity to feed off whatever host will best nourish him, even if he must abandon or betray his master.

The sodomitical tenor of Volpone's household becomes especially prominent in allusions to monstrosity, foreignness, and nonreproductive (or prodigiously reproductive) sexuality. Mosca's claim that Volpone conceived his three monstrous servants with Gypsies, Jews, and Moors recalls the belief that sodomites were the offspring of unnatural unions, usually between witches and devils.[39] Nano himself parodies reproduction in narrating the degenerate transmigration of Pythagoras' soul into an ass (among other beasts) and finally into Androgyno. Moreover, the play's overall dependence on animal lore might suggest bestiality and its monstrous products.[40] Whether Volpone is actually childless or the "true father" of his three servants, he clearly rejects orderly heterosexual reproductivity and chaste sexuality. When Volpone boasts that "The *Turke* is not more sensuall, in his pleasures, / Then will Volpone" (1.5.88–89), we should recall that the English typically held that the Turkish are "not more inclined to any one sinne, than to this sin of lechery . . . they are not contented with the abuse of women, for the satiating of their beastly humours: but they are so outragiously given over to the abominable sin of Sodomie, that it is impossible without horror to be uttered."[41]

Like the stereotypically lustful Turks, Volpone indulges a "beastly humour" that is not contented with the abuse of women. One of the ironies of *Volpone* is that the celebrated invitation to heterosexual sex, the song "Come, my Celia," is preceded by what can be read as an explicit reference to homoerotic role-playing:

> I am, now, as fresh,
> As hot, as high, and in as joviall plight,
> As when (in that so celebrated *scene*,
> At recitation of our *comoedie*,
> For entertainement of the great Valoys)
> I acted yong Antinous; and attracted
> The eyes, and eares of all the ladies, present,
> T'admire each gracefull gesture, note, and footing.   (3.7.157–64)

There is reason to interpret this Antinous as the beautiful male favorite of the Emperor Hadrian, since Volpone played the role to entertain

Henri III, who was notorious for keeping favorites.[42] David McPherson detects in the extravagant festivity mounted for Henri III and in the general atmosphere of Volpone's household the "lavishness, theatricality, and sexual exhibitionism" characteristic of Nero's Rome. Concluding that Volpone has a penchant for classical travesty and "decadent" theatrical roles, McPherson fails to mention that Volpone's reference to Antinous makes his attractiveness to women dependent on his attractiveness to men.[43] And as for his own attraction to Celia, watching Mosca act gives Volpone greater pleasure than the "pleasure of all womankind" (5.2.11). Volpone's desire for Celia is motivated less by heteroerotic lust than by the pleasures of role-playing, shape-changing, and mastery over another man's wife who is as "lovely, as [his] gold" and "kept as warily, as is [his] gold" (1.5.114, 118).

Like ancient Rome, Venice was reputed to be a city of sexual licentiousness, famous for its "cunning curtizan[s]" and its witty sodomites (3.5.20). Lady Would-be mentions the notorious sodomite Aretino, the "desperate wit" with the "obscene" pictures who celebrated the freedoms of Venice (3.5.96–97). She later accuses her husband of hiring a transvestite prostitute, a "female devill, in a male out-side" (4.2.56), whom she calls "Your Sporus, your *hermaphrodite*" in an oblique reminder of Volpone's sexually unruly servants (4.2.48). Guido Ruggiero notes that late fifteenth-century Venetians expressed concern about "a growing trend of some prostitutes to hawk their services in masculine garb and with a masculine manner."[44] This trend seems to have become an institution. To explain the scene in *The Merchant of Venice* when Jessica feels ashamed to disguise herself as a page, Marjorie Garber cites a late sixteenth-century account of clever Venetian prostitutes who wear "a somewhat masculine outfit" to attract customers. One of these prostitutes, according to Aretino, was always available for anal intercourse, whether she was dressed as a pageboy or as a woman.[45] Volpone and his servants are certainly at home among the gender and sexual transgressions of Venice, and they use such transgressions, like the resourceful transvestite prostitutes and the self-promoting Aretino, for their own profit.

In *Volpone*, the homoerotic theatricality that inextricably binds master to servant is inextricably bound to the central project of achieving mastery over gulls. Thus, when the bond between master and servant dissolves, so does the witty mastery that it enabled. At the apex of his wit, Volpone feigns death in order that Mosca, his heir, may conclusively vanquish the legacy seekers. Having witnessed this conquest, which he punctuates with rapturous commendation of his servant, Volpone warmly exclaims:

> my wittie *mischiefe*,
> Let me embrace thee. O that I could now
> Transforme thee to a Venus – Mosca, goe,
> Streight, take my habit of *Clarissimo*;
> And walke the streets.   (5.3.102–6)

Volpone transforms his servant *not* into a Venus (or courtesan) for his private use but into a public streetwalking version of himself – and "[o]ut of mere wantonnesse," as he later realizes (5.11.4). Precisely this moment marks their mutual decline. Once Mosca cross-dresses above his station, hence publicly taking on the "dead" Volpone's own status and authority, the homoerotic dominance of master over servant is irrevocably displaced. It might be relevant to note that when Jonson revised the 1601 quarto *Every Man in His Humor* for the 1616 folio, he removed the final stage exit in which Justice Clement rewards Brainworm by dressing him "in [his] owne robes" (5.5.445). Did Jonson wish to disassociate the festively homoerotic inversion between master and servant in the earlier play from the disastrously homoerotic inversion between master and servant in *Volpone*?

Volpone's betrayal by an erotically empowered servant and ultimate conviction in court oddly anticipates the notorious trial of the Earl of Castlehaven, who was accused of sodomizing his servants and encouraging them to rape his wife. Although Castlehaven's servants testified against him, they, like Mosca, were nevertheless convicted as contributors to the social disorder that their master authorized. Frances Dolan's description of the judgment against Castlehaven applies as well to Volpone's social transgression: "In the view of those who try him, he has scandalously coerced his servants to take up the master's position, and he cannot resume it."[46] Proleptically, the moment in which Volpone coerces Mosca to take up his own social position is preceded by a punitive anal reference, as Mosca dismisses the last gull, the "costive" Voltore, with the advice to "go home, and purge" (5.3.101). Here purged at disastrous cost, the homoerotic bond between master and servant is finally resumed at the moment of Mosca's prospective marriage – "I am Volpone, and this is my knave" (5.12.89) – only for the sake of a mutual punishment, a literal bondage they are to share with other men in the galley or the prison. Transplanted from a disorderly all-male household to all-male places of discipline, Mosca and Volpone are sentenced to grimly ironic fates.[47]

The Alchemist, in significantly reconfiguring the master–servant dynamics of *Volpone* and *Epicoene*, achieves a more orderly version of master–servant solidarity. When Lovewit first appears in act 5, his unexpected return threatens to spoil all the clever schemes of his servant.

That Captain Face must shave his beard to become "smooth Jeremie" (4.7.131), the dutiful butler, at first seems to symbolize his imminent submission to his master's will. Smoothness is characteristic of boys: in Middleton's *A Mad World, My Masters* (1606), Sir Bounteous describes his grandson as an "*Imberbis juvenis*" (beardless youth) and "Ganymede" (2.1.142, 146). Yet Face does *not* become a ganymede, another Epicoene for his master to direct as he pleases: he retains his brazen wit. Neither does he become another Mosca who tries to out-master the master: he begs pardon for his deception. Lovewit may be an "indulgent master" who loves wit but he is not another Volpone, whose reckless homoerotic indulgence of a servant precipitates their mutual ruin (5.3.77).

In contrast to *Volpone*, therefore, the relationship between master and servant in *The Alchemist* succeeds because it achieves an orderly balance: the master retains his social mastery; the servant retains his intellectual mastery. When combined, Lovewit's status and Face's wit easily vanquish all rivals and foes, and (unusual in Jonson) permit the concluding marriage between Lovewit and Dame Pliant. The belated teamwork between Lovewit and Face has all the theatrical brilliance of Volpone's and Mosca's masquerades, but none of the sodomitical consequences. And it adds to the virtuosity of Dauphine's and Epicoene's victory a much greater sense of warm friendship and mutual profit. When Lovewit appreciatively declares, "I will be rul'd by thee in any thing, Jeremie" (5.5.143), he is indulging his servant, not abdicating his rule. As *The Alchemist* ends, we might recall not the final act of *Volpone*, in which a witty servant's rule is disastrously played out, but the final action of *Every Man in His Humor*, in which a witty servant is allowed to "rule" for the duration of his walk off the stage.

In Jonson's satiric comedies, homoerotic relations between masters and servants may promote or disrupt social order. In *Every Man Out of His Humor*, the effeminate courtier and base upstart who employ servants for social advancement become easy satiric targets. The masculine playwright whips deficient men by exposing the excesses of their homoerotic modes of self-promotion: Briske's sexual use of a page, Sogliardo's grotesque friendship with an impostor, even Carlo's boorish praise of a fellow critic. Transferring master–servant erotics from the city streets into the household, *Volpone* gives the servant a different role and status. The play suggests that, when transgressive of marriage, inheritance, and hierarchical authority, a sustained partnership between master and servant can be powerful and profitable, even attractive, but is liable to be unstable and self-destructive. Authorized by his wanton master to violate social propriety, Mosca eventually overturns the master–servant hierarchy itself. On the other hand, because it is a temporary and orderly relationship, Dauphine's maintenance of a well-born boy gives him intellectual mastery without the risks of personal intimacy and affection that undo Volpone. Lovewit combines Dauphine's social and intellectual mastery with Volpone's witty use of an intimate household servant. In *Every Man Out of His Humor* and *Volpone*, then, erotically disorderly relations between masters and servants threaten the social order with class mobility and the nonreproductive (or monstrously reproductive) household. The erotically orderly relations between masters and servants in *Epicoene* and *The Alchemist*, on the other hand, bolster the social order by helping to reestablish an heir's proper inheritance, proper gender relations between men and women, and a master's proper authority over his household.

Crafting friendship: Chapman's homoerotics of mastery

Like *Epicoene*, Chapman's *The Gentleman Usher* concerns the attempt of a man of high rank to establish a temporary homoerotic relationship with a servant. Chapman's play may be distinguished from Jonson's plays by its representation of a traditional romantic love plot. As I demonstrated in chapter 2, however, homoeroticism may be as important a factor in plots of courtship and marriage as in plots, like Jonson's, in which heteroerotic desire plays a minimal role. Moreover, although originally entered in the Stationer's Register as "*A Book Called Vincentio & Margaret*," Chapman's play was published in quarto as "*The Gentleman Usher*," the change in title shifting focus from the romantic male–female couple to the "ass" who is an essential component of satire (4.5.45).[48]

The homoerotic bond between master and servant in *The Gentleman Usher* is crucial in uniting Prince Vincentio, son of Duke Alphonso, with Margaret, daughter of the nobleman Lasso. The eponymous gentleman usher is Bassiolo, a high-level servant in Lasso's household. In rivalry with his father for Margaret, Vincentio convinces Bassiolo to facilitate his own secret correspondence and assignation with Margaret, and in turn their secret betrothal. Securing Bassiolo's help by offering his intimate friendship, Vincentio elevates his social inferior to a position of nominal equality. This contradiction in social status is registered in the very name of the service position that names the play: "usher" connotes the social and erotic submission appropriate to a servant, yet "gentleman" implies a relative class parity and a capacity for the intellectual and moral virtue appropriate to a "friend."[49] In *Epicoene*, Jonson reveals neither how Dauphine convinces the boy to play a woman's part nor what the conditions of their four-month partnership are. In *The*

Gentleman Usher, on the contrary, Chapman thoroughly stages – and exposes to an audience – how Vincentio accomplishes his goals by exploiting the homoerotic conventions and contradictions of service. Despite his success, Vincentio, like Volpone, is finally unable to extricate himself from the sodomitical effects of his own homoerotics of mastery.

The disorderliness of Bassiolo's advancement is signaled in several ways. Elevated to the status of "friend," Bassiolo familiarly addresses his prince as "Vince," at times using the epithets "sweet" and "dear." Ironically, the nickname that closes the gap in status between them punningly reinscribes the mastery of *Vince* (from *vincere*) over *Bassiolo* (from *base* and *ass*?). This indecorous exchange of names is only the most concise sign of an inappropriate intimacy. Although Vincentio does not hire Bassiolo in the urban marketplace, his feigned friendship with an usher recalls contemporary reference to the decline in the honor of personal service, a degeneration often blamed on changes caused by market economics and the general decline of the feudal aristocratic household.[50] Beier notes that "dependency declined in the period and was increasingly replaced by short-term hirings on a cash basis."[51] In Marston's *Histrio-Mastix*, for example, two extravagant courtiers dismiss the retainers who had served their fathers. Astounded, the discharged servants blame the impudent pages and costly outfits that have made them obsolete; one of them tersely recounts the decline of noble households:

> For service, this is savage recompense.
> Your Fathers bought lands and maintained men?
> You sell your lands, and scarce keep rascall boyes,
> Who Ape-like jet, in garded coates; are whipt
> For mocking men? though with a shamlesse face,
> Yet gracelesse boyes can never men disgrace.[52]

The Host of Jonson's *The New Inn* (1629) protests that the "nurseries of nobility" in which pages once learned "all the blazon of a gentleman" are no longer virtuous (1.3.46). The current function of a page, he insists, is to "play sir Pandarus . . . / And carry messages to Madam Cressid; / Instead of backing the brave steed o' the mornings, / To mount the chambermaid" (1.3.70–73).

According to such commentators, the decline in militaristic and noble training establishes an effeminate and undisciplined role for the male servant, whether a boy page or an adult usher. That Braithwayte's *A Strappado for the Devil* (1615) makes "Ushers, Panders" adjacent in a catalog of deviants suggests their association in contemporary minds.[53] Indeed, this association is made explicit in John Mason's play *The Turk* (1607), in which a gentleman usher procures for others but abstains himself: "he is sir the preface to your compoundresse of mans flesh, and Ushers her to imployment: and is a creature of singular patience; contenting himselfe with the Theory, when others are the Practique."[54] In Jonson's *The Devil is an Ass*, the offices of the gentleman usher have been even more drastically feminized. Those duties deemed "fit for a gentleman [servant], not a slave" include carrying "all the deare secrets" of cosmetic treatments from one gentlewoman to another (4.4.149, 141). Although Bassiolo has important administrative duties in Lasso's household, Vincentio directs him into becoming just such a pander and bearer of secrets.

The secrecy between Vincentio and Bassiolo is not the kind deemed essential to the conventional bond between master and servant or between male friends. As a symbol and support of orderly intimacy between men, secrecy grounds the Renaissance discourse of friendship: in Jeremy Taylor's wonderfully resonant phrase, "secrecy is the chastity of friendship."[55] According to the manuals and treatises examined by Richard Rambuss and Jonathan Goldberg, the secretary, his office etymologically derived from "secret," should be linked to his master through private counsel and a "friendlie knot of love."[56] Following Alan Bray, Rambuss argues that the assertion of friendship or equality would protect the intimacy between master and servant from appearing sodomitical. Yet I would argue, much as Goldberg does, that homoerotic intimacy between a master and a subordinate does not necessarily imply social disorder or sodomy.[57] For instance, the homoerotics of service are treated as commonplace in Thomas Middleton's *A Mad World, My Masters*, when Sir Bounteous asks Lord Owemuch (actually his grandson Follywit in disguise) to employ Follywit: "Shall I be bold with your honour to prefer this aforesaid Ganymede to hold a plate under your lordship's cup?" The Lord agrees to "reserve a place for him nearest to my secrets"; Sir Bounteous replies, "I understand your good lordship, you'll make him your secretary."[58] The Cambridge editor of the play makes explicit the homoerotics of secretaryship by glossing the Lord's "secrets" as his "private affairs / private parts." Middleton's text registers no anxiety about this homoerotic intimacy, no fear that this secretary will abuse his master's "secrets," perhaps because Sir Bounteous has described Follywit as a beardless – that is, a powerless – Ganymede.

In Chapman's play, however, secrecy between master and servant promotes not trust, obedience, and friendship, but distrust, disobedience, and self-interest. Vincentio's friend Strozza first suggests that Vincentio "[s]uborn some servant of some good respect" who has access to Margaret. Vincentio "need not fear / His trusty secrecy, because he dares not / Reveal escapes whereof himself is author" (1.1.91, 96–98). Having, in his own words, "corrupted" the usher to deceive his actual employer, Vincentio stresses Bassiolo's enforced secrecy: "Well, he is mine, and he being trusted most . . . / And being thus engag'd dare not reveal" the assignation with Margaret (3.2.211–13). Strozza and Vincentio prove right. When Lasso threatens Margaret with punishing whatever "close traitor 'tis / That is your agent in your secret plots" and a shaken Bassiolo determines to reveal her secret affair (4.5.13–15), Margaret threatens not only to expose his instrumentality in the plot, but to use as evidence the love letter he has himself written for her to Vincentio. Vincentio has seen to it that the obedience Bassiolo owes his true master has been violated in the very name of the "secrecy" and "friendship" that are supposed to ground orderly relations between master and servant.

Therefore, what could look like orderly master–servant intimacy in another context looks disorderly here. And this disorder takes a distinctly erotic form with Bassiolo's bodily interpolation in the secret courtship of Vincentio and Margaret. Since Vincentio must actively woo Bassiolo to be his friend, Bassiolo not only mediates between Vincentio and Margaret, but serves as a substitute or temporary replacement for her. Vincentio boasts, "I made him embrace me, / Knitting a most familiar league of friendship" – a friendship that in turn helps "[k]nit" the lovers in marriage (4.2.110–11, 142). Vincentio's "sacred oath" to his eternal friendship with Bassiolo foreshadows his actual wedding vows (3.2.193); the oath also temporarily displaces Margaret, as, in Shakespeare's *Othello* (1604), Iago's oath of love to Othello permanently displaces Desdemona. If "love's ushering fire" (4.2.156), or beauty, unites Vincentio and Margaret spiritually, it is the usher's role as substitute lover that unites them materially.

The masque staged within *The Gentleman Usher* draws attention precisely to the sexual substitution of role-playing male servants for actual women. Of course, such substitutions were targeted by the strain of English antitheatrical discourse that held that transvestite boy players incited sodomitical desire. Chapman's play was produced by a boy's company in a private theater; as the display of "fine enghles" in *Cynthia's Revels* suggests, the elite theaters may have provided a more explicitly homoerotic venue than the popular theaters.[59] It is also worth restating that the reopening of the boys' playing companies in 1599 and 1600 coincides with the expansion of satiric discourse, much of it homoerotic, in print and on stage.[60] In the masque staged within Chapman's play, the female roles are played by "pages made, for need, / To fill up women's places / By virtue of their faces / And other hidden graces" (2.1.221–24). This erotically provocative description of pages' ability to fill in for women recalls the masque that Gaveston plans for Edward II in

Marlowe's play, featuring boys dressed as nymphs with leaves to "hide those parts which men delight to see."[61] A more crass sexual role is played by the page in Middleton's *Black Book* (1604), who "fills up the place of an ingle."[62]

The sexual – and sodomitical – connotations of Bassiolo's "filling up" Margaret's place are further strengthened by the play's representation of what Patricia Parker has called "preposterous events," its inverted substitutions not only between males and females, but between fronts and backs.[63] The very gratuitousness of these instances warrants our attention. The play opens with Pogio protesting that he is not an "ass," but his asinine inversions earn him the epithet "cousin Hysteron Proteron" (1.1.18, 26). The foolish pedant Sarpego can not determine "which is the part precedent of this nightcap / And which the posterior" (2.1.125–26). When Bassiolo instructs Vincentio to appreciate Margaret's posterior part, the erotic significance of the play's inversions becomes clear. In putting what's behind in front, the sexually preposterous (or "arsyversy") inappropriately foregrounds the ass: "if she turn her back, / Use you that action you would do before / And court her thus: / 'Lady, your back part is as fair to me / As is your forepart.'" Bassiolo reasons that "the worst part / About your mistress you must think as fair, / As sweet and dainty as the very best" (4.2.56–60, 63–65). Vincentio exacerbates the absurdity of the compliment by informing Margaret, "[Y]our back part is as *sweet* to me / As all your forepart" (4.2.96–97; my emphasis). Bassiolo's interference reduces Vincentio's courtship of his future wife to a sodomitical and scatological joke.[64]

Vincentio's erotically disorderly wooing of his servant, therefore, leads to erotically disorderly wooing of his wife, coded as sodomy. In early modern England, the possibility of heterosexual anal intercourse was acknowledged with both humor and horror.[65] In Middleton's *Michaelmas Term*, a servingwoman, advocating a hairstyle that gives a woman a "mock-face behind," wryly notes: "'tis such an Italian world, many men know not before from behind."[66] To such men who might desire a woman's behind as well as a boy's, object choice may not have been as important to their sexual taste as the particular physical activity usually associated with the ingle. Jean Howard reads in this way the reference in *The Roaring Girl* (1611) to wives who "ingle" for favor with their husbands.[67] Educated Renaissance readers could find a classical panegyric of heterosexual ingling in the pseudo-Lucianic *Erotes*, in which Charicles, a lover of women, and Callicratidas, a lover of boys, express different responses to a naked statue of Aphrodite. Charicles admires the statue's front while Callicratidas admires its backside, comparing it to Ganymede's buttocks. Whereas the pederast can appreciate a female body only as a substitute for a boy's body in the practice of anal sex, Charicles boasts that a female body can be penetrated in more ways than a male body: "a woman . . . may be used as a boy, so that one can have enjoyment by opening up two paths to pleasure, but a male has no way of bestowing the pleasure a woman gives."[68] Taking a less sanguine view of the variety of heterosexual sex, an epigram from 1620 may punningly figure the "two paths" of female anatomy as the signs of a woman's false means and bad end:

> Rosa being false and periur'd, once a friend,
> Bid me contented be, and marke her end.
> But yet I care not, let my friend go fiddle,
> And let him marke her end, Ile marke her middle.[69]

In *Volpone*, the jealous Corvino threatens to punish Celia's false means or "middle" by marking her "end": "Then, here's a locke which I will hang upon thee; / And, now I thinke on't, I will keepe thee backe-wards; / . . . and no pleasure, / That thou shalt know, but backe-wards" (2.3.57–58, 60–61). The appropriate punishment for his wife's whorish openness, Corvino implies, is restriction to sodomitical pleasures.[70]

Given the possibility that both men and women could fill the sexual place of an ingle, it is remarkable that Margaret calls Bassiolo an "ingle." Does she perceive him to be taking her place in Vincentio's disorderly affections? The Regents editor glosses *ingle*, bizarrely, as "fire"; accurately, as "catamite"; predictably, with the disclaimer that it is "merely a pejorative epithet" (5.1.112n.). It is true that Margaret also derides the usher as a "beagle," a "servile coward," and a "cockscomb" (5.1.35; 4.5.47; 4.5.113); but would she use "ingle" merely as another term for the usher's servility and stupidity?

On the contrary, Chapman seems to endow Margaret with the contemporary satiric understanding of gentleman ushers not only as panders but as erotic objects for their masters and mistresses. These servants may be eroticized more frequently than others because the activity of ushering evokes various sexual connotations.[71] Ushering produces strong legs, a major criterion of male beauty in the Renaissance. In *Every Man Out of His Humor*, Shift advertises his services as a gentleman usher furnished with "little legges of purpose, and a black satten sute of his owne, to goe before her in" (3.3.37–39). In Chapman's *The Widow's Tears* (1605), the Governor is pleased to find his new usher "tressel-legged": "The better; it bears a breadth, makes room o' both sides."[72] After watching him "stalk," the Governor promises the usher's former employer, a widow, that he will "accept this property at your hand, and wear it bare for your sake" (5.5.281–82). Is there a sexual innuendo in this master's admiration of his usher's widespread legs? The Governor might be compared to Ferdinand in *The Duchess of Malfi* (1614), who fantasizes about the "strong-thighed barge-man" or the "lovely squire / That carries coals" to his sister.[73]

The sexual connotations of ushering are legible not only in the servant's eroticized body, but in the position of that body in relation to others. Paradoxically, the sign of the usher's subservience is going before other people. In performing his duty the usher is seen from *behind* – a perspective from which he is subordinated and potentially eroticized. When perceived to be disorderly, the implicit eroticism of such positioning can be explicitly articulated as sodomy. The usher in Mason's *The Turk*, ordered to *follow* a ghost, complains, "S'foot my office is italianated, I am faine to come behinde" (5.1.170–71). The social chaos depicted in Mason's play is neatly epitomized here by an inversion of the usher's social and sexual role. The usher's disorderly "coming behind" echoes an earlier sodomitical joke based on William Lyly's Latin grammar in which a Madame Fulsome remarks of verb declensions that "*Lilly* was a beastly knave to put *pono* [I put in] behind *gigno* [I beget]" (3.2.18–19). As Leonard Barkan observes of jokes about the humanist proclivity for flogging and sodomy, "grammatical instruction is still a business of dominance, and the audience can still hear how close paideia is to pederasty." Because the relations of social dominance and subservience are posed in erotic terms, the sodomitical humor leveled at lecherous pedagogues who position themselves behind their students is just as applicable to disruptively positioned gentleman ushers.[74]

Finally, the erotic connotations of ushering may be traced to the mythological Ganymede, who is an usher of sorts. In his dictionary, Thomas Cooper defines *Ganymedes* as "A Troiane childe, which was feigned to bee ravished of Jupiter, and made his butler."[75] Ganymede's office as a "butler" or cupbearer is refigured in less prosaic contexts as an ushering in of sensual pleasures. The Revels editor of *The Roaring Girl* explains the name "Sir Beauteous Ganymede" by noting that it "suits this character's function in assisting the marriage": he ushers in the bride on his arm.[76] In Dekker's *Satiromastix*, the King remarks of his wedding banquet: "Why so, even thus the Mercury of Heaven, / Ushers th'ambrosiate banquet of the Gods," where "Joves page / Sweet Ganimed fills Nectar" (5.2.1–2, 5–6). And in Jonson's *Poetaster* (1601), where courtiers literally dress as the Olympian gods for a luxurious banquet, the page playing Ganymede supplies the wine that inspires lusty words and deeds. One reveler says of Vulcan, who calls for amity through drunkenness, "His tongue shall bee gent'man-usher to his wit, and still goe before it"

(4.5.143–44). As Ganymede's functions indicate, to usher is to create the circumstances in which sexual activity can flourish.

When Margaret calls Bassiolo an "ingle," therefore, she seems aware of the homoerotic potential implicit in Bassiolo's role as usher and actualized by Vincentio's manipulation of that role. Moreover, she understands her own compromised position within Vincentio's scheme: "Men work on one another for we women" (3.2.377). Bassiolo mediates between Vincentio and Margaret; Margaret mediates between Vincentio and Bassiolo. Because she understands that Vincentio's scheme has placed both Bassiolo and herself in the position of interchangeable ingles, Margaret simultaneously identifies with and distinguishes herself from the usher. That is why she can at once pity the "poor creature" and scorn the "cockscomb" (4.2.115; 4.5.113). Even when sarcastically distinguishing herself from Bassiolo, Margaret describes herself in terms that recall their mutual involvement in Vincentio's disorderly exchanges: "Every woman cannot be a gentleman usher; they that cannot go before must come behind" (3.2.504–5).

Vincentio, on the contrary, seems unable to recognize the compromised role he plays within his own scheme. Denouncing to Bassiolo those dishonorable lords "who will cog so when they wish to use men / With 'pray be cover'd, sir,'" Vincentio asks with mock indignation, "Where's the deeds? The perfect nobleman?" (3.2.75–76, 78–79). Of course, Vincentio deliberately flatters Bassiolo in just the way he denounces, but the moral issues he raises ironically undermine his actual friendship with the nobleman Strozza.[77] The Regents editor mentions Vincentio's "perversion of Renaissance concepts of friendship," but claims, wrongly I think, that the deceptions "do little to complicate his character" (p. xxvi). In early modern drama, noble male friendship is always represented by deeds, usually of self-sacrifice, as in *Damon and Pithias* (1565), *The Two Gentlemen of Verona* (1590), and *The Case is Altered* (1597). Vincentio performs no deeds at all for his ostensible "true friend" (4.3.81). When Strozza is shot, Vincentio visits him briefly and coolly reiterates his concern for his health; he never makes an effort to seek justice from his father, and next appears in carefree amorous play with Margaret. In contrast, when Vincentio is stabbed, Strozza, "burning in zeal of friendship," dares to accuse Duke Alphonso of being a "tyrant" and a "pagan Nero" who has devoured his own son (5.4.39–40, 42). Given the evidence of Vincentio's feigned friendship with Bassiolo and without any counterindication of substantial deeds performed on behalf of Strozza, an audience might well question Vincentio's capability for noble friendship.

Why might Chapman undermine Vincentio's integrity? A second son,

Chapman himself served in the household of a nobleman, Sir Ralph Sadler, for at least two years, and in 1604 was appointed to the position of sewer in ordinary to Prince Henry, a position quite similar to that of gentleman usher.[78] Chapman's familiarity with service of such high rank (and, given his chronic patronage problems, with its discontents) might well have put an edge on his representation of Vincentio's misuse of a servant. Chapman also criticizes the self-interest behind the rhetoric of friendship in the earlier play *All Fools* (1599), in which the Knight Gostanzo cynically advises his son not to honor a promise made by "debt of friendship":

> Tush, friendship's but a term, boy. The fond world
> Like to a doting mother glazes over
> Her children's imperfections with fine terms.
> What she calls friendship and true, humane kindness,
> Is only want of true experience.[79]

In Vincentio's case, friendship is a term that "glazes over" not naivete, but a clever scheme to achieve sexual mastery at a servant's expense. Although Margaret assures Bassiolo that Vincentio "dotes on thee," the usher in a moment of lucidity "half suspect[s]" this mystifying dotage to be the "crafty friendship" – both crafty and crafted – it really is (4.5.50, 38,37).

If Chapman's satire is necessarily directed against the servant, it is sufficiently directed against the master. That is, if it is slightly ungenerous to consider Bassiolo an "ass," it is equally unclear that Vincentio can be considered a "wit." Lying down with Bassiolo onstage, the future Duke Vincentio advises him to "lay about for state / Worthy your virtues: be the minion of some great king or duke" (3.2.92–94). The irony of Vincentio's situation suggests that Bassiolo is *already* a minion, a disorderly servant who, like Mosca, might use his favored status to promote his own ambitions, perhaps at his master's cost. In early modern England, a master who slept with and had sex with his servant would likely not consider his socially orderly activity, that is, his dominance of an inferior, as "sodomy," which named social disruption.[80] But physical intimacy between master and servant could also work to the advantage of the *servant*. In his conduct book *Galateo*, Giovanni Della Casa makes explicit the link between homoerotic intimacy and the social advancement of a servant:

Besides, let not a man so sit that he turne his tayle to him that sitteth next to him: nor lye fottering with one legg so hygh above the other, that a man may see all bare that his cloathes would cover. For such parts be never playde, but amongst those to whome a man needs use no reverence. It is very true, that if a gentleman should use these fashions before his servants, or in the presence of some friende of meaner condition then him selfe: it would betoken no pride, but a love and familiaritie.[81]

The "love and familiaritie" signified by a gentleman's display of his "tayle" or secret parts to a social inferior is precisely what Vincentio offers Bassiolo, to the diminution of his own rank and power.

The threat involved in social advancement through homoerotic intimacy is suggested by Jonson's epigram "To Captayne Hungry," who is instructed to save his tales for "your yong States-men (that first make you drunke, / And then lye with you, closer, then a punque, / For newes)."[82] In *Volpone*, Mosca may use a similar strategy to steal the clothes of a Venetian commandadore. Mosca elliptically explains to Volpone, "Him will I straight make drunk, and bring you his habit" (5.1.243). In Middleton's *Michaelmas Term*, the citizen Quomodo directs his servant to seduce a gentleman into losing his lands:

> Give him a sweet taste of sensuality;
> Train him to every wasteful sin, that he
> May quickly need health, but especially money;
> Ravish him with a dame or two, be his bawd for once,
> I'll be thine forever;
> Drink drunk with him, creep into bed with him,
> Kiss him and undo him, my sweet spirit. (1.1.122–28)

Here the erotic enchantments of women are hardly distinguished from those of men, and the language of sin and waste evokes the satiric type of the hollow, diseased sodomite.[83] To gloss this passage by explaining that "Elizabethan men slept together as a habit of friendliness," as Richard Levin does, completely fails to account for the unfriendliness motivating a servant's sexual undoing of a gentleman in Middleton's play (1.1.127n.).

Encouraged by Vincentio's homoerotic flattery, Bassiolo threatens to become just such a self-promoting servant. Acting as a secretary, he identifies too strongly with Margaret, composing and inditing a love letter "from" her to Vincentio. He also identifies too strongly with Vincentio, instructing him, "And thou dost love me, kiss her," and warning Margaret, "Were I as Vince is, I would handle you / In rufty-tufty wise" (5.1.29, 33–34). He ultimately claims authority over both lovers, his social superiors: "Ah, I do domineer and rule the roast" (5.1.11). Because Bassiolo never fully realizes that Vincentio's love for him has been contrived, he continues to assert the claims of his prior "marriage" to the prince, a marriage that the prince himself had condoned:

VINCENTIO. And are not two friends one?
BASSIOLO.   Even man and wife. (3.2.135)

In his last action of the play, Bassiolo, embracing Vincentio, declares: "Here in thy bosom I will lie, sweet Vince, / And die if thou die, I protest by heaven" (5.4.172–74).

Vincentio attempts to contain the disorder offered by his servant, but he is unable to because he himself has authorized and contributed to it. Vincentio wants to believe that, unlike his capricious father, he is an orderly master and that, unlike his father's favorite, Medice, Bassiolo is an orderly servant. Immediately after advising Bassiolo to become a royal minion, Vincentio laments: "There's Medice, / The minion of my father – O the Father! / What difference is there!" (3.2.94–96). Strozza similarly differentiates between orderly and disorderly servants when, advising Vincentio to employ a trustworthy servant, he subsequently evokes Medice. Both men describe Medice as a crass social opportunist, Vincentio derogating him as that

> parcel of unconstrued stuff,
> That unknown minion rais'd to honor's height
> Without the help of virtue or of art
> Or, to say true, of any honest part.
> O, How he shames my father! (1.1.109–13)

The sexual transgression alluded to in these lines is supported by Strozza's claim that Medice has committed "adultery with nobility" (1.1.123). In the masque, moreover, Medice plays the part of Sylvanus, the uncivilized, possibly sodomitical, wood god, and he demonstrates his beastly nature by influencing a "trusty servant" to shoot Strozza.[84] This episode, however, shows Medice using the same strategy that Vincentio uses to seduce Bassiolo: "Be secret, then, / And thou to me shalt be the dear'st of men" (3.1.1, 13–14). In demonizing Medice, therefore, Vincentio and Strozza misrecognize the similarities between Medice and Bassiolo (as ambitious servants), between Medice and Vincentio (as deceptive masters), and between Alphonso and Vincentio (as sodomitical masters).

The play ends with a double ordering that attempts to undo the sodomitical effects of Vincentio's homoerotics of mastery. Alphonso legitimates the secret marriage between Vincentio and Margaret, and Medice is exposed as a fraud, as Mendice, "king of the gypsies," who learned from "an old sorceress, that [he] should be great / In some great prince's love" (5.4.260–62). Through his past association with gypsies and witches, Mendice is tainted with the religious, sexual, and linguistic disorder of the Renaissance sodomite. He is banished from the court and condemned to "live a monster, loath'd of all the world" (5.4.275). Pogio evidently refers to the sodomitical desire that will lure Mendice away from the newly ordered court when he announces that he will "get boys and bait him out o'th'court" (5.4.276); yet the bait is Mendice, who is beaten away by a group of pages.

With the ritual expulsion of the sodomitical servant, Vincentio's mastery over his wife and father, recently challenged by Bassiolo's affectionate embrace, might seem more secure. Significantly, however, Bassiolo is virtually the only character onstage who has escaped some form of punishment: Strozza and Vincentio have been seriously injured by Mendice; Margaret, distraught, has disfigured her face; and Alphonso has confessed his responsibility for the "unnatural wounds" afflicting his state (5.4.85). At the play's close, Margaret is still wearing a medicinal mask over her face. "Love's ushering fire," her beauty, has been temporarily quenched; it is the actual usher who, unscathed, passionately embraces Vincentio. Bassiolo – the substitute "wife," expendable friend, and eroticized servant – remains silently onstage to reflect, and to generate audience reflection on, the dangerous consequences of Vincentio's homoerotics of mastery. Like Volpone, Vincentio cannot fully master the servant he has eroticized. Hence, as the future duke he has recreated the potential for "sodomy," the social and political disruption produced by Duke Alphonso's indulgence of a disorderly minion. Vincentio's homoerotics of mastery reveals the dangers, in early modern England, of an insufficiently witty mastery of homoeroticism – the failure to keep master–servant intimacy distinct from sodomy, the inability to control the ambitious servant one has erotically empowered.

Embracing wits: Middleton's homoerotics of mastery

What role do women play in the male homoerotics of mastery? Margaret may appreciate more than Vincentio does the dangers of Bassiolo's homoerotic advancement, but she nevertheless submits to her future husband's scheme. In two plays by Thomas Middleton, *Michaelmas Term* and *No Wit, No Help Like a Woman's*, women with greater independence play greater roles in the homoerotics of mastery. In *Michaelmas Term*, the greedy citizen Quomodo and his shape-changing servant Shortyard join forces to cheat Richard Easy, an Essex gentleman, out of his lands. Like Volpone, Quomodo feigns death, consequently abdicating his authority and losing all. But unlike Volpone, Quomodo has a wife. The more Quomodo ensnares Easy, the more his wife Thomasine pities and loves Easy. When Quomodo feigns death, she instantly seizes the opportunity to marry the gentleman her husband has ruined. Her new alliance in turn ruins both Quomodo and Shortyard. Engrossed by his schemes for mastery over Easy, Quomodo does not realize the disorder of his own marriage: he has failed to maintain an appropriate degree of mastery over his own wife. Significantly, it is the seizure of his authority by his wife, not his servant, that ultimately puts an end to Quomodo's homoerotics of mastery. Quomodo's mistake is treating a treacherous, eroticized servant too much like a partner, and a witty, sexually neglected wife too much like a subordinate.[85]

In *Michaelmas Term*, the male homoerotics of mastery fails because a husband fails to take into account his own wife's wit and erotic desire. In *No Wit, No Help Like a Woman's*, on the contrary, a wife's witty help does not destroy a male homoerotics of mastery but establishes a *female* homoerotics of mastery. As part of a witty plot to defeat the rich widow Lady Goldenfleece, whose husband financially ruined her own, Kate Low-water poses as a young gallant, then woos and marries the widow. Kate is assisted in this scheme by her husband, who plays the role of her servant. Thus, from the perspective of the other characters and of Middleton's audience, Kate's homoerotics of mastery might initially appear to threaten a triple inversion of sexual order: a wife's mastery of her husband (Kate – Master Low-water); a marriage between two women (Kate – Lady Goldenfleece); a disorderly marriage between a "boy" and a lusty widow (Kate-as-Gallant – Lady Goldenfleece).

Kate's homoerotics of mastery succeeds precisely because none of these three scenarios actually transpires. Kate does not master her husband; nor, of course, is she really the "boy" who marries the widow. And her marriage to Lady Goldenfleece is not "sodomitical" according to the particular construction of female homoerotic desire in early modern England. Because female–female sex *per se* did not have the potentially disorderly social consequences of male–female sex (an illegitimate or adulterous pregnancy), and because it was not included in the legal or religious discourse of sodomy (as was male–male sex), it was relatively unthreatening and could even be figured as "chaste."[86] Female homoeroticism threatened social order inasmuch as it granted women autonomy from male rule, traditional gender roles, and reproductive sexuality: hence the threats posed by Spenser's monstrously separatist Amazon nation; by the antireproductive erotic pleasures of Catholic nunneries in *Measure for Measure* (1603) or Marvell's "Upon Appleton House"; by a female community's refusal of marriage and reproductive sexuality in *Love's Labour's Lost* (1594); or by actual women who sexually took "the man's part" through transvestism or use of an artificial phallus.[87] Against the frightening specter of a female homoeroticism independent from male control, a woman's desire for a woman could be safely represented as a harmless, temporary dalliance preceding or subsumed under her orderly desire for and subordination to a man.

Valerie Traub concludes that "the absence of outcry against 'feminine' homoeroticism" in early modern England "suggests that it posed very little gender trouble at all."[88] For these reasons, the sodomy that compromises the homoerotics of mastery for Vincentio in Chapman's play does not do the same for Kate in Middleton's play.

No one in the play ever questions why it is Kate and not her husband who takes on the disguise of the gallant. Kate is clearly the stronger and smarter of the Low-waters. In a speech reminiscent of the outspoken title character of *The Roaring Girl*, Kate vehemently denounces the injustice of her dilemma as a poor woman: "Must I to whoredom, or to beggary lean, / My mind being sound?"[89] Whereas Kate is passionate, her husband is passive and needs his wife's encouragement to take action: "I crave no more of thee than a following spirit" (1.2.159). Perhaps the name "Low-water" refers not only to the husband's low fortunes, then, but to the wife's ability to play the man's part. Kate is not one of the typically incontinent "leaky" women found by Gail Paster in city comedy.[90] Beveril, Kate's scholar-brother, insists that allegorically speaking "water certainly should be a woman" (3.1.249), yet Kate is no ordinary woman, being particularly low in the watery qualities of "weakness and inconstancy" (4.3.119).

Despite the fact that her scheme requires Master Low-water to obey his wife and "fill the cup" like Ganymede, Kate's witty self-mastery prevents any imputation of disorder to this arrangement. There are no references to sodomy, no ganymede jokes about Master Low-water's role, because Kate is careful not to master her husband as a shrewish wife might:

> MISTRESS. I'll have a trick for 'em; look you second me well now.
> MASTER. I warrant thee.
> MISTRESS.   I must seem very imperious, I can tell you;
> Therefore, if I should chance to use you roughly,
> Pray, forgive me beforehand.
> MASTER.   With all my heart, Kate.
> MISTRESS. You must look for no obedience in these clothes;
> That lies in the pocket of my gown. (2.3.19–24)

As Master Low-water later recognizes in a comforting aside, "How few women are of thy mind; she thinks it too much to keep me in subjection for one day, whereas some wives would be glad to keep their husbands in awe all days of their lives" (2.3.211–14). There is no sodomy without social disorder.

By contrast, Kate's appearance as a young gallant immediately provokes disorderly sexual desires in Weatherwise, one of the widow's four suitors. Struck by the feminine beauty of the supposed youth,

Weatherwise exclaims to himself, "A proper woman turned gallant! If the widow refuse me, I care not if I be a suitor to him. I have known those who have been as mad, and given half their living for a male companion" (2.1.180–83). The foolish Weatherwise has already been associated with disorderly homoeroticism, when, in reading his almanac, he recalls, "'the sixth day, backward and forward' – that was beastly to me, I remember" (1.1.262–63). His outburst is nevertheless remarkable for the analogy it draws between wooing a widow and wooing a "male companion," a figure who seems to combine the sexual availability of the ingle with the mutuality of the male friend. The aside creates audience complicity with Weatherwise, implying that they, too, know men who have left off wooing recalcitrant widows to pursue more available and equally desirable young men.

Weatherwise's appreciation of the wooable youth may say more about the competitive activity of mastering an object of desire, of being a suitor, than it does about the gender of object choice. Throughout the play, the widow's *suitors* are figured as phallic *shooters*, a common Renaissance pun explicitly drawn out in *Love's Labour's Lost* (4.1). Curiously, *No Wit, No Help* presents the ass as the target of these suitors' phallic aim. Sir Oliver Twilight rejects Weatherwise as a suitor to his daughter because a rival suitor can produce more attractive female offspring: a "chopping girl with a plump buttock, / Will hoist a farthingale at five year's old" (1.1.244–45). Weatherwise notes of his rivals for the widow, "Here are more shooters, / But they have shot two arrows without heads; / They cannot stick i'th'butt yet" (2.1.22–24). The mastery of a male suitor over his male rivals and his (male or female) object of desire can be figured as a phallic penetration "in the butt" because the ass is common to both sexes and because it is associated with both eroticism and domination. When Kate achieves such mastery, Pickadille remarks that "all the old shooters . . . have lost the game at pricks" to the "last arrow" (3.1.76–79). This pervasive phallic/anal imagery may explain the seemingly gratuitous comic scene in which Pickadille chastises Lady Goldenfleece's servants as "ponderous beef-buttock'd knaves" and calls for "the flesh-color velvet cushion now for my lady's pease-porridge-tawny-satin bum" (4.2.1–4). Besieged by "shooters" engaged in homosocial and homoerotic rivalry for her sexual favor, the widow may well require a shield.

Initially, Kate's marriage to Lady Goldenfleece appears to produce various kinds of erotic disorder. The audience of the play sees a woman "married" to another woman; those characters ignorant of Kate's actual sex perceive a marriage between a lusty widow and a "beardless domineering boy" (5.1.261). Significantly, it is Kate's insufficient masculinity as a "boy" husband, not as a "female" husband, that produces the strongest effect of a disorderly, even sodomitical, marriage. As either a woman or a boy, Kate is an insufficiently phallic suitor/shooter. To Kate's bowling metaphor – "I've a clear way to th'mistress" – Master Low-water responds, "You'd need have a clear way, because y'are a bad pricker" (2.3.77–78). While Kate and her husband joke lightheartedly about her female lack of a "prick," the rejected suitors use the wedding masque to condemn Lady Goldenfleece of a monstrous violation of marital norms:

> Rich widows, that were wont to choose by gravity
> Their second husbands, not by tricks of blood,
> Are now so taken with loose Aretine flames
> Of nimble wantonness and high-fed pride,
> They marry now but the third part of husbands,
> Boys, smooth-fac'd catamites, to fulfill their bed,
> As if a woman should a woman wed.   (4.3.64–70)

Gratifying herself with a womanish boy, this conventionally lusty widow imitates the sodomitical Italians and urban gallants of satire: *catamite* is not a "homosexual boy" but a boy hired for sexual services, usually, of course, by men. In their masque's allegorical depiction of the four elements, the male quartet of suitors conveys via the discourse of the unnatural the sodomitical embraces of Lady Goldenfleece's unruly marriage to a catamite: "And now to vex, 'gainst nature, form, rule, place, / See once four warring elements all embrace" (4.3.147–48).

Sir Gilbert condemns the disorderliness of Lady Goldenfleece's marriage to a boy most strongly by comparing it to the almost unthinkable marriage of women: "As if a woman should a woman wed." Although a woman has "wed" a woman in this play, I have already shown that it is the simulated marriage between a widow and a boy and not between two women that provokes anxieties about unnatural sexuality. Yet if a hypothetical marriage between women epitomizes social and erotic disorder to Sir Gilbert's mind, then how can Middleton represent such a potentially transgressive union between Kate and Lady Goldenfleece while managing to maintain Kate's virtue and attractiveness and concluding the play harmoniously? How, in other words, does the play preserve the marriage of Kate and Lady Goldenfleece from the taint of monstrous sexuality imagined by Sir Gilbert?

Examining some of the rare representations of female homoeroticism in early modern texts reveals Middleton's use of a common strategy for containing the threat of female homoerotic desire: the conditional. In Nicholas de Nicholay's travel narrative, *Navigations into Turkie* (1585), as in *No Wit, No Help*, female homoerotic activity occurs when witty wives break away from their husbands' control. Nicholay claims that Turkish wives, jealously restricted by their husbands, frequent the baths as an excuse for leaving their homes. But other enticements await these women at the baths, and here Nicholay picks up on English culture's common belief in Turkish sexual excess:

[They] do familiarly wash one another, wherby it commeth to passe that amongst the women of Levan, ther is very great amity proceding only through the frequentation & resort to the bathes: yea & somtimes become so fervently in love the one of the other *as if it were with men*, in such sort that perceiving some maiden or woman of excellent beauty they wil not ceasse until they have found means to bath with them, & to handle & grope them every where at their pleasures so ful they are of luxuriousnes & feminine wantonnes: Even as in times past wer the Tribades, of the number wherof was Sapho the Lesbian which transferred the love wherwith she pursued a 100. women or maidens upon her only friend Phaon. And therfore considering the reasons aforesaid, to wit, the clening of their bodies, health, superstition, liberty to go abroad, & lascivious voluptuousnes, it is not to be marvelled at that these baths are so accustomably frequented of the Turks.[91]

In this passage, as well as in *No Wit, No Help* and, as I have shown, *As You Like It*, the threat of female homoerotic desire is contained by an identical rhetorical strategy: the incredulous "as if." A woman's desire for a woman can be more safely represented within the confines of a conditional statement that suggests her "proper" desire for a man. Dekker's *Satiromastix* deploys a similar containment strategy. As the play opens, a gentlewoman asks her "bedfellow" why people furnish weddings with flowers; she responds:

> 2. One reason is, because tis – O a most sweet thing to
>   lye with a man.
> 1. I thinke tis a O more more more more more sweet to lye
>   with a woman.
> 2. I warrant all men are of thy minde.   (1.1.17–21)

Clearly, the second gentlewoman does not interpret her friend's emphatic preference for her own sex as a sign of maidenly chastity, since her reference to men eroticizes the sweetness of lying with a woman. But her response also serves to erase or subsume female homoeroticism by shifting the terrain away from any consideration of a female desiring subject towards the heteroerotic desire felt by "all men."

In these examples, a woman's desire for another woman is, to use Nicholay's term, finally "transferred" onto a man. Although a man like Weatherwise in Middleton's play might have a "male companion," it is virtually inconceivable within this cultural construction of female sexuality that a woman would "marry" another woman. Sapho leaves 100 women for a single man; each of the Turkish wives returns from the homoerotic bathhouse orgy to her own husband; Celia, Rosalind, and Phoebe are all furnished with a husband at the end of *As You Like It*. As Valerie Traub argues, Renaissance writers "pose eroticism between women as an option, only to displace it through the force of a seemingly 'natural', ultimately more powerful heterosexual impulse."[92] This process of displacement is clearly dramatized in Chapman's *Monsieur D'Olive* (1605), in which Eurione desires to remain a virgin in memory of a dead friend, her "dear Sister vow'd." Her friend Vandome cannot understand her devotion: "Now heaven forbid; women in Love with women . . . Well well, there is some other Humor stirring, / In your young bloud then a dead womans Love."[93] Vandome exaggerates the strangeness of female homoeroticism by projecting one woman's love for her friend into an imagined community of female lovers: "women in Love with women." This threat is erased when Eurione confesses that she has fallen in love with her friend's husband because he "lov'd / His Wife so dearely, that was deere to me" (2.1.169–70).

Whereas in Eurione's case a woman's love is transferred from a woman to a man, a seventeenth-century satire raises the possibility of female lust traveling the same route. In William Goddard's *A Satirical Dialogue* (1615), three sisters amuse each other by relating their erotic dreams. The eldest sister begins by complaining of her small incentive for going to bed:

> Alas, alas, what pleasure and delight
> Takes one mayde with an other in the night?
> But smale god knowes it, for my owne part I
> Ne're tooke anie with whom I e're did lie.
> For love, noe revells in that bedd doth keepe
> Where one girle, by an others side doth sleepe.
> For trulye (sisters) there is none that can
> Give maydes delight in bedd, but a young man.[94]

By having the sister insist so strenuously on the futility of female–female sex, Goddard raises the possibility of just such "pleasure and delight," especially for the younger, less experienced, sisters. Yet any speculation about the "revells" girls keep in bed might well be dispelled by the youngest sister's pornographic account of the man of her dreams, who is graced with "snowe-white armes," a "full-broade manlie some-what-downye cheste," "prettie fruiteles teatlinges," a "soft slender waste," and something that "grewe beneathe his plump-round bellie" (sigs. C2r–v). Despite the possible homoerotic charge produced by the circulation of sexually explicit tales among these women, the youngest sister's dream

seems to prove that only a young man is equipped to give sexual delight
to a maid.

What do these representations of female homoeroticism reveal about
the female homoerotics of mastery in *No Wit, No Help*? In all of the texts
cited above, female homoeroticism is both raised and razed, as a
woman's desire for another woman is transferred onto the husband or
male lover, real or imagined, who is deemed the appropriate object of her
desire. The transferal may not be complete, or it may reveal the
ideological traces of its erasure as in Goddard's *Dialogue*; nevertheless,
there is a strong cultural imperative to anchor female desire onto a single
man. The female homoeroticism of Middleton's play is already extenu-
ated by the fact that Lady Goldenfleece does not consciously know that
her husband is really a woman. For these reasons, Kate's homoerotics of
mastery is less socially disruptive and hence more successful than
Vincentio's homoerotics of mastery. Kate undoubtedly triumphs: she
scorns Lady Goldenfleece's love, publicly accuses her of adultery with
Beveril, acquires £5,000 in their divorce settlement, and requires her to
choose her next husband. As the final blow, Kate informs Lady Goldenfleece that their marriage is invalid, for "he" is already married, and
Lady Goldenfleece chooses Beveril for her new husband. It is only at this
point that Kate, having accomplished all her goals, can reveal her true
sex, bringing her homoerotics of mastery to a triumphant close.

In a triangulation familiar from *Twelfth Night*, Lady Goldenfleece's
disorderly desire for a woman disguised as a boy is simply transferred to
that woman's brother.[95] The homoerotic bait-and-switch is especially
smooth in *No Wit, No Help* because its parallel romantic plot depends on
the switched identities of two women, the wife and the sister of Philip
Twilight. At the end of the play, Philip learns that his wife Grace is his
long-lost sister. Just as Middleton redeems the disorderly marriage of
Lady Goldenfleece and Kate, he redeems the incestuous marriage of
Philip and Grace. The final revelation of the play is not, in fact, Kate's
declaration of her female sex, but Lady Goldenfleece's declaration that
Jane Twilight and Grace Sunset were switched at infancy. With Lady
Goldenfleece's help, Philip escapes a truly incestuous marriage to Jane
and is cleared of incest with Grace. Similarly, it is only after Kate has
transferred Lady Goldenfleece's desires onto her brother that she can
safely reveal her bosom, thus revealing the secret of their dissolved
disorderly marriage.

Middleton signals the transferal of Lady Goldenfleece's desires from a
female to a male object of desire through a sequence of carefully staged
embraces. Throughout the play, embracing signifies desire and harmony.
In the first scene of the play, for instance, Philip and Sandfield are

transformed from enemies into "embracing friends" (1.1.145). Lady Goldenfleece's wedding-night embraces are far less chaste:

> LADY GOLDENFLEECE.
>   Now, like a greedy usurer alone,
>   I sum up all the wealth this day has brought me,
>   And thus I hug it.
>   [*Embracing her*]
> MISTRESS LOW-WATER. Prithee!
> LADY GOLDENFLEECE.   Thus, I kiss it.
>   [*Kissing her*]   (5.1.1–3)

Lady Goldenfleece's reformation at the end of the play is appropriately
symbolized by more orderly signs of affection, when she hugs Kate and
kisses Beveril: "[T]hus I'll revenge this, / With an embracement here, and
here a kiss" (5.1.377–78). Thanks to Kate's wit, revenge dissolves into
accord and the disorderly homoerotics of mastery yields to orderly
marriage.

Through a female homoerotics of mastery – getting the widow "in the
end" – Kate appropriates the male roles of witty gallant and phallic
suitor to make enemies into embracing friends. These embraces are
redemptive, not disorderly, because Kate has carefully avoided mastering
her husband and has effectively transferred Lady Goldenfleece's unruly
desires to a male object. There is no wit and no help like a woman's
because the potential threat female homoeroticism posed to the early
modern social order could be relatively easily dispelled. By contrast, the
lingering effects of disorderly male homoeroticism are not as easily
banished as Mendice is from the court in *The Gentleman Usher*. Unlike
the welcome embraces that conclude Middleton's play, Bassiolo's unwel-
come embrace of his prince at the end of Chapman's play epitomizes the
volatility of hierarchical male bonds. The lingering sodomy of satiric
comedies such as *The Gentleman Usher*, *Volpone*, and *Michaelmas Term*
attests to the palpable threat that homoerotic relations between masters
and servants could pose to the normative social structures of early
modern England.

The sodomitical subject of tragedy

For understanding the politics of male homoerotic relations in early
modern England, Chapman's *The Gentleman Usher* (1602) offers a simple
but crucial lesson: some homoerotic intimacies are more threatening to
social order than others. With his administrative responsibilities and
authority over other servants, a gentleman usher or steward, if corrupt or
incompetent, could impede the smooth functioning of a noble household.[1] Bassiolo may represent just such an ambitious and disorderly
household servant, but it is Mendice, the court favorite, who is finally
banished from the play. Although both Bassiolo and Mendice have
disruptive access to the bodies of their social superiors, Mendice's access
is more dangerous because his master is the Duke.

In early modern Europe, favorites could acquire tremendous power
through their closeness to the body of the prince. The correlation
between political power and physical proximity to the monarch's body
was complexly negotiated in the court of Queen Elizabeth. Elizabeth's
domestic intimates were women and therefore not holders of political
office, although they did wield considerable influence with the queen in
matters of patronage.[2] Throughout her reign, Elizabeth had various male
favorites such as Leicester, Ralegh, and Essex, who provides the most
notorious example of one who pressed to the limit of treason his
privileged closeness to the queen. As for courtiers and statesmen, new
historicist and feminist scholars have explored how Petrarchan conventions shaped political relations generally in the Elizabethan court.[3]
Although these conventions elicited the public performance of erotic
desire for Elizabeth, however, the access of courtiers to her body was
always mediated by the sexual unavailability of the virgin queen as
acknowledged, for instance, in Ralegh's poems addressing her as chaste
Diana or Cynthia.

Given the importance and visibility of relations between the queen and
her favorites, why do Elizabethan playwrights depict relations between

male monarchs and their male favorites? One reason is that the Elizabethan court functioned through the expression not only of heteroerotic
but also of homoerotic desires, as in the patronage bonds between male
favorites, courtiers, and clients. With the exception of the queen herself,
power in the Elizabethan court circulated among men. Another explanation is provided by Simon Shepherd, who argues that theatrical representations of favoritism primarily concern not gender or eroticism but
power. According to Shepherd, an "Elizabethan dramatist who wished
to explore the contradictions of personal rule used a male monarch and
male favourites. For the power sought by the favourite is always possible
to achieve within the conditions of personal rule as stressed by the
ideology of absolutist monarchy."[4] Drawing largely from English,
French, and Roman history, both Elizabethan and Jacobean playwrights
return to the relation between male monarch and favorite as a means of
dramatizing issues of contemporary political and ideological relevance:
the limits of sovereign power and of resistance to it; the means by which
political authority is established, maintained, transferred, and delegitimized; the dangers of flattery, misgovernment, corruption, and civil war;
the interdependence among sovereign, peers, courtiers, subjects, and
foreign powers; the conflict between sovereign will and sovereign duty;
the place of sexuality and favoritism in court culture and politics.

Some Renaissance playwrights use the bodily intimacies of the early
modern court as a source of satirical or bawdy humor. In Marston's
satirical *Parasitaster* (1606), for instance, a courtier mocks Dondolo's
closeness to the duke's body: "Thou art private with the duke; thou
belongest to his close stool."[5] Although Dondolo's privacy with the duke
gives him valuable access to news, it also associates him with the base
function of the duke's privy. Marston's satire is even more pointed when,
in *The Malcontent* (1603), he has Mendoza rapturously describe the
power of a favorite:

O sweet God! O pleasure! O fortune! O all thou best of life! what should I think,
what say, what do to be a favourite, a minion? to have a general timorous respect
observe a man, a stateful silence in his presence, solitariness in his absence, a
confused hum and busy murmur of obsequious suitors training him; the cloth
held up, and way proclaimed before him; petitionary vassals licking the pavement
with their slavish knees, whilst some odd palace-lampreels that engender with
snakes, and are full of eyes on both sides, with a kind of insinuated humbleness,
fix all their delights upon his brow. O blessed state! what a ravishing prospect
doth the Olympus of favour yield![6]

Observing his prince's body, the minion is observed in turn by suitors
deformed by their obsequious fawning. The "ravishing prospect" af-

forded the minion by the bodily mortification of suitors depends on the power invested in his own favored body.

Despite the temptation to treat satirically the favorite's mediation between the bodies of prince and courtiers, Renaissance playwrights more frequently represent the spectacle of court favoritism in a tragic mode. *The Gentleman Usher*, for instance, approaches the concerns of contemporary tragedy in its depiction of a sodomitical favorite who injures noblemen and subverts political order. Yet the fact that dramatists represent intimate relations between princes and favorites in a tragic mode does not mean that homoerotic desire was inevitably associated with sodomitical death and destruction in the early modern period. On the contrary, Renaissance writers present desire between princes and favorites neither as inherently sodomitical nor as the sole cause of tragedy. Homoerotic relations of favoritism frequently produce tragic disorder because the favorite's proximity to the prince's body creates a volatile political situation with enormous consequences. In his essay "Of Wisdom for a Man's Self," Francis Bacon observes that princes "themselves are not only themselves, but their good and evil is at the peril of the public fortune."[7] The favorite's access to the prince's body affects the body politic, for good or for evil. Yet the fact that the unmatched term "peril" breaks the rhetorical symmetry of Bacon's formulation suggests an excess anxiety about the evils that might accompany the prince's division into personal and corporate "selves." Early modern tragedies of state represent as "sodomy" the various perils arising from physical intimacy between princes and favorites.

Of course, the tragedies written during King James's reign appear to have particular topical reference to his notorious promotion of male favorites. James's highly visible affection for his favorites was noted and discussed throughout the seventeenth century, and contemporary scholarship acknowledges the homoerotic relationships he pursued both in Scotland and in England, both before and after his marriage to Anne.[8] Men who were at once personal favorites and political office holders enjoyed direct access to James's body. Not only were the gentlemen of the bedchamber James's personal servants, but unlike Elizabeth's gentlewomen, they were involved as well at the highest levels of court patronage, bureaucratic administration, and policy formation.[9] In an important connection to the theater, seventeenth-century observers compared James's relations with his favorites to the mythological and historical paradigms of favoritism (Jupiter and Ganymede, Edward II and Gaveston, Tiberius and Sejanus) that populate Renaissance tragedy.[10]

Nevertheless, it would be at best reductive to claim that playwrights deliberately modeled their characters after the personal example of James. Jacobean court tragedies do not simply materialize as a direct "response" to the monarch's homoerotic behavior; rather, they constitute interventions in a sustained cultural discourse about power and desire – a discourse that was also available to, and just as compelling to, Elizabethan playwrights.[11] James is not the origin of a homoerotic political practice that the plays imitate or reflect; rather, sovereign, favorites, court commentators, and poets participate in and collectively shape the various practices and discourses of the early modern court. Unavoidably, then, the representation of historical kings in poetry or drama has relevance to the erotic practices of the English court.[12]

Before turning to the drama, it will be instructive to consider in more detail the intertwining of discursive and material practices of homoeroticism in the Jacobean court. Since even a text as "static" as an emblem can usefully open up a tangle of interpretive and ideological considerations, I will begin with the figure of Ganymede that appears in Henry Peacham's emblem book *Minerva Britanna*, published in 1612 and dedicated to Prince Henry. In sixteenth-century emblem books, the image of Ganymede lifted to the heavens by an eagle commonly symbolizes transcendent spirituality.[13] Significantly, Peacham recasts Ganymede as a sodomite. Titled *"Crimina gravissima,"* the text of the emblem reads:

> Upon a Cock, heere *Ganimede* doth sit,
>   Who erst rode mounted on *JOVES* Eagles back,
> One hand holdes *Circes* wand, and joined with it,
> A cup top-fil'd with poison, deadly black:
>   The other Meddals, of base mettals wrought,
>   With sundry moneyes, counterfeit and nought.
>
> These be those crimes, abhorr'd of God and man,
> Which Justice should correct, with lawes severe,
> In *Ganimed*, the foule Sodomitan:
> Within the Cock, vile incest doth appeare:
>   Witchcraft, and murder, by that cup and wand,
>   And by the rest, false coine you understand.[14]

Peacham's emblem illustrates the passage from *Basilicon Doron* in which James instructs Prince Henry that a king must never forgive the crimes of witchcraft, poisoning, and sodomy. James evidently did not regard his own licensed behavior with favorites as the disorderly sodomy he proscribed as the unforgivable crime of a subject.[15] The seeming contradiction between his proscription of sodomy and his homoerotic relations with favorites exposes not James's disavowal or repression of his "homosexual desire," but the practices and significations available to him from the specific subject-position of early modern kingship – in the particular case of James including a belief in absolute rule that made him accountable only to God. From his perspective, his behavior was not "sodomy."

When we turn from Peacham's emblem to James's court, will we find a criminal Ganymede or a "foule Sodomitan?" Whereas James may not have viewed his homoerotic desires as disorderly, certain observers who did not subscribe to his mystification of kingship did. Rebecca Bushnell describes the double-edged sword honed by James's political rhetoric: "For James, identification with the Roman emperors offered a way of styling himself as a god; for his antagonists, the comparison would suggest a less complimentary association with depravity and cruelty."[16] Under the "specious titles" of classical friendship, claimed the French ambassador in 1622, James "endeavours to conceal scandalous doings, and because his strength deserts him for these, he feeds his eyes where he can no longer content his other senses."[17] A contemporary poem by William Browne describes how the king's sensual vision transforms worthless parasites into great luminaries:

> So if a King behold such favourites
> (Whose being great, was being *Parasites*,)
> With th'eyes of favour; all their actions are
> To him appearing plaine and regular:
> But let him lay his sight of grace aside,
> And see what men hee hath so dignifide,
> They all would vanish, and not dare appeare,
> Who *Atom-like*, when their *Sun* shined cleare,
> Danc'd in his beame; but now his rayes are gone,
> Of many hundred we perceive not one.[18]

Feeding his eyes with the sight of handsome favorites instead of using his perspicacious "sight of grace" to discern their true inner qualities, such a king sees "plain actions" where a keener observer sees parasitical deceptions. Whereas the French ambassador registers dismay at royal indecorum and Browne criticizes the king's poor judgment and administration, Simonds D'Ewes speculates that the "sinne of sodomye" is "as wee had probable cause to feare, a sinne in the prince as well as the people."[19]

Why is James's homoerotic desire intelligible from certain perspectives not as royal patronage – the epitome of social order – but as sodomy – the epitome of social disorder? The French ambassador's account describes not just erotic desire, but the ridiculous and shameful desire of an impotent old man for an attractive youth. Roger Coke explains the political absurdity of James's dependence upon a young and flighty minion:

Neither was it any great wonder, that *Edward* the II*d*, a young Man, should be governed by *Pierce Gaveston*, a Person of far more accomplished Parts than *Buckingham*, for *Gaveston* was bred up with *Edward* ... But for an old King, having been so for above fifty one Years, to dote so upon a young Favourite, ... and to commit the whole Ship of the Common-wealth, ... to such a *Phaeton*, is a Precedent without any Example.[20]

Coke makes no mention of sexual relations between these kings and their favorites. In fact, he seems to feel much as do the peers in Marlowe's *Edward II* (1592), who do not find a king's love for a favorite objectionable in itself: far from wonderful, the government of a king by an equally accomplished favorite might even serve, Coke implies, as a precedent.[21] What Coke objects to is the folly of letting an inexperienced man like Buckingham run the commonwealth. When Sir Henry Yelverton likewise compared James's court to that of Edward, the king responded angrily to the slur: "To reckon me with such a prince is to esteem me a weak man, and I had rather be no king than such as one as King Edward II."[22] James would rather be a subject than a weak king, because to be a weak king is in a sense to be no king at all.

As James recognized, what these accounts find disturbing are the ostensible signs of his political weakness, variously expressed as an undignified and impotent sexual indecorum, the illness that debilitated him as an old man, the virtual abdication of regal power to an ambitious Phaeton, or the inability to manage powerful favorites. It was not the homoerotic nature of James's attachments so much as the excessive power his desire bestowed on male favorites that provoked censure of his sexual behavior. Francis Bacon identifies the single favorite as a sign of political vulnerability: "To be governed (as we call it) by one is not safe, for it shows softness, and gives a freedom to scandal and disreputation."[23] It was the scandalous softness of the court, according to Alan Bray, that was the main focus of antisodomitical invective against it:

It was the Court – the extravagant, overblown, parasitic Renaissance Court – not homosexuality which was the focus of their attention. What homosexuality provided was a powerfully damaging charge to lay against it; at what should have been the stronghold of the kingdom there was only weakness, confusion and disorder.[24]

Bray is certainly right when he argues that in Renaissance England homosexual practices were not identified apart from the larger social practices in which they took place. Yet he implies that a distinct thing called "homosexuality" *could be* identified and distinguished from a distinct thing called "the court" when he claims that "it was the Court . . . not homosexuality" that provoked political antagonism. Bray thereby renders homosexual disorder peripheral to social disorder: not intrinsic to court politics, homosexuality is merely "laid against" the court.

The early modern monarch's "sexual" and "political" practices, his "private" and "public" selves, could not be so easily distinguished, and any attempt to do so would appear ideologically motivated. In *The True Law of Free Monarchies* (1598) James himself tendentiously tried to distinguish his public duties from his personal desires, which he considered "private matters."[25] According to his contemporaries, however, the king's personal desires directly interfered in his public duties by empowering the undeserving and by diminishing the symbolic dignity of his own estate. Precisely the *intersection* of "the Court" and "homosexuality" – in less reified and spatial terms, of court practices and homosexual practices – generated political struggle around the legitimacy of the sovereign's desires. That a text caricaturing James as a weak old man leaning on his favorites' shoulders was published as antiroyalist propaganda after the Civil Wars reveals how much is at stake in representations of homoerotic court practices.[26]

Given this ideological conflict within the Jacobean court, Peacham took a risk in casting the generic "sodomite" of James's *Basilicon Doron* as "Ganymede," a figure that could be interpreted as the royal favorite. Although the term "ganymede" might signify in this period any erotically subservient male, it could also be used in the sense most proximate to that of its mythological source: the favorite servant of a king. As a cupbearer in James's Privy Chamber early in his career, George Villiers (later Duke of Buckingham) fulfilled exactly Ganymede's role. A contemporary poem that seems to pick up imagery from Peacham's emblem makes Buckingham confess, "I that my country did betray, / Undid that King that let me sway / His scepter as I pleased."[27] Controlling the phallic scepter, the favorite "undoes" the king politically as well as sexually. In a Caroline manuscript poem, Alexander Gill the Younger asks God to preserve his "sovereign from a Ganymede / Whose whorish breath hath power to lead / His Majesty which way it list."[28] Peacham's emblem unites these sexual threats in the image of Ganymede as a whore/witch who sways a scepter, "Circe's wand," symbol of the degrading lust that transforms men into beasts.[29] Moreover, his poison cup links Ganymede with Circean women such as the Whore of Babylon and Cleopatra. An emblem book published in 1591 depicts a similarly elaborate cup with the motto "Filthy love constraineth men to commit all wickednesse." The tale that illustrates the motto condemns Cleopatra, a "shamelesse woman," who prevents Antony from drinking poisoned wine to prove her power over his life.[30] Mixing "filthy love" with death, whorish boys and whorish women offer cups of poison to the weak princes they control.[31]

Although Peacham's composite figure of Ganymede richly illustrates the incoherent category of "sodomy" – the subversion of gender, religious, sexual, economic, and political order – it does so under the guise of order, indeed of rule.[32] Peacham does not explain what has transformed the pure Ganymede who "erst" climbed to heaven on "Jove's eagle's back" into a wicked creature who descends to earth astride an incestuous Cock. Nevertheless, the emblem can be read as a subversive allegory of how an aspiring courtier degenerates into a dangerously powerful favorite. Enjoined to find in the emblem an image of crimes *against* the state, Peacham's reader might see there crimes *of* the state, namely the monstrous regiment of a "foule Sodomitan" – whether that figure is taken to be favorite, king, or both. The monstrosity of this sodomitical figure may be most powerfully manifested in its very blurring of the boundaries between ruler and ruled, king and favorite. The emblem can therefore be read as the *antithesis* of the court (hence an illustration of *Basilicon Doron*) or as an *illustration* of the court (hence the antithesis of *Basilicon Doron*).

The more subversive reading is corroborated by the two Latin quotations accompanying the emblem, which seem more applicable to King James than to Peacham's nominal patron, Prince Henry. The first quotation warns, "O flee the foolish effeminacy of boys, who as trusting a whirling top, always have passions for an unjust cause"; the second admonishes, "By that vice which you do not correct you will be punished, O King."[33] Peacham's emblem was published when James was promoting his second favorite, Robert Carr (the first, Esmè Stuart, died in 1583; the last and most notorious, George Villiers, was not to appear for several years). Coincidentally, a few years later Carr (now Earl of Somerset) was indeed convicted of employing his "passions for an unjust cause": his wife's murder of Thomas Overbury, a scandal which caused James to relinquish his favorite to judicial proceedings and advance Villiers instead.[34] Because Peacham's emblem is not easily reducible to a single interpretation – does it praise or admonish the king? – or even a single referent – does it concern a particular favorite or favorites in general, as the Latin citations might suggest? – it succinctly illustrates the overdetermined representation of homoeroticism within the early modern court.

Redeeming wanton kings: *The Massacre at Paris* and *Edward II*

The difficulty of interpreting the political significance of homoerotic courtly relations is a central problem in two tragedies by Christopher Marlowe. In both *The Massacre at Paris* (1593) and *Edward II*, precariously situated kings promote favorites who become the focus of political animosity. Nevertheless, the plays suggest that not the royal favorites but Machiavellian rivals for the throne pose the greatest danger to the monarch and state. "Sodomy" emerges not only when kings support disorderly favorites, therefore, but when nobles use violent and treacherous means to obtain access to the body and power of the king.

Marlowe structures *The Massacre at Paris* along the erotic trajectory of King Henry III's political career. Primarily responsible for the massacre of Protestants depicted at the beginning of the play, the Catholic Duke of Anjou assumes the throne as Henry III, a weak king who promotes civil discord. Despite his Machiavellian beginnings, however, Henry develops into a dignified monarch who upholds true (Protestant) religion and procures the stability of his nation. Favorites hold a symptomatic place in Henry's progress towards orderly rule: whereas the wanton king at the center of the play is surrounded by a group of disorderly favorites, the virtuous king at the conclusion of the play favors only one man, the loyal and wise Epernoun. Henry thereby redeems himself from the taint of weakness and false counsel associated with his earlier patronage of favorites. Moreover, as the promoter of civil war, it is the papist and overreaching Guise who represents the greatest threat to the king's personal and political safety. *The Massacre at Paris* redeems royal favoritism by replacing a group of wicked favorites with a single good favorite and by locating the threat of political usurpation not in Henry's erotic relation with this minion but in his manipulation by a powerful and violent faction leader.[35]

In *Edward II* Marlowe's depiction of favoritism resembles the lesser-known partnership between Henry III and Epernoun. The political conditions and consequences of Edward's love for Gaveston have been discussed at length in much excellent recent scholarship.[36] While my own interpretation is informed by this work, I find it necessary to demonstrate in more detail the significance of bodily intimacy among monarch, favorites, and peers in Marlowe's play. Such an analysis reveals that by shifting our attention away from the disorderly intimacy between Edward and Gaveston, the ambitious favorite, and towards the disorderly intimacy between Edward and Mortimer, the ambitious peer, Marlowe partially defends Edward's relationship with his favorites. "Sodomy," understood not as a sexual act but as a politically transgressive relation between men, occurs most damagingly not between Edward and Gaveston but between Edward and the peers.

Although it becomes the occasion for rebellion against the king, Edward's patronage of Gaveston is not as unequivocally sodomitical as the peers within the play, and some recent critics of the play, would have it. In his first lines, Gaveston reveals that the newly crowned king has invited him to "share the kingdom with [his] dearest friend."[37] Edward's invitation evokes the classical discourse of favorites as *participes curarum*, or "sharers in care" of the state. Francis Bacon discusses the contradictory implications of this role in an essay titled not "Of Sodomy" but "Of Friendship":

It is a strange thing to observe how high a rate great kings and monarchs do set upon this fruit of friendship whereof we speak; so great, as they purchase it many times at the hazard of their own safety and greatness. For princes, in regard of the distance of their fortune from that of their subjects and servants, cannot gather this fruit, except (to make themselves capable thereof) they raise some persons to be as it were companions and almost equals to themselves, which many times sorteth to inconvenience. The modern languages give unto such persons the name of favourites, or privadoes, as if it were matter of grace or conversation. But the Roman name attaineth the true use and cause thereof, naming them *participes curarum*, for it is that which tieth the knot.[38]

Although Bacon is silent on how the monarch's raising of inferiors might become a "hazard" or "inconvenience," the Roman name he attaches to favorites is telling, for *participes curarum* was the name Tiberius gave to Sejanus, who not only participated in the rule of Rome, but began to usurp it.[39] Ben Jonson remarked in his *Discoveries* the danger that ambitious favorites pose to tyrannical princes, whose "fortune is oftentimes to draw a Sejanus to be neere about 'hem; who will at last affect to get above 'hem, and put them in a worthy feare, of rooting both them out, and their family."[40] The prince hazards his safety due to the favorite's intimate involvement not only in household matters "of grace or conversation" – a private function signified by the label *privadoes* – but in the very public affairs of state.

Nevertheless, Bacon makes it clear that kings will "purchase" such friendship even to their peril. The language of economic exchange subtends a central tension in the bond between king and favorite, namely the king's dependence on a man whom he has raised to near equality. Although Jonson implies that only a tyrant need fear the treachery of a powerful favorite, Bacon explains that "servants" have been raised to the status of royal friend "not by weak and passionate princes only, but by the wisest and most politic that ever reigned."[41] In the similarly comprehensive statement of Marlowe's Mortimer Senior, "The mightiest kings have had their minions" (1.4.393), and not because they have always had the authority to gratify their sensual desires, but because they have always needed political allies. Simon Shepherd sees the undeserving favorite precisely as a sign of the Renaissance monarch's power over the gentry:

The threat of the favourite is as much economic as political, in so far as the monarch's desire cannot be accommodated within the marital and kinship systems which guarantee the security of the state. Such systems stabilise property ownership within individual hands; but, in a logical reversal, the favourite who is personally desired thus gains a power base which did not come from inheritance. Hence James I's public indulgence of favourites was a perhaps not unconscious display of the power of the absolute monarch, from whom come all benefits, however fanciful.[42]

A wise and mighty monarch might use a favorite to display his power; in so doing, however, his power becomes partially dependent on the favorite's own power of display. Patronizing favorites sustains the king's power yet reveals that power to be based not in "absolute" right but in structures of political and economic interdependence.

Aside from presenting an economic and political obstacle to those vying for power with the sovereign, the favorite may also fulfill a more personal need. Bacon ends the essay "Of Followers and Friends" with the acknowledgment that hierarchical friendships may be the only kind still possible in his society: "There is little friendship in the world, and least of all between equals, which was wont to be magnified. That that is, is between superior and inferior, whose fortunes may comprehend the one the other."[43] Aristotle's definition of friendship required the complete absence of self-interest; in modern times, Bacon implies, the mutual interests of social unequals may foster the most satisfying bonds. Whereas the inferior receives social and financial "fortunes" from his superior, the superior receives not only the personal gratification of bestowing these fortunes but also the material obligations of loyalty and service they incur on the dependent. A prince who raised an inferior to the status of favorite might be presenting himself as the munificent ruler and friend that an idealizing strand of early modern political ideology said he was supposed to be.[44]

An epistemological problem arises in identifying the kind of favorite who can be bound to act as a friend rather than a rival to his king. Early modern definitions of the "good favorite" and the "good king" are troubled by a similar contradiction. As Rebecca Bushnell and Alan Sinfield have shown, Renaissance political theorists confronted both the need and the inability to distinguish between the "king" and the "tyrant." Sinfield argues that King James tried to protect his absolutist rule from the stigma of tyranny by polarizing the "lawful good king" and the "usurping tyrant" in *Basilicon Doron*. Yet Shakespeare's *Macbeth* (1606) reveals that the supposedly metaphysical distinction between the good king and the bad king is based on an ideological distinction between legitimate (state-sponsored) violence and illegitimate violence. Likewise, Bushnell remarks the difficulty Renaissance political theorists faced in maintaining the etymological and rhetorical distinctions between king and tyrant.[45] If the absolutist ruler and the tyrant ideologically slip into one another, then the "good" and the "bad" favorite are in no less danger of categorical collapse. The king needs intimate companions to share in the administration of the state. But when do participants in care become rivals in power? Who determines at what point the favorite's beneficial services have become harmful to the sovereign's safety and status? Marlowe's *Edward II* implicitly raises the question in these terms: who or what distinguishes the "friend" from the "parasite?"

The notoriety of Marlowe's Gaveston and the historical Duke of Buckingham has distorted our notions of Renaissance favoritism with the stigma of sodomy. Before considering the differences between the good and the bad favorite, therefore, it is necessary to establish what Bacon might have meant by the kind of favorite kept by the "wisest and most politic" princes. An excellent example of the worthy favorite can be found in a Jacobean poem based on the biblical story of Joseph. In Robert Aylette's *Joseph; or Pharoh's Favourite* (1623), Joseph becomes an ideal sharer in the cares of state. Raised by Pharaoh from prisoner to prime counselor, Joseph uses his privileged access to the king for the public interest, not his own profit: "Nor sought I mine owne honour, wealth, and praise, / But his, who did me from the Dungeon raise, / And therefore, first take care for publike good."[46] His unjust imprisonment by his former master taught Joseph that favorites, despite or even because of their virtues, are continually subject to the whims of their superiors:

> Great *Favorites* in Court have suddaine falls,
> By their owne faults, or others accusation,
> Or by their Lords dislike and alteration
> Of Favorites.[47]

Despite the precarious position of favorites, Joseph achieves a permanent place in his monarch's "grace" because he has learned to direct his obedience first to God and only then to his temporal lord.

Although Aylette, following his biblical source, does not suggest a homoerotic bond between Pharaoh and Joseph, this does not imply that orderly relations of favoritism were incompatible with homoerotic desire in early modern thinking. The absence of homoerotic desire in Aylette's poem can be attributed to the fact that the poem's dedicatee, the Lord Bishop of Lincoln and Keeper of the Great Seal, was not, despite Aylette's flattery, the "Joseph" of the Jacobean court. In 1623 it was Buckingham who undeniably enjoyed "in Realm the second place" next to King James.[48] Unlike Joseph, Buckingham was widely judged to have used his intimacy with the king for his own "honour, wealth, and praise." The desire to flatter his patron may have influenced Aylette not to describe Pharaoh's relationship with Joseph in the erotically explicit terms that would have evoked James's disorderly patronage of Buckingham.

What Aylette does describe is a paradigm of the mutual and publicly beneficial bond between king and favorite. In having Edward II invite Gaveston to "share the kingdom" with him, Marlowe opens his play by evoking this paradigm of the favorite as friend. Gaveston's opening monologue repeatedly returns to an apparent concern for the king's welfare. He loves London because "it harbours him I hold so dear, – / The king, upon whose bosom let me die" (1.1.13–14). Gaveston wishes to experience the sexual consummation that will express his status as the king's favorite, but the intimacy he seeks requires his own absolute loyalty, which he expresses here as a willingness to perish alongside his patron. These are not the sentiments of a man motivated entirely by cynical self-interest, despite the intention to "draw the pliant king which way I please" (1.1.53). Gaveston does not declare his objectives in so manipulating Edward, yet the king's *pliancy* and the favorite's *pleasure* are clearly in harmony, even alliteratively. Howsoever Edward is being "drawn," it is not against his will.

Against the model of the favorite as friend, the peers promote the alternative model of the favorite as parasite. Significantly, Marlowe does not directly represent the wasteful actions for which the peers repeatedly attack Gaveston. We hear about but do not see Gaveston flattering the king or manipulating him with "lascivious shows" (2.2.157), mocking the peers' attire, or squandering the realm's treasure on extravagant ornaments and masques for Edward's entertainment. In the aggregate, these accusations of Edward's mismanagement of royal household and realm gain credibility, and they corroborate what we see of Edward's extravagant and irresponsible behavior. Nevertheless, the truth of the accusations is never conclusively demonstrated. Emily Bartels makes the cogent point that "the sexual/social transgression is the crucial framing source and subject of obfuscation" in the play.[49] Frequently, the charges against Gaveston proceed from Mortimer, whom Marlowe increasingly reveals to be an interested party in the favorite's demise and therefore an unreliable commentator.

The inappropriate bodily intimacy between Edward and Gaveston is more frequently described by Mortimer than actually represented on stage, and this discrepancy has the effect of highlighting Mortimer's obsession with Edward's "wanton humor," despite his long disclaimer to the contrary (1.4.404–20).[50] Mortimer repeatedly calls attention to the bodily display between Edward and his minions.[51] The usual strategy of the peers is to construct images of parasitical male bodies. Lancaster protests that "arm in arm, the king and he [Gaveston] doth march" as if they were equals (1.2.20). Mortimer makes explicit Lancaster's image of parasitical intertwining when he slurs Gaveston as "a night-grown mushrump" and fashions for his own chivalric emblem a "lofty cedar tree" besieged by a "canker" grown equally high (2.2.16–18). Gaveston is compared to the promiscuously erring body of "the Greekish strumpet" Helen; Spenser is condemned as "a putrifying branch / That deads the royal vine" (2.5.16; 3.2.165–66). The peers' imagery of parasitical corruption obscures the fact that Renaissance emblems of intertwined limbs and branches do not transparently or even primarily signify disorder. To the contrary, the vine embracing the elm is a common emblem of mutual love within marriage or male friendship.[52] The rebellious peers translate this image of virtuous love into a putative sign of Gaveston's parasitical sodomy.

Yet Edward's body is tormented not by his "parasitical" favorites but by his peers.[53] Not only do Mortimer's agents Matrevis and Gurney shave off Edward's beard in filthy puddle-water, symbolically emasculating and rechristening him as a subject, they imprison him in "the sink / Wherein the filth of all the castle falls" (5.5.58–59). Mortimer's tortures of Edward are scatological: they take place in, and allude to, the lower regions of the castle and the body. In contrast to the grotesquely specific architectural and anatomical siting of Edward's torments, Edward and Gaveston have figured their love in high terms borrowed from Ovidian erotic narratives and romantic love poetry. Like Leander, Gaveston would swim across the ocean merely to receive a "smile" and hug from the king (1.1.9). Edward and Gaveston sentimentally exchange pictures upon departing, and Edward remembers his friend as the "sweet favorite" to whom his "soul was knit" (3.3.43–44). Even according to their antagonists, physical intimacy between Gaveston and Edward occurs in the upper bodily regions: Lancaster notes their passage "arm in arm" (1.2.20); Warwick discovers Gaveston "leaning on the shoulder of the king" (1.2.23); Isabella complains that her husband "claps his cheeks, and hangs about his neck, / Smiles in his face, and whispers in his ears" (1.2.52).

While Gaveston and Edward are described, or imagined, as walking arm in arm, embracing, laughing out from a window, and frolicking together in a distant corner of the realm, Marlowe does not rely on anatomical or architectural specification to underline a sense of sodomitical disorder within the royal household. The play's descriptions of household intimacy suggest not the physical manifestations of "sodomy" (as nonreproductive sex) so much as a physical affection in which it becomes impossible to tell if king and favorite are whispering amorous blandishments or state secrets as they pass conspicuously through chambers and halls. Moreover, the dominant language of the play describes Edward's desire abstractly as a dotage (1.2.50), a lovesickness (1.4.87), a wanton humor (1.4.201), a vain toy (1.4.403), or simply love (1.4.76). In this, Edward does not resemble the King James described by an unsympathetic commentator who accused him of always "fidling about his cod-piece" in public.[54] Mortimer reduces Edward's affection to an image of lower bodily filth, so translating a homoerotic bond that in socially orderly contexts is deemed acceptable – for "the mightiest kings have had their minions" (1.4.393) – into the literal terms of a disorderly anality.

Most significantly, in authorizing Lightborn to murder Edward, which he accomplishes with an anally inserted poker, Mortimer enacts both regicide and sodomy.[55] Regarding the unpointed letter with which Mortimer commands Edward's death, John Archer observes that regicide as much as sodomy becomes a crime not to be named. In *Edward II*, Archer continues, the sovereign is a sodomite, but so, I would add, is the regicide.[56] Mortimer – the courtier most familiar with the bodily intimacy between Edward and Gaveston; the speaker of the parasitical and scatological aspects of homoerotic patronage; the leader of an "unnatural" and sexually disorderly rebellion; the architect of Edward's parodically sodomitical death – he most resembles the sodomite condemned in James's *Basilicon Doron* and in Peacham's corresponding Ganymede emblem. That Mortimer's scatological and sodomitical tortures of the king's body occur at one remove, through his various agents, does not imply his absolute difference from Gaveston, the minion who has direct access to the body of the king. Rather, it shows that "sodomy" is a category dependent as much upon a social relationship as upon a bodily relationship. Sodomy is a matter of *degree*, in both senses of the term. Bodily access to the king is secured, for Gaveston, by his erotic and political status as favorite, for Mortimer, by his military and political leverage as peer. Not only Gaveston but Mortimer, as if playing Gaveston in a sadistic register, had aspired to rule by having exclusive access to Edward's body: "And none but we shall know where he lieth" (5.2.42). Tellingly, Mortimer's power and knowledge converge to murder Edward as he lies in bed. From Edward's perspective, the sodomite is not Gaveston but Mortimer.

Embodying the unruly rule of the murderous Ganymede depicted in Peacham's emblem, Mortimer comes to resemble the disorderly favorite he defines and destroys as such. When the play opens, the death of the king (Edward I) enables Gaveston to manipulate the new king (Edward II); Mortimer wishes to punish Gaveston's presumption by striking off his head (1.1.123–24). By the end of the play the situation has repeated itself with Mortimer in the role formerly played by Gaveston. The death of the king (Edward II) enables Mortimer to manipulate the new king (Edward III), who finally strikes off Mortimer's "accursed head" as punishment for his "monstrous treachery" (5.6.95–96). The play opens with Gaveston expressing his willingness to die on the king's bosom but it concludes with Edward III's command that the traitorous Mortimer's head be displayed alongside the murdered king's hearse.

In one of the more provocative interpretations of *Edward II*, Jonathan Goldberg insists that "Marlowe is defending sodomy, not an idealized friendship or some spiritual relationship."[57] Although the relationship between Edward and Gaveston is both erotic and disorderly, Marlowe emphasizes the danger to the throne posed by the unnatural traitor who, in condemning the favorite's access and the monarch's patronage, acquires an even more destructive access to the monarch's body and power. The concept "unnatural" may indict Edward, but it does so abstractly, and indicts as well those who oppose him. In all these ways, then, Marlowe partially redeems the relationship between king and favorite from the stigma of "sodomy" and defends it from exclusive responsibility for the political disorder afflicting England.

Originally performed and published during the reign of Elizabeth, *Edward II* intervened in the political debates of its time. Yet Marlowe's play was also published and performed during the reign of James. A quarto appeared in 1612, the year in which Peacham's Ganymede emblem appeared and in which James appointed Robert Carr, Viscount Rochester, to the Privy Council. In 1613 James named Carr Earl of Somerset and sponsored his marriage to Lady Frances Howard after engineering her divorce from the Earl of Essex. By 1615, following the scandal surrounding the murder of Sir Thomas Overbury, Somerset had fallen from the king's favor and George Villiers began his rapid climb to power. When Marlowe's play was performed at the Red Bull and published yet again in 1622, the notorious Buckingham had acquired tremendous financial and political influence with James. As I indicated above, a variety of seventeenth-century sources attest that James's favorites were easy targets for censure of the monarch's personally and politically scandalous behavior. Nevertheless, like Peacham's emblem, Marlowe's play could have been read during James's reign as a defense of as well as an attack on homoerotic court politics. For no matter how disorderly, how scandalous, how improvident the homoerotic relations between Edward II and his favorites might be, it is Mortimer's access to the body of the king that the legitimate authority of Edward III finally constructs, and visibly punishes, as a sodomitical transgression against the body politic.

Penetrating the body politic: *Richard II* and *Sejanus*

Whereas *Edward II* evokes images of the parasitical male body, Shake-speare's *Richard II* (1595) and Jonson's *Sejanus* (1603) more thoroughly develop a discourse of parasitism. In these plays, the discourse of parasitism constructs kings and favorites as penetrating and penetrable bodies, and it is revealed as instrumental in achieving specific, and contradictory, political agendas. Whereas charges of sexual and political parasitism are used to justify the usurpation of the sovereign's power in *Richard II*, parasitic male relations sustain and even augment the sovereign's power in *Sejanus*.

In *Richard II*, Richard's critics attribute the injustices perpetrated by his government more to the flatterers who have misled the young king than to his own caprice or absolutism. York, for instance, complains that the king's ear

> is stopped with other flattering sounds,
> As praises, of whose taste the wise are fond,
> Lascivious meters, to whose venom sound
> The open ear of youth doth always listen,
> Report of fashions in proud Italy,
> Whose manners still our tardy-apish nation
> Limps after in base imitation.
> Where doth the world thrust forth a vanity –
> So it be new, there's no respect how vile –
> That is not quickly buzzed into his ears?
> Then all too late comes counsel to be heard,
> Where will doth mutiny with wit's regard.[58]

Here and elsewhere, Richard is accused of succumbing not to wanton-ness, the repeated charge against Edward II in Marlowe's play, but to flattery.[59] If Edward is most himself – and most kingly – when allowed to frolic uncontrolled with his base favorite, not so Richard, according to Northumberland: "The king is not himself, but basely led / By flatterers" (2.1.241–42). Such accounts remove agency from Richard, implying that his misgovernment proceeds not from a willful "mutiny" of his sexual "will," but from a youthful and characteristically English inclination to imitate the manners of haughty Italians.

Although Shakespeare mitigates Richard's responsibility for misrule by not directly staging his indulgence of favorites, we can nevertheless detect a hint of sexual transgression when York criticizes the king for delighting in "lascivious" meters and vile fashions "thrust forth" by foreign cultures. While certainly sartorial, the strange fashions so appealing to Richard may also be erotic, especially given their Italian origin. Gaunt brings out what York had only intimated regarding Richard's mutinous sexual will:

> And thou, too careless patient as thou art,
> Committ'st thy anointed body to the cure
> Of those physicians that first wounded thee:
> A thousand flatterers sit within thy crown,
> Whose compass is no bigger than thy head,
> And yet, incaged in so small a verge,
> The waste is no whit lesser than thy land.   (2.1.97–103)

York had focused on Richard's abused ear as a synecdoche for his dangerously open body; Gaunt's metaphor of disease initially encompasses the king's entire "anointed body" only to hone in on the image of a thousand flatterers crammed inside the king's "crown" or "head." Like physicians who "ever have been near the king" (2.2.134), the favorites use their access to explode the boundaries of the king's physical and corporate bodies, wounding and wasting both his literal and figurative crowns.[60]

In Bolingbroke's denunciation of Bushy and Greene, the site of transgression against the king's two bodies expands yet again from the "small verge" of the crown to the actual bedchamber:

> You have misled a prince, a royal king,
> A happy gentleman in blood and lineaments,
> By you unhappied and disfigured clean;
> You have in manner, with your sinful hours,
> Made a divorce betwixt his queen and him,
> Broke the possession of a royal bed,
> And stain'd the beauty of a fair queen's cheeks
> With tears, drawn from her eyes by your foul wrongs.   (3.1.8–15)

Bolingbroke implies that the "sinful hours" the favorites have spent with Richard have kept the royal couple from harmoniously occupying their bed. This charge resonates with the connotation of sexual expenditure in the Gardener's reference to Richard as "the wasteful king" whose "waste of idle hours" cost him the crown (3.4.55, 66). That Richard never produces an heir with either wife certainly undermines national stability, whatever its negative consequences for his conjugal life. Bolingbroke therefore detects sexual disorder at the microcosmic and macrocosmic levels, for by disfiguring Richard's "blood and lineaments" the favorites have disfigured a king's noble "blood" and lineage. Evoking the once immaculate sovereignty of the "royal king" and "royal bed" the favorites have violated and of the "queen" and "fair queen's cheeks" they have stained, Bolingbroke demonizes the favorites as disrupters of a *political* marriage – and hence raises the specter of sodomy.

Bolingbroke's interpretation of the marital crisis precipitated by the favorites, however, contradicts the evidence of marital harmony within the play. Shakespeare would have read in Holinshed that in Richard's time "there reigned abundantlie the filthie sinne of leacherie and fornication, with abhominable adulterie, speciallie in the king."[61] Accordingly, the contemporary tragedy *Thomas of Woodstock* (1592) depicts a bitter sexual competition between Richard's minions and the noble women of the court. The play thereby emphasizes the destruction incurred when the king replaces men and women of the nobility with sodomitical minions who by weakening his body weaken the realm. In *Richard II*, on the contrary, Isabella reveals to Bushy and Bagot not a longstanding estrangement from her husband but a new grief at "bidding farewell to so sweet a guest / As my sweet Richard" (2.2.8–9). Bidding farewell to her deposed husband, whom she has described not as the head of the household but as a transient guest, the queen plaintively asks, "And must we be divided? must we part?" (5.1.81).

By omitting any representation of antagonism between Isabella and the favorites, or between Isabella and Richard, Shakespeare makes Bolingbroke's charges against Bushy and Greene sound contrived. The conjugal division that Bolingbroke blames on the favorites occurs only after he himself has removed them from their king. Evoking Gaunt's image of flatterers who invade the royal crown, Richard accuses Bolingbroke of the same sin that Bolingbroke had attributed to the favorites: "Doubly divorc'd! Bad men, you violate / A two-fold marriage – 'twixt my crown and me, / And then betwixt me and my married wife" (5.1.71–73). Just as in *Edward II* Mortimer destroys Gaveston by casting him as the parasitical favorite that he himself comes to resemble, so Bolingbroke condemns the favorites for the erotic and political divorce for which he is directly responsible. Despite his rhetorical lament over the broken royal bed, what Bolingbroke deplores about the favorites' erotic power over Richard actually increases his own power, since Richard's lack of an heir bolsters Bolingbroke's claim to the throne. Bolingbroke does not simply reveal an undeniable truth about Richard's sodomitical favorites (no more than Mortimer does about Edward's); rather, he evokes the favorites' transgression against the king's two bodies to justify his own usurpation of Richard's power.

The transferal of political power is naturalized by the conventional trope of favorites as parasites, which moves the action symbolically from the enclosed royal household into the enclosed garden or orchard. Tropes of parasitical invasion and growth are conventional in the early modern discourse of favoritism. In *The Tragedy of Tiberius* (1607), for instance, Tiberius meditates while strolling through his orchard: "These

Poppies too much aspire, they are too high, / I must needes make them headlesse for their pride."[62] In *Richard II* Bolingbroke likewise swears to "weed and pluck away" Richard's proud followers, "noisome weeds which without profit suck / The soil's fertility from wholesome flowers" (2.3.165–66). During an extended rumination on the "disordered spring" unleashed by the king's misgovernment, the Gardener confirms that "[t]he weeds which his broad-spreading leaves did shelter, / That seem'd in eating him to hold him up, / Are pluck'd up root and all by Bolingbroke" (3.4.48, 50–52). Imagined as harmful weeds, political rivals may be eradicated with an incontrovertibly natural authority.

The weeds that devoured Richard's body are plucked up, however, only to make room for new growths nourished by the new king. "Who are the violets now / That strew the green lap of the new-come spring?" (5.2.46–47), the Duchess of York wonders regarding Bolingbroke's newly blossomed followers. Bolingbroke's indulgence of favorites resembles Richard's own. Similarly, the Gardener attributes Richard's downfall to his failure to prune "[s]uperfluous branches" (3.4.63), yet the same metaphor informs the Duchess of Gloucester's panegyric on the sons of Edward III as "seven fair branches springing from one root" (1.2.13). The homoeroticized body of one king produces male favorites, who share synchronically the space of his royal household; the procreational body of another king produces male offspring who share diachronically the name of his royal "house." Thus the play reveals "illegitimate" political affiliation and "legitimate" biological filiation to be parallel processes. The conflation of Richard II's stigmatized body with Edward III's celebrated body troubles Bolingbroke's own claims to legitimacy: are any of Edward III's "fair branches" actually "superfluous branches?" If Richard's line must be pruned for the Lancastrian line to flourish, then what guarantees that Bolingbroke's own branch will not in turn be deemed parasitical?

By raising these contradictions, *Richard II* suggests that homoerotic parasitism and favoritism are the conditions not merely of Richard's disorderly reign but of the reign that supplants it, that of Henry IV. The play exposes the parasite discourse as an ideological strategy used to naturalize a usurper's deposition of the legitimate king. Representations of the royal household as a locus of "unnatural" (antimarital or sodomitical) sexuality and of the royal garden as an image of the "natural" growth and extirpation of parasites have been instrumental in constructing an interested narrative of the favorites' and monarch's "private" responsibility for public disorder.

In no Renaissance play are sodomy and parasitism so constitutive of national politics as in Jonson's *Sejanus* (1603). Jonson conveys the disorder of the ancient Roman court by representing the male body as an amorphous, permeable organism equipped to facilitate homoerotic power negotiations. Although keeping his body "open" allows Sejanus to obtain political power, it finally renders him vulnerable to a political ruin that takes the form of literal dismemberment. Paradoxically, Tiberius survives political adversity by deploying his own grotesquely open body in sodomitical stratagems. Unlike Edward II and Richard II, Tiberius triumphs over hostile rivals and parasitical favorites. For a ruthless and canny sovereign, Jonson implies, sodomy can become a source of power.

In Tiberius's Rome, bodily intimacy greases court politics. In the first speech of the play, Sabinus reminds Silius why they fail as courtiers:

> We have no shift of faces, no cleft tongues,
> No soft and glutinous bodies, that can stick,
> Like snails, on painted walls; or on our breasts,
> Creep up.[63]

Polymorphous, malleable, and adhesive, the courtier's body accommodates itself to other forms. Sejanus's clients not only praise him "if he spit, or but piss fair, / Have an indifferent stool, or break wind well" (1.39–40), they actually share a bodily sympathy with their patron: they can "sweat when he sweats; / Be hot and cold with him" (1.33–34). Aside from providing a moment of scatological humor, Silius's disgusted account of sycophancy recalls just how much real political power a Groom of the Stool or Gentleman of the Bedchamber could have in the early modern court.

The power of intimate court positions is underlined by Sejanus's attempts to suborn figures who enjoy proximity to royal bodies. Seeking access to Livia, Sejanus asks the physician Eudemus to reveal which of his patients is the most "pleasant lady, in her physic" (1.302). Denying any interest in the scent of urine or habits of defecation, Sejanus crudely broaches the physician's familiarity with "ladies' privacies" or lower bodies (1.301). Because he knows that physicians "by the favour of their art, / Have still the means to tempt, oft-times the power" (1.368), Sejanus evokes the "open" female body to remind Eudemus of his power to open Livia to temptation. These rhetorical strategies evidently succeed in convincing Eudemus and Livia to poison Drusus, Livia's husband. To administer the poison, Sejanus seduces Lydgus, a cupbearer and a "eunuch Drusus loves" (2.13). Lydgus enjoys his master's "free access and trust" because his anatomical status renders him sexually nonthreatening to Livia (2.17). Lydgus is nevertheless susceptible to erotic manipulation: by "work[ing]" on the "wanton, light" eunuch's body,

Sejanus pursuades him to poison Drusus's body (2.22, 24). Sejanus gets ahead by manipulating the openness of noble bodies and the access of trusted favorites to them.

Having transcended his base origins by keeping his own body open, Sejanus intimately knows the mechanisms of political advancement in Rome. According to Arruntius, Sejanus's early career of homosexual prostitution required the sacrifice of his body to cannibalistic clients:

> I knew him at Caius' trencher, when for hire
> He prostituted his abused body
> To that great gourmand, fat Apicius,
> And was the noted pathic of the time.   (1.213–16)

Sejanus not only abuses his body as a "pathic" prostitute, he can imagine a hypothetical punishment for himself in which "Egyptian slaves" and Hebrews "print [his] body full of injuries" (2.140, 142). Given the association of Jews with "inverted" writing, Sejanus might be imagining sodomitical "prints" on his body. Unlike the honorable wounds of battle Silius receives on his breast, Sejanus's hypothetical wounds, "the backward ensigns of a slave" (3.262), mark him as both coward and catamite. Paradoxically, this self-abusive submissiveness promotes his ascent to power, which he secures through a network of parasitical spies: the "greedy vultures," "horse-leeches," and "bloodhounds, whom he breeds / With human flesh" (4.140; 4.366; 3.376–77). Sejanus achieves an exalted place by treating the male body as flesh to be eaten, penetrated, manipulated.

Not only does Sejanus employ bloodsucking parasites, he feeds off his patron, the most exalted body in the state. Just as Sejanus once provided his body for the ingestion of fat Apicius, so Tiberius nurtures the "mongrel" Sejanus with "his own blood" (4.366–67). When Agrippina describes Tiberius's body as "stuck with eyes" (2.450), she imagines a ruler at once universally observant and penetrated by the gaze of all. The object of courtly observation, Tiberius perversely submits to the "strokes and stripes of flatterers, which within / Are lechery to him, and so feed / His brutish sense with their afflicting sound" (1.413–15). If Tiberius's network of spies penetrates into the secret thoughts of his subjects, his own body is pierced by the erotic and invasive gaze of his rivals and subjects, Sejanus first among them.[64]

As Sejanus's appropriation of Tiberius's authority becomes more complete, Tiberius's body is increasingly described in terms of the grotesque: as filthy, libidinous, and open. At Capreae, for instance, Tiberius reportedly submits beautiful boys and girls to "strange and new-commented lusts, / For which wise nature hath not left a name"

(4.400–1). To his observers, Tiberius's sodomitical exploits become the cause and the sign of his imminent political downfall. "Bogged in his filthy lusts," Tiberius supposedly "sleeps" at conspiracies and has "disarmed / Himself of love" (4.217, 462–63). Moreover, Arruntius continues, "(what most strikes us, and bleeding Rome) / He is, with all his craft, become the ward / To his own vassal, a stale catamite – " (4.402–4). The syntax here is as equivocal as Agrippina's image of a Tiberius stuck with eyes: the "stale catamite" might refer to either Sejanus or Tiberius. If Tiberius is Sejanus's catamite, then "bleeding Rome" may allude metonymically to the penetrated body of the sovereign as well as of the state. Who is the sodomite here – the sovereign, the favorite, or, indistinguishably, both?

Whereas Tiberius might well be a catamite and employ catamites for his personal pleasure, his critics wrongly assess his political vulnerability, for he is well aware of Sejanus's parasitical designs. Sejanus imagines that his "charms" will seize upon Tiberius's epicurean senses as if he "hadst snuffed up hemlock, or ta'en down / The juice of poppy and of mandrakes" (3.595, 597–98). On the contrary, Tiberius intends to prove the proverb that "while two poisons wrestle, we may live" (3.654) and recognizes that the "prince that feeds great natures, they will sway him; / Who nourisheth a lion must obey him" (3.659–60). Setting Macro against Sejanus, Tiberius does not deny that his royal body absorbs poisons and nourishes lions; instead he sets dangerous poisons and lions against each other. Jonson endows Tiberius with the astonishing ability to pursue his erotic pleasures and acknowledge his dependence on his favorite without experiencing any real diminution of power. Because he recognizes that his own bodily openness represents political advantage as well as liability, Tiberius effectively detects and disarms his favorite's treachery.

Significantly, the language used to describe Tiberius as a grotesquely "struck" and "stuck" body comes to mark the political decline of Sejanus. For instance, upon hearing a report of the favorite's decline, Arruntius declares, "Till I see / Sejanus struck, no sound thereof strikes me" (4.504–5). Having hinted to Sejanus of a great honor in store, Macro explains that his discretion was meant to make the reward appear "more full and striking" (5.344); Sejanus flirtatiously objects, "You take pleasure, Macro, / Like a coy wench, in torturing your lover" (5.360–61). While it may be characteristic of Sejanus to imagine himself as a tortured lover, Tiberius's equivocal letter, like Mortimer's unpunctuated letter condemning Edward in *Edward II*, produces the literal torture of his body. "Mingling his honours and his punishments" (4.449), Tiberius acts in accordance with the mingling of sexual pleasure and pain, glory and degradation, that define his favorite's career.

Though Tiberius's grotesque body may not retain its erotic integrity, it is Sejanus's body that is grotesquely devoured and dismembered. Tiberius's scheme to ruin his favorite intensifies and magnifies the violence characteristic of both erotic and political practice in Jonson's Rome. Having first torn down statues of Sejanus like "so many mastiffs, biting stones" (5.777), the "rude multitude" rend his body "limb from limb," leaving the once great man "torn and scattered" (5.818, 840). The multitude that tears Sejanus's body into parts is itself a collection of anatomical parts: "A thousand heads, / A thousand hands, ten thousand tongues and voices" (5.821–22). Himself the subject of erotic pleasures so various that they lack a name, Tiberius reproduces his power by multiplying the threats to it: one poisonous favorite expells another, a pack of mastiffs devours the "mongrel" who devoured his blood, a "thousand heads" brutally destroy his "dearest head" (3.501). The label of "monster" (4.372) likewise travels from the singular "loathèd person" (4.375) of Tiberius to the abstract "monster" of the anarchic "multitude" that executes Sejanus (5.889–90).[65] To destroy the favorite who has sodomitically threatened his power, Tiberius unleashes what might be called the monstrously *reproductive* power of sodomy.

Sejanus exposes an important contradiction within the early modern discourse of favoritism. Tiberius is not necessarily weakened in his role as host, despite claims that he has abdicated his power by indulging his voluptuous body with parasitical minions. Literal or figurative openness to penetration, in either early modern or modern contexts, should not be equated automatically with powerlessness.[66] In *Richard II*, the king weakens his power by disseminating it among favorites whose "sodomitical" social and erotic practices provide a rival nobleman with the justification for deposing his sovereign. Delegitimized by his sodomitical patronage, Richard becomes the object, not the subject, of sovereign knowledge, a distinction central to James's condemnation of sodomy in *Basilicon Doron*. Tiberius, on the contrary, successfully negotiates *as a sovereign* the contradiction of political supremacy and dependency. John Archer reminds us that Jonson's Tiberius does not accurately represent "the strong personal monarch of absolutism" but is rather "an impossible combination of absolute power and nearly absolute self-effacement."[67] Tiberius may not represent a politically or psychologically viable early modern sovereign; nevertheless, he exists in (or as) the embodied space in which early modern discourses of royal homoeroticism and parasitical favoritism intersect.

Despite the diligent observance of his open, lustful body by antagonistic rivals, favorites, and potential successors, Tiberius demonstrates that sodomitical sexuality, when located in the sovereign's body, may act as a source of power. Rebecca Bushnell argues that "the ruler's sexuality is unrelated to his rule" in the case of Tiberius, and that he triumphs because "his lust has nothing to do with his power."[68] I have been arguing the opposite case: *Sejanus* insists that the ruler's sexuality is inextricably related to his rule, and that his lust has everything to do with his power. Tiberius retains his authority precisely because Jonson appreciates that the ruler's spectacularly displayed homoerotic desire may function not only as a *sign* of his power but as the very *means* through which power circulates in a court system based on interdependence among and privileged access to male bodies. Jonson's daring innovation with *Sejanus* lies in so absolutely embodying sodomy in the person of the sovereign. Even *Edward II* stops short of this point, for the homoerotic interdependence between king and favorite in Marlowe's play becomes intelligible in part through the orderly conventions of male friendship.[69] Like Peacham's "foule Sodomitan" who might symbolize both Ganymede and king, Tiberius is a symptomatic collection of ideological contradictions: at once emperor and catamite, vigilant and voluptuous, a grotesque body and a bodily cipher, observer of all and observed by all, nourisher and annihilator of parasitical bodies, source of Rome's blood and Rome's bleeding source. Unlike Edward II, Tiberius retains his pleasure and his power by strategically embodying, rather than being disembodied by, the contradictions of sodomitical favoritism.

Courting the favorite: Chapman's tragedies of the French court

Chapman appears to invert the direction of political struggle depicted in the tragedies of Marlowe, Shakespeare, and Jonson, for his tragedies set in the early modern French court depict princes who compete for access to a particular favorite, not favorites who compete for access to a single monarch. As their titles reveal, the four tragedies Chapman produced between 1604 and 1610 center not on kings but on great favorites who are raised and destroyed by rival princes. In *Bussy D'Ambois* (1604) Bussy is promoted first by Monsieur and then by Henry III; in the double play *The Conspiracy and Tragedy of Charles Duke of Byron* (1608) Byron wavers between the Duke of Savoy and Henry IV; in *The Revenge of Bussy D'Ambois* (1610) Clermont D'Ambois finds himself caught between the Duke of Guise and Henry III.[70] In each play a favorite's service to a patron dangerously alienates him from a former or rival patron with a competing claim to his service. Stubborn and stoical figures, the favorites generate further conflict by denying their dependence on the homoerotic court patronage system that promotes their careers.[71]

Chapman exceeds his contemporaries in developing an exceptionally rich language to describe the erotic and political dependency between patron and favorite. The princes in his plays passionately express their desires to possess the love and loyalty of a favorite. While such language establishes the normative homoeroticism of early modern patronage practices, the bitter rivalry between patrons evokes an alternative rhetoric of sodomitical disorder that signifies the corruption of these practices. In important ways, then, Chapman returns us to the central conflict of Marlowe's *Edward II*: the struggle between two powerful political factions to define and thereby either legitimize or delegitimize homoerotic patronage relations. Whereas Marlowe places the prince between rival nobles and favorites who compete for his patronage, Chapman places the favorite between rival princes who compete for his service. Through the discourses of homoerotic devotion and sodomitical inversion, Chapman's tragedies illuminate and critique the erotic rivalries of court favoritism that conspire to destroy valiant, if flawed, soldiers and courtiers.

Bussy D'Ambois begins with disorder and inversion. An impoverished soldier "discontent with his neglected worth," Bussy enters declaring that "Fortune, not Reason, rules the state of things, / Reward goes backwards, Honour on his head" (1.1.47, 1–2). The statement is not only reflective but proleptic, for the erotically disorderly court Bussy is about to enter could accurately be described as a system that rewards "backwards" or sodomitical practices. Tempting Bussy to serve as his follower, Monsieur, the brother of King Henry III, compares the court's splendor to the sun's radiance and the source of a pure spring. Bussy demystifies this idealizing rhetoric, wondering instead if he must "(like a strumpet) learn to set my looks / In an eternal brake, or practise juggling, / To keep my face still fast, my heart still loose," to "gain being forward," but "believe backwards" (1.1.86–88, 98, 100). Bussy realizes that survival at court requires the brazenness of a strumpet and the looseness of a catamite, who goes "forward" (gains favor) by going "backwards." Finally convincing Bussy to "be rul'd" by him, Monsieur calls his new favorite the "Favourite" of Fortune (1.1.116), thus identifying himself with the force that rules by inversion and rewards in reverse. Even before he depicts the court, Chapman conveys its political disorder through the terms of disorderly sexuality.

Introducing Bussy into the court, Monsieur treats his favorite with homoerotic affection and patriarchal possessiveness: "Come mine own sweetheart I will enter thee" (1.2.56). Henry III compares his brother's new sweetheart to a prize mistress or wife – "If you have woo'd and won, then Brother wear him" – an objectified role which Monsieur encourages Bussy to accept: "Th'art mine, my love" (1.2.69–70). Bussy, however, continually resists the position of dependence prescribed by the code of patronage. For instance, insisting that he "to himself is law" (2.1.203), Bussy declines Henry's pardon for his participation in a fatal duel. Despite Bussy's rhetoric of self-legitimation, Monsieur obligates his favorite to "quite" his love and protection: "Be true to the end: / I have obtain'd a Kingdom with my friend" (2.1.210–11). With characteristic equivocation, Monsieur describes his personal friendship with Bussy as a "kingdom" that will help him obtain the actual kingdom of France.

Bussy D'Ambois points to the potentially treasonous collusion of a faction leader and a favorite, only to recuperate this danger by representing Bussy's eventual shift of allegiance from Monsieur to Henry III. The French King Henry IV is similarly threatened by the conspiracy of a favorite in *The Conspiracy and Tragedy of Charles Duke of Byron*, which I would like to consider here briefly. The two Byron plays depict the seduction of an influential warrior and royal favorite by the enemies of his sovereign. In the courtly world of these plays, the language of power is the language of eroticism; the practices of power are consequently eroticized.

Early in *The Conspiracy* Chapman reveals a crucial dimension of Byron's character: "his blood is not voluptuous / Nor much inclined to women" (1.1.66–67). To seduce Byron away from King Henry IV, therefore, the Duke of Savoy administers the "physic" of flattery with the aid of La Fin, a disgraced French Lord (1.1.93–94). Rebuking La Fin as a "drone" who "witchest with [his] smiles, suckst blood with praises, / Mockest all humanity, society poisonst" (1.1.114, 154–55), Henry might be describing Peacham's emblem of Ganymede. In *The Tragedy*, Byron will indeed accuse La Fin of witchcraft: "He bit me by the ear and made me drink / Enchanted waters" (5.2.161–62). Both "witch" and "whore" (5.4.88–89), La Fin poisons and enchants Byron with his flattering bite.

Even before he encounters La Fin in *The Conspiracy*, Byron is susceptible to sensual manipulation. Greeted at Archduke Albert's court with rich carpets and sweet music, Byron experiences rapture:

> The blood turns in my veins; I stand on change,
> And shall dissolve in changing; 'tis so full
> Of pleasure not to be contained in flesh.   (1.2.27–29)

Here and elsewhere, Byron imagines power as dissolution. A courted favorite, he aspires to have access to power without being "contained" by it. When Albert finally enters the court, however, he reveals that his patronage will touch Byron with the utmost intimacy: "Would we might grow together and be twins / Of either's fortune, or that, still embraced, / I were but ring to such a precious stone" (1.2.167–69). The image of anatomically joined male bodies represents the unbreakable political bond between the favorite and his patron. A gemstone is not only set off but fixed by the ring that embraces it. Recalling Jove's deadly erotic embrace of "happy Semele / That died compressed with glory!" (1.2.37–38), Byron ironically foreshadows his own destruction by these homoerotic embraces.[72] In the Byron plays, the signs of erotic treachery reveal political treachery: embracing the enemies of his king, Byron commits a sodomitical crime of tragic proportions.

Tragedy in *Bussy D'Ambois* has a different source, for Bussy betrays not his king but Monsieur, the king's rival. Like the fickle strumpet he describes at the beginning of the play (or the whorish La Fin in the *Byron* plays), Bussy leaves his former patron to "[s]tand like an Atlas underneath the King" (3.1.98–99), although he would attribute his inconstancy not to feminine vice but masculine virtue. Suddenly placed at a political disadvantage by his raising of Bussy, Monsieur "turns his outward love to inward hate: / A Prince's love is like the lightning's fume, / Which no man can embrace, but must consume" (3.1.111–13). Like Byron, Bussy is cast here as Semele; Monsieur plays both Jove, who destroys with his erotic embrace, and Juno, who jealously engineers her rival's destruction. J. W. Lever has described the two *Bussy* plays as "revenge tragedy in reverse, where the revenge is taken not by the challenger of the order but by the order itself, exercising its built-in sanctions against the man who defies it."[73] Although Lever is not concerned with the erotics of tragedy, the revenge of the order against the man who defies it is also registered in the sexual realm. In *Bussy D'Ambois*, the order takes the form of Monsieur and the Guise, and the revenge takes the metaphorical form of sodomy.

As a royal favorite, Bussy bolsters Henry against the peers through his plain speech, refusal of flattery, and habit of demolishing the pretensions of the great. When Monsieur chastises him for quarreling with the Duke of Guise, Bussy boasts, "His greatness is the people's, mine's mine own" (3.2.75). Yet Bussy's former poverty and subsequent advancement are common knowledge in the court: Monsieur, Tamyra recalls, "was but yesterday his maker," his "raiser and preserver" (3.1.102–3). Who owns the favorite's greatness? Does Bussy rise through the homoerotic attentions of his patrons or simply by his own virtue? Politically compromised by his favorite's defection, Monsieur compares Bussy to "a spirit rais'd without a circle, / Endangering him that ignorantly rais'd him" (3.2.300–1). Henry acknowledges that his own sovereign authority depends on the very scarcity of men of such bold "spirit" (3.2.97). Moreover, although he wants to possess Bussy like a "brave Eagle" or rich "jewel" hanging in his ear (3.2.4, 6), Henry also recognizes that "these definite terms of Mine and Thine" characterize the fallen state of nature (3.2.100). Demystifying the foundations of sovereign power through his open dependence on Bussy, the king simultaneously uses his favorite's great spirit to sustain his material power.

Bussy's paradoxical function as royal favorite – bolstering Henry's power while revealing the material and contingent foundations of that power – constitutes a political challenge too great for Monsieur and the Guise to let pass unpunished. Monsieur knows that "[t]here is no second place in numerous State / That holds more than a cipher: in a King / All places are contain'd" (1.1.34–36). Having "grown all one" with his king, that is, Bussy threatens not only to displace Monsieur to the empty "second place" of power but to dismantle precisely those mechanisms of patronage that would allow Monsieur to advance a new favorite (4.1.113). Significantly, Monsieur's revenge exploits not the homoerotic relationship with Henry that has empowered Bussy but the heteroerotic relationship with Tamyra that has made him vulnerable; moreover, it is the incontinent speech of a woman that reveals this vulnerability. Courting Tamyra's maids to gather intelligence, Monsieur converts Charlotte's declaration of their chastity – "ye must gather us with the ladder of matrimony, or we'll hang till we be rotten" – into a bawdy innuendo regarding their incontinence: "Indeed that's the way to make ye right open-arses" (3.2.237–39). Monsieur intimates that great men have the means to open their inferiors, whether male or female, to their sexual and political advances. Despite Bussy's declarations of integrity and self-sufficiency, Monsieur treats him as an "open-arse," a mere instrument opening his way to the crown, and he continues to address his former favorite, perhaps with sly irony, as his "sweetheart" and "Love's glory" (4.1.52, 93). Bussy may think he has achieved independence, or at least ascendance above the lords and incorporation with the king, but Monsieur refuses to relinquish his destructive, sodomitical embrace.

Bussy's ruinous affair with Tamyra serves a symbolic as well as a dramatic function, for if Tamyra has betrayed her husband with Bussy, Bussy has likewise betrayed his former patron with Henry. Of course, the relation between husband and wife is not isomorphic with that between prince and favorite, not least because gender difference allows Montsurry physically to abuse Tamyra "with beastly odds of strength" (5.1.12). Yet the system on which this court thrives demands that all its dependents – wives, court ladies, maids-in-waiting, male favorites, courtiers – be open-arses, at the same time that it punishes them for being so on their own terms, at their own volition. Montsurry represents his wife's sexual betrayal through the discourse of inversion that signified the "backwards" court practices at the play's start: "The too huge bias of the

World hath sway'd / Her back-part upwards, and with that she braves / This Hemisphere" (5.1.155–57). To have a back-part open to the machinations of powerful men is required of dependents, whether male or female; to flaunt and brave with it is deemed monstrous and worthy of revenge.

Monsieur's assassination of Bussy from behind represents a sodomitical punishment for Bussy's refusal to remain properly, submissively, open. To Bussy, the very word "murder" is "Hebrew" (5.3.76), a language he can not understand because it is read in the same "backwards" direction that corrupt clergymen "vent" their bowels of luxurious meals (3.2.46). The association of Jewish reading practice with preposterous inversion appears in a sixteenth-century emblem that illustrates "Preposterous and overthwarte doinges" with the image of a man setting the cart before the horse:

> Arse varse he goes to worke,
>   he dothe all oute of qune:
> He stemes the malte above the wheate,
>   he readethe like a Jue.[74]

Penetrated from behind, Bussy regards his murder as an "arse varse" violation of his great spirit: "Guise and Monsieur, Death and Destiny / Come behind D'Ambois: is my body then / But penetrable flesh?" (5.3.124–26). Indeed, the metaphor Montsurry uses to express his separation from Tamyra might apply equally well to the fatal divorce of Bussy and Monsieur: the candle that "being thus turn'd down / (His natural course of useful light inverted) / His own stuff puts it out" (5.3.259–61). Because Bussy has inverted and denied the erotic structures of dependence that have raised him, trusting instead in the self-sufficient virtue of his "own stuff," Monsieur extinguishes him in a corresponding act of sodomitical inversion. No longer a "useful light" in Henry's court, Bussy fades in the manner of a "falling star / Silently glanc'd" (5.3.191–92).

Bussy D'Ambois and *The Revenge of Bussy D'Ambois* approach a similar destination from opposite paths. Whereas Bussy is destroyed by his defiance of a corrupt homoerotics of favoritism, his brother Clermont is destroyed by his adherence to an idealized homoerotics of favoritism. On the surface *The Revenge* imitates the pattern of favoritism established in *Bussy D'Ambois*. Just as Bussy leaves Monsieur for Henry, so Clermont leaves Monsieur and "hangs upon the ear of the Guise, / Like to his jewel" (*The Revenge* 1.1.152–53). Clermont's stoical philosophy and contempt for riches give the impression that the "Guise, embracing him, / Is thought t'embrace his virtues" (1.1.173–74), yet Monsieur bitterly describes the Guise's patronage as a political rape:

> Come, you two,
> Devour each other with your virtue's zeal,
> And leave for other friends no fragment of ye:
> I wonder, Guise, you will thus ravish him
> Out of my bosom that first gave the life
> His manhood breathes, spirit, and means, and lustre.   (1.1.184–89)

The Guise's theft of his "dear minion" not only angers Monsieur but "hath possess'd the King / (Knowing his daring spirit) of much danger / Charg'd in it to his person" (1.1.146, 129–31). Despite his virtues, Clermont's advancement constitutes a political threat to his sovereign.

Because it reveals the king's complicity in destroying the loving bond between Clermont and his patron, *The Revenge* presents an even stronger indictment against political corruption than *Bussy D'Ambois*. *The Revenge* focuses less insistently than *Bussy D'Ambois* on the erotic politics of court rivalry and more on the abuses of an unscrupulous spy, Baligny, whom Henry III employs to investigate Clermont. Nevertheless, Chapman represents the disorder of Henry's court through an erotic idiom familiar from *Bussy D'Ambois*. For instance, Clermont considers his betrayal by Baligny a "common / And more than whore-like trick of treachery / And vermin bred to rapine and to ruin" (4.1.100–2).

More significant than this linguistic similarity between the plays is Clermont's difference from Bussy as a subject of erotic desire. Clermont's interest in the Countess of Cambrai, despite her profound devotion, seems even less erotic than Bussy's interest in Tamyra.[75] Although Clermont can feel sexual passion for a woman, after "the desire and the delight be gone" reason overcomes his affection and enamors him to inner goodness (5.1.162). Urged by the Guise to marry the Countess, Clermont strenuously denies that "any man doth love, / Affecting wives, maid, widows, any women," since

> what excites the bed's desire in blood,
> By no means justly can be constru'd love;
> For when love kindles any knowing spirit,
> It ends in virtue and effects divine,
> And is in friendship chaste and masculine.
>
> GUISE. Thou shalt my mistress be; methinks my blood
> Is taken up to all love with thy virtues.
> And howsoever other men despise
> These paradoxes strange and too precise,
> Since they hold on the right way of our reason,
> I could attend them ever.   (5.1.184–94)

Transvaluing conventional terms, Clermont equates heteroerotic desire, even within marriage, with base physical lust; male friendship epitomizes true love.

Does the play endorse Clermont's view that male friendship, "chaste and masculine," eschews physical desire? The Guise compensates for his former hatred of Bussy with "ten parts more love" for Clermont (5.1.108) and acknowledges that Clermont does not return his extraordinary affection: "How strangely thou art lov'd of both the sexes: / Yet thou lov'st neither, but the good of both" (5.1.154–55). Clermont's overall devaluation of erotic desire prevents him from acknowledging that the system of royal patronage that sustains him is *openly* and *normatively* homoerotic. To see that Clermont's advocation of de-eroticized masculine love is not inevitable but ideological, one need look no further than the Guise, who does not shun "desire in blood" as Clermont advises; instead he sees in his masculine instructor a "mistress" who agitates his "blood." What constitutes a foundational lesson of masculine self-sufficiency for Clermont becomes for the Guise a set of "strange and too precise" paradoxes. When he simply declares "Clermont is my love," the Guise speaks out of more "blood" than Clermont would approve (2.1.80).

In *The Revenge* the discourse of blood signifies the life-sustaining homoerotic bond between patron and client. At the end of the play, having revenged Bussy's death with Montsurry's death, Clermont learns of the Guise's death, which requires yet another death – not Henry's, as the genre of revenge tragedy would suggest, but Clermont's own, after the manner of a romantic tragedy like *Romeo and Juliet*. When Clermont asks, "Shall I live, and he / Dead, that alone gave means of life to me?" (5.5.149–50), he refers not so much to the material means by which the Guise raised him to favor, but to the shared blood that animates his spirit. He explains that "friendship is the cement of two minds, / As of one man the soul and body is, / Of which one cannot sever, but the other / Suffers a needful separation" (5.5.157–60). If the soul and body are indivisible, then friendship must "cement" two bodies as well as two minds. Hence Clermont understands death as a corporeal disrobing that will give him access to the Guise's spirit:

> The garment or the cover of the mind,
> The human soul is; of the soul, the spirit
> The proper robe is; of the spirit, the blood;
> And of the blood, the body is the shroud.
> With that must I begin then to unclothe,
> And come at th'other.   (5.5.170–75)

Clermont's suicide expresses the urgency of his desire to be reunited with his master: "I come, my lord! Clermont, thy creature, comes."

(5.5.192–93). The Countess of Cambrai enters upon this tragic scene to articulate the symmetry between her absolute love for Clermont and Clermont's for the Guise: "It must be so; he liv'd but in the Guise, / As I in him" (5.5.206–7). Both Clermont's suicide and the Countess's interpretation of it suggest a deeper physical dependence on his patron than Clermont was willing to admit.

The different trajectories of the favorite's career in *Bussy D'Ambois* and *The Revenge of Bussy D'Ambois* trace two different relationships between male homoeroticism and political patronage in the early modern court. In *Bussy D'Ambois* homoerotic favoritism becomes a dangerous but necessary means to power in a court shot through with rivalry and faction. Bussy's tragedy proceeds from an underestimation of the claim that Monsieur's patronage has on his political advancement. Denying his openness to Monsieur's advances, he nevertheless rises from them and is finally brought down, sodomitically, by them. Bussy is destroyed not because he enters into a homoerotic patronage relation but because he misjudges the danger of rejecting the erotic and political patronage of an ambitious, ruthless lord. In *The Revenge* Chapman distinguishes a mutual bond between patron and favorite from the rivalry, surveillance, and injustice of the court, the locus of an erotic and political disorder that claims the Guise as its chief victim. Clermont is destroyed because he openly accepts his essential spiritual and somatic dependence upon his friend and master, even though he seems to deny the specifically erotic aspects of such dependence. Unlike Bussy, then, Clermont dies not as the unwilling victim of disorderly court intrigue but in willing self-sacrifice based on an orderly love for his patron. Clermont's virtuous love has no place within a dishonorable and disorderly court.

The significance of Chapman's departure from the more familiar tragedies of Marlowe, Shakespeare, and Jonson should be evident. Because he shows sodomitical patronage relations to be corruptions of otherwise orderly homoerotic bonds, Chapman dissociates male homoeroticism from an inevitable connection with sodomy and tragedy. Moreover, his plays deploy an explicitly erotic language to convey the intense desire that motivates both orderly and disorderly male patronage relations. Chapman's tragedies therefore help us recognize that contemporary representations of the sodomitical reigns of Edward II, Richard II, and Tiberius do not imply a universal or monolithic condemnation of homoerotic favoritism in early modern England. Not only do *Edward II*, *Richard II*, and *Sejanus* each advance a different interpretation of the causes and effects of sodomitical disorder, but Chapman's French tragedies offer still other perspectives on homoerotic court politics. For instance, as minions of the great, Sejanus and Clermont possess extremely dissimilar political goals, moral philosophies, and erotic inclinations. And their deaths, while perhaps equally tragic, suggest very different constructions of the relation between homoerotic desire and political disorder.

If we turned only to plays like *Sejanus* and *Edward II* for evidence, it would be difficult to deny the equation of homoerotic desire and sodomy in early modern representations of favoritism. The extremity of *Sejanus* – in which all homoeroticism is sodomitical – and the critical prominence of *Edward II* – which has been read as a "homosexual" tragedy (hence, the tragedy of homosexuality) – can obscure a crucial political dynamic illuminated by a play like *The Revenge of Bussy D'Ambois*. When read alongside and against the tragedies of Marlowe, Shakespeare, and Jonson, Chapman's tragedies reveal that it is the exploitation and abuse of the homoerotic intimacy between male favorite and prince, not homoerotic favoritism itself, that generates sodomitical disorder.

5   The homoerotics of masculinity in tragicomedy

Soldiers, lovers, and Renaissance gender ideology

Although women play only a minor role in the predominantly male world of Chapman's tragedies, anxieties about effeminacy pervade his depictions of the erotically disordered early modern court. The resentment Chapman's soldiers feel about the effeminacy of a pacifist courtly culture was frequently voiced in late sixteenth- and early seventeenth-century English texts. A good example of such a text is Barnabe Riche's *Farewell to Military Profession* (1581), to which I would like to turn momentarily before considering how similar concerns are manifested in the drama.

In his dedicatory epistle to "Right Courteous Gentlewomen," Riche describes his transformation from a soldier and former author of military books into a writer of "very pleasant discourses fit for a peaceable time: gathered together for the only delight of the courteous gentlewomen."[1] A belated discovery of courtly pleasures explains why Riche, "having spent [his] younger days in the wars among men and vowed [himself] to Mars, should now, in [his] riper years, desire to live in peace amongst women and to consecrate [himself] wholly unto Venus" (123). Although the swearing of vows to both Mars and Venus implies Riche's devotion to men of war no less than to women of pleasure, his gendered antithesis is neither as stable nor as foundational as first appears. For he goes on to confess that he finds "more sound sleeping under a silken canopy close by a friend than under a bush in the open field within a mile of our foe." The prior distinction between male and female collapses here into a more fundamental distinction between friend and foe: it is clearly preferable to sleep at home with a companion of either sex than to sleep outdoors among the enemy. In early modern England neither the military world nor the courtly world precludes the expression of male homoerotic desire, although the form such expression takes may well differ within martial and peacetime contexts.

When home from the wars, Riche might sleep comfortably with either a male or female friend, but he is no friend of men who act like women and women who act like men. Riche's more polemical second dedicatory epistle to "Noble Soldiers" unfolds the gender anxiety managed with considerable poise and humor by the epistle to the gentlewomen. Addressing his male peers, Riche laments the currently low "estimation" of military men and scorns the fashionable breed of man who in assaying to please women becomes a woman himself: "How many gentlemen shall you see at this present date that, I dare undertake, in the wearing of their apparel, in the setting of their ruffs and the frizzling of their hair, are more newfangled and foolish than any courtesan of Venice" (128). This satirical portrait deflates English gentlemen by demoting their gender, social, and national status, and by implying their sexual subservience to other men. Effeminacy makes a courtier degenerate into a courtesan. Moreover, in an associative train of thought common to Renaissance gender satire, Riche recasts his scorn of male effeminacy into scorn of female masculinity.[2] Recalling his disgust at encountering a gentleman riding through London brandishing "a great fan of feathers," Riche reasons that "it is as fond to see a man with such a bauble in his hands as to see a woman ride through the streets with a lance in hers" (129). Riche claims to have initially mistaken this ridiculously womanish man for a cross-dressed woman. Although the gentleman's beard finally reveals his actual sex, his virility can not match that of the phallic lance-wielding woman Riche imagines as his parallel in absurd comportment.

Satiric accounts of gender inversion in London and in the court were a staple of English writing from the *Farewell* until 1620, which saw the publication of the counterpoised pamphlets *Hic Mulier; or, The Man-Woman* and *Haec Vir; or, The Womanish Man*. The relation between gender disorder and erotic disorder in these texts is often quite complex. The effeminate men who appear in the *Farewell* and *Haec Vir* usurp female attributes and ornaments as a consequence of *heteroerotic* desire: Riche's fop dresses like a gentlewoman because he wants to attract a gentlewoman. In *Haec Vir*, the "Man-Woman" Hic Mulier objects that the "Womanish Man" Haec Vir "court[s] his Mistress with the same words that Venus did Adonis."[3] Just as Riche implies that the effeminate English courtier might imitate not only the dress but also the sexual practices of the Venetian courtesan, so Hic Mulier's mythological allusion to Venus and Adonis raises the possibility of erotic disorder in Haec Vir's courtship. But is this disorder of a heteroerotic or homoerotic stamp? Haec Vir's gender transitivity defies erotic taxonomy: does his courtship express the desire of a man (the Petrarchan wooer) or of a woman (Venus)? Is this desire for a woman (the Mistress) or for a man (Adonis)? More confusing still, the mythological figures offered as models of Haec Vir's identification and desire are themselves cross-gendered: in *Venus and Adonis* (1593) Shakespeare depicts Venus as an aggressively "masculine" woman and Adonis as a passively "feminine" boy. This highly queer situation at once asserts and subverts male/female gender difference, as cross-gender identification elicits the performance of both heteroerotic and homoerotic desires. One thing, however, is clear: the source of confusion resides in "Venus," the disorderly passion that afflicts unruly women and womanish men.

In contrast to Haec Vir's disorderly identification with Venus, Riche himself represents the male desire to live among and be appreciated by other socially normative men; hence the reluctance of his farewell to the military. Riche is not idiosyncratic in this regard, for it is a commonplace of early modern English drama that military men form enduring emotional and erotic attachments to each other. For instance, Alexander and Hephestion are cited as a famous male couple in Marlowe's *Edward II* (1592) and appear as the main characters in John Lyly's *Campaspe* (1584).[4] In Lyly's play, Hephestion employs Riche's strategy of distinguishing male from female spheres to shame Alexander into abjuring his effeminizing desire for Campaspe:

Remember, Alexander, thou hast a camp to govern, not a chamber; fall not from the armour of Mars to the arms of Venus, from the fiery assaults of war, to the maidenly skirmishes of love.[5]

The crisis is resolved only when Alexander renounces heteroerotic desire altogether, reasserting the bond with Hephestion that undergirds his imperial power: "when all the world is won, and every country is thine and mine, either find me out another to subdue or, of my word, I will fall in love."[6] Although the eroticism of Alexander's friendship with Hephestion is not as explicit in Lyly's play as it is in Marlowe's, the conqueror's debilitating love for women clearly interferes with more important masculine pursuits.

In *The Golden Age* (1610), Thomas Heywood emphasizes the particularly erotic dimension of military companionship by representing Ganymede not in his usual guise as a shepherd boy, but as a soldier. Having captured Ganymede in battle, Jupiter vows to keep him as a "prisoner to [his] love" and "bosome friend": the homoerotic Ganymede myth familiar from Ovid suggests an erotic component to Jupiter's love and friendship.[7] In transposing Ovid's pastoral Ganymede myth into a military setting, Heywood may be following William Warner's *Albions England*, a poem published first in 1586 and popular in the post-Armada years, when it was reprinted in editions of 1589 and 1592. Warner's nationalistic history of England encompasses biblical and classical mythology, including the story of Saturn's war against Jupiter:

> Ganymedes, King Troys sonne, was sent in Saturnes ayde:
> A worthy knight, and, valiant warre to Iupiter he made.
> But he and his were chased backe even to their cittie walles,
> For whoso stoode with Iupiter, by Jupiter he falles.
> And theare the Troyan Paragon Ganymedes was taine,
> Twixt whome and Iupiter thenceforth sound friendship did remaine.[8]

For Jupiter and Ganymede, homoerotic friendship promotes honor, courage, and national strength. According to the post-Armada tract *A Tipe or Figure of Friendship* (1589), without friendship "no Countrey [can be] safe preserved, no State long continued, no nor anie thing in the use of man rightly ordered." As with Jupiter and Ganymede, orderly masculine love bolsters the nation in peace and functions as "a treasure abroad in the warres."[9]

Not surprisingly, the primary focus of critical attention regarding the conjunction of homoeroticism and militarism in Renaissance literature has been Shakespeare's *Troilus and Cressida* (1602). Recent interpretations of Shakespeare's play have productively examined how discourses of male homoeroticism intersected in early modern England with discourses of political power, disease, violence, and masculine honor.[10] Yet the most sustained dramatic representations of military homoeroticism appear not in this one play by Shakespeare but in the less frequently discussed body of works by John Fletcher and his collaborators.[11] Like *Troilus and Cressida*, Fletcherian tragicomedies have been labeled "problem plays" due to their mixed genre and sexually frank subject matter.[12] Whereas *Troilus and Cressida* may be regarded as atypical of Shakespeare's usual concerns and tone, however, the explicit representation of "extreme" sexual situations throughout the Beaumont and Fletcher canon has frequently distressed modern critics. Writing in 1978, Denzell Smith deemed the overall state of Beaumont and Fletcher criticism during the past century "tediously repetitive":

The "characteristics" of the plays are described nearly identically by critic after critic, followed by a favorable or unfavorable assessment depending on the critic's sensitivity to the "morality" of the plays, or to the critic's attachment to the idea of "decadence" in Jacobean drama.[13]

Surveying in 1973 the long history of critical discomfort with Fletcher's "low sexual morality," Nancy Cotton Pearse observed that most twentieth-century critics object that in these plays "extreme issues – rape, adultery, impotence – are introduced primarily as topics for brilliant and clever debate"; others dismiss the plays outright as deliberately prurient or obsessed with "abnormal" sexuality.[14] With few exceptions, it seems, critics have evaluated the plays of Beaumont and Fletcher based on their putative sexual ethics or, perhaps in an effort to avoid sex altogether, on their formal qualities. They have not appreciated the plays as texts that articulate historically specific gender and sexual ideologies.

It is only in the past decade that critics of various persuasions have taken seriously the cultural and dramatic significance of sexuality to the Beaumont and Fletcher canon.[15] Nevertheless, even materialist accounts of tragicomedy as astute as those provided by Walter Cohen and Kathleen McLuskie may fail to focus sharply enough on the specificity of the (homo)erotic. In Cohen's usage, "sexuality" refers to the construction of gender difference in a heteroerotic context. For instance, he attributes the "sexual" problems of royal figures in tragicomedies to the "irreducibly political character of *gender* relations" in the seventeenth century.[16] While McLuskie's feminist methodology more sharply tunes her reading to the homoerotic dynamics of tragicomedy, her emphasis understandably falls on the representation of women and gender ideology. Moreover, she limits her analysis of homoeroticism to *Philaster* (1609), a play that concludes with the revelation that a page apparently smitten with love for his master is actually a woman in disguise. In early modern drama, cross-dressing plots can provide an important vehicle for representing homoerotic desire; yet the drama includes other kinds of same-sex relations, such as male friendship, which do not depend upon the theatrical manipulation of sartorial gender difference.[17]

I want to propose that both feminist and queer theoretical interests can be productively served by examining how Fletcherian tragicomedies refract homoerotic desire through the discourses of masculinity and effeminacy. Both orderly and disorderly manifestations of male homoerotic desire inform these plays, and the relation between them needs to be understood in terms of a carefully historicized Renaissance gender ideology. As Jonathan Dollimore, Linda Woodbridge, and Jean Howard have argued, the construction of the female cross-dresser or "masculine woman" as a threatening figure in the early decades of the seventeenth century reveals a pervasive anxiety about social, economic, and sexual dislocation.[18] As evidence of this anxiety, Dollimore offers John Chamberlain, who in a single letter of 1620 mentions two disturbing social developments: the perceived upsurge in female cross-dressing, and "the selling of honours and abasing ancient nobility, by new advancements."[19] Although Dollimore does not pursue the connection, interrelated anxieties about gender definition and male "honor" comprise an important ideological dimension of Fletcher's contemporary plays.

Performed at Blackfriars for a relatively elite audience, Fletcher's tragicomedies staged plots about militarism and male honor during a period when aristocratic militarism and honor were perceived to be in decline. Before his death in 1612, Prince Henry's cultivation of a warrior identity "awakened the immediate interest both of the old Elizabethan war party and of those who had graced the tiltyard in Gloriana's reign."[20] Henry's early death quelled hopes for a revival of more masculine military displays and policies. According to Lawrence Stone, the nobility's participation in military service greatly declined during the reign of James, the *Rex Pacificus*:

Another twenty years of peace after 1604 meant that they were now almost entirely absorbed in private and civilian pursuits, and no longer looked to war as a natural outlet for their energies. The movement of the aristocracy out of the countryside into London and about the Court greatly accelerated this shift by providing alternative fields of competition, intrigue, and pleasure. By 1640 the bellicose instincts of the class had been sublimated in the pursuit of wealth and the cultivation of the arts.[21]

Along with the gradual decline of militarism as a means of acquiring honor, James swiftly debased the nobility by creating the new rank of baronet in 1611 and by initiating the "direct cash sale of titles" in 1615. Between 1615 and 1619 James created an average of 120 knights per year; hence, the rank "fell into contempt, and men began seeking some further title of distinction."[22] As a social status and a chivalric practice – in essence, as a signifier of masculine identity – knighthood was losing its distinction in the second decade of the century.

In a related development, Jacobean satires and tragedies registered the perception that male servants and courtiers were performing increasingly ceremonial, ornamental, or "effeminate" functions in the great household and court. Karen Newman argues that the development of "femininity" as an ideological category during the Renaissance was connected to the "sartorial extravagance" and proliferation of consumer goods in Jacobean London.[23] Conspicuous display and consumption – not only of goods but of people – signaled the erotic disorder and "effeminacy" of the London gallant.

The various social and economic developments of seventeenth-century England – the open struggle over gender definition; the decline of militarism; the financial and erotic extravagance of courtiers and aristocrats; the emerging consumerist ideology of femininity – all help to explain the recuperative agenda of Jacobean tragicomedies with regard to male gender definition. Philip Finkelpearl posits that the soldier figures who populate the plays of Beaumont and Fletcher speak to the "frustration and desperation" of the "young would-be heroes" in the audience who had few opportunities to distinguish themselves in Jacobean London. Moreover, in 1620 Fletcher himself expressed the wish that James would declare war on Spain.[24] Although Fletcher's witty heroines may well have appealed to the women who comprised a significant proportion of the Jacobean theater audience,[25] Beaumont and Fletcher frequently cater to the desires and identifications of a gentle male audience by proffering heroes who define standards of masculine honor against effeminate cowards and foolish lovers. In the epilogue to *The Humorous Lieutenant* (1619), for example, the cowardly lieutenant teaches male playgoers how to cure his foolish sexual humors: "As you are good men helpe me, a Carowse / May make me love you all, all here i'th'house, / And all that come to see me doatingly."[26] If the male playgoers dote on the players by applauding them, that is, they will transform the Lieutenant's improper love into a proper love of "good men." Like Barnabe Riche's romances, addressed to gentlewomen readers as well as neglected soldiers, Fletcher's plays seem calculated to please both sophisticated women and worthy men.

In Fletcherian tragicomedy, male worth is measured by masculinity, an attribute easily compromised by various behaviors ideologically coded as "feminine." As Riche's *Farewell to Military Profession* and *Haec Vir* indicate, an effeminate man might resemble a woman in his vanity, passivity, lack of discipline, cowardice, or sensuality. Effeminacy is frequently the result of disorderly passion. Regarding the unmanly behavior of Achilles in Shakespeare's *Troilus and Cressida*, Gary Spear rightly concludes that "[e]ffeminacy is a trait of excessive male desire regardless of object choice."[27] Nevertheless, Fletcher's tragicomedies usually associate male effeminacy with excessive heteroerotic desire, since even the most masculine soldier may become effeminate when afflicted by passion for a soft and weak woman.

In what follows I will focus on Fletcher's critique of male heteroerotic passion in three plays: *The Nice Valour, or, The Passionate Mad-man* (1615–16); *The Humorous Lieutenant*; and *The Mad Lover* (1617). Connecting male heteroerotic desire to disorderly homoeroticism and effeminacy, these plays contrast disorderly male lovers to masculine soldiers who either feel no heteroerotic desire or who finally renounce it for the sake of stable male bonds. Although each play concludes with a marriage, in each a central male character remains unmarried or renounces women altogether, his social and erotic energies redirected towards other men and their common military pursuits. The plays differ in the intensity with which they problematize male heteroerotic desire: *The Nice Valour* generally explores the social and sexual consequences of disorderly male gender behavior (effeminacy and hypermasculinity); *The Humorous Lieutenant* more directly links male heteroeroticism to disorderly homoeroticism; *The Mad Lover* presents the strongest case against heteroerotic desire and reproductive sexuality. Despite these variations, the three plays concur that socially orderly male homoerotic bonds offer an attractive alternative to the disruptive effects of hetero-erotic desire.

Having shown the incompatibility of heteroeroticism and masculinity in these plays, I reverse perspective, focusing instead on a play that successfully incorporates male heteroerotic desire into the masculine imperatives of military conquest. It is the centrality of racial difference and colonialist ideology to *The Island Princess* (1619–21) that accounts for its particular treatment of masculinity. Because colonial ideology valorizes the "masculine" European conquest of a "feminine" Indian nation, heteroerotic desire and masculine honor mutually reinforce each other for the Portuguese soldiers in the play. Such an empowering conjunction of sexuality and gender ideology eludes the soldiers in *The Nice Valour*, *The Humorous Lieutenant*, and *The Mad Lover*, who remain unable to reconcile their heteroerotic impulses with their responsibility to uphold the masculine ideals of noble friendship and military discipline.

Passions, humors, mad loves: heteroerotic desire and disorderly homoeroticism

The title of *The Nice Valour, or, The Passionate Mad-man* identifies two men who embody different forms of disorderly masculinity. The "Nice Valour" refers to Shamont, the Duke's favorite, who is known by some for "strength of manly merit" and extreme jealousy of "honours losse, or reputations glory," and by others as "a vainglorious coxcombe."[28] The play distinguishes Shamont from a character known only as the Passio-nate Lord (the "Passionate Madman" of the title), so named because he "runs through all the Passions of mankind" (1.1.51). Shamont's hyper-masculine egotism sharply contrasts to the effeminate antics of the Passionate Lord. For instance, believing a certain gentleman to be his mistress in disguise, the Passionate Lord absurdly woos him as "the fairest, yet the falsest woman, / That ever broke mans heart-strings" and then refuses responsibility for her pregnancy (1.1.205–6). Ironically, the Passionate Lord has already transgressed in just this fashion, having impregnated and then abandoned a woman he promised to marry. Disguised as Cupid, this woman pursues the Passionate Lord throughout the play, performing masques and songs intended to "draw all his wilde passions" to the point of honorable married love (3.1.12).

While Shamont disdains the Passionate Lord's homoerotically charged spectacles of effeminate passion, the ideal of masculinity he promotes does not reject all signs of affection. Warmly embracing his brother, known only as the Soldier, Shamont enjoins him to cherish La Nove, an "absolute friend" who "loves a Souldier far above a Mistris, / Though excellently faithful to 'em both. / But love to manhood, owns the purer troath" (1.1.261–64). Though masculine love for a soldier may be superior to love for a woman, heteroerotic desire can quickly destroy the orderly bonds of love between men. When he discovers his brother courting the Duke's sister (the "Lady"), Shamont experiences a betrayal of male identity: "Why can a thing, / That's but my selfe divided be so false?" (2.1.51–52). The Soldier's indulgence of heteroerotic desire not only represents a degeneration from pure "love to manhood" but threatens Shamont's patriarchal investment in the Lady's virginal purity. Exacerbating the disruption in normative male relations, the Passionate Lord mocks the Soldier's manner of wooing, provoking him to vow revenge. The Soldier's desire for the Lady thus not only alienates him from his overly "nice" brother but pits him against an effeminate lover on whom he wastes his martial prowess and masculine honor.

From this point, the play unfolds the disorderly consequences of passionate male behavior. Whereas the Soldier manifests a disruptive heteroerotic passion, Shamont displays a devotion to masculine honor so excessive that it paradoxically approaches effeminacy. The Duke means no offense when he taps Shamont's shoulder with a switch, but Shamont nevertheless feels irredeemably shamed and vows never again to love or serve his patron. Ruefully observing that his favorite "knows no difference between contempt and manhood," the Duke replaces his Gentlemen of the Chamber with mere Grooms who will be less sensitive of dishonor (2.1.309). A mutual sense of injured manhood threatens to explode into violence between Shamont and the Soldier, despite the claims of male friendship and kinship:

> SOULDIER. Provoke me not; for I've a wrong sits on me,
> That makes me apt for mischiefe; I shall lose
> All respects suddainly of friendship, Brother-hood,
> Or any sound that way.
> SHAMONT.   But 'ware me most;
> For I come with a two-edg'd injurie;
> Both my disgrace, and thy apparent falshood,
> Which must be dangerous.   (4.1.45–51)

The excessively passionate pursuit of heteroerotic desire and male honor has converted what should be loving bonds between men – brother and brother, friend and friend, patron and favorite, soldier and lord – into relations of enmity and revenge.

The violent excesses of masculine honor are exposed, somewhat paradoxically, by another male character who epitomizes shameful effeminacy, the coward Lapet. Lapet's unflinching acceptance of physical abuse contrasts with the absurd fastidiousness that prevents Shamont from enduring even the slightest tap:

> Why, what's a kicke? the fury of a foote,
> Whose indignation commonly is stampt
> Upon the hinder quarter of a man;
> Which is a place very unfit for honour,
> The world will confesse so much:
> Then what disgrace I pray, does that part suffer
> Where honour never comes?   (3.2.3–9)

The hinder quarter of a man is a dishonorable "part" because it is commonly "stampt" by the parts of other men, not only the foot but the penis. Far from keeping the stamping of his ass a private matter, Lapet publishes a book cataloging various types of kicks, thus publicly circulating his own dishonorable reputation via the common stamp of the printing press. Evoking the familiar association of Italy with sodomy, he instructs the Clown to have the printer set the kicks "All in Italica, your Backward blowes / All in Italica, you Hermaphrodite" (4.1.236–37). La Nove remarks of Lapet himself that "his Buttock's all black Lead, / He's halfe a Negro back-ward" (4.1.217–18). According to the play's ideology of masculinity, men who are beaten and sodomized become monstrously deficient, either half-woman or half-black. Even worse, some of the male figures illustrated in Lapet's book willfully submit to backward blows: "here's a fellow stands most gallantly, / Taking his kick in private behinde the hangings, / And raising his hips up to't" (4.1.343–45). Does the gallant receive his kick in private because he wants to protect his honor or because he wants to facilitate whatever else may happen "behinde the hangings" to that part where honor never comes?

Despite Lapet's contemptible effeminacy, *The Nice Valour* implies the desirability of a society in which men graciously accept a certain degree of physical and social humiliation.[29] Because he so parodically rechannels and absorbs male violence, Lapet provides an alternative outlet for the passionate masculinity that threatens the stability of the court. His book, "The up-rising of the kick, / And the downfall of the Duello," promises to replace a lethal with a relatively mild form of male aggression, an accomplishment for which "young blouds / Will thank [him] then, when they see four-score" (4.1.22–23, 25–26). Presumably, Lapet's treatise will discourage hot-headed young men from killing each other and will teach them instead merely to abuse the author and his cowardly peers.[30]

The lesson of Lapet's book is incorporated into the apex of the play's tragic plot, which attempts to defuse the more injurious violence of revenge with the therapeutic hostility of kicking. Earlier in the play, the Passionate Lord had capriciously exchanged his effeminate courtly demeanor for the "more manly" humor of hurting other men (3.3.14). In the climactic tragic scene, as he perversely enjoys an account of the brutal beating he arranged for the Soldier, the Passionate Lord is confronted by the Cupid, who leads six fools in a masque of kicks based on Lapet's book. Because the Cupid intends the masque for the Passionate Lord, its ostensible message might be that dishonorable heteroerotic desire makes men into fools. Yet because it also presents a Cupid presiding over the spectacle of men striking each other from behind, the masque appears to enact the eroticization of a carefully delimited, ritualized form of male aggression. Michael Moon's analysis of a similarly "perverse" male sadomasochistic ritual in David Lynch's film *Blue Velvet* (1986) may help to explain the function of the masque's eroticized violence. Structured through the tension between pleasure and pain, desire and disavowal, male sadomasochistic rituals have the potential, Moon argues, to "disorient" supposedly fixed categories of sexual orientation.[31] Although he is concerned with deconstructing modern categories of heterosexual and homosexual orientation that were not established in early modern England, Moon's queer analysis speaks to the way that the ritually eroticized violence of the masque attempts to disorient and reconfigure male relations in Fletcher's play. Intervening directly in male homosocial structures, the female Cupid's masque advocates a more controlled, safer alternative to the random and dangerous fury the Passionate Lord unleashes against the Soldier.

That the Soldier interrupts the masque to stab the Passionate Lord in a nearly fatal "work of honour" (5.2.43) reveals the fragility of the accommodation between masculinity and violence that the Cupid tries to achieve. Both Mervyn James and Lawrence Stone have remarked the characteristic violence of the male code of honor in early modern England. According to James, honor "could both legitimize and provide moral reinforcement for a politics of violence." Yet Stone notes that when duels peaked in the second decade of the seventeenth century, the government attempted to assert its control over interpersonal combat.[32] In Fletcher's play, the conflict between the claims of family honor and lawful civility arises when Shamont finds himself "torne in pieces between love and shame" for his brother (5.2.66). Although *The Nice Valour* explicitly criticizes arbitrary violence and pointless dueling, then, it hesitates fully to condemn the use of deadly force to redress an injury against masculine honor.

For this tragic turn of events to conclude in comedy requires the reformation of the disorderly effeminacy and masculinity that have compromised orderly male relations. In exchange for Shamont's promise to rejoin his court, the Duke forgives the Soldier whose bloody deed has worked to "cure" Shamont of his hypermasculine sense of disgrace: "Never could wrongs boast of a nobler end" (5.3.193, 195). Having survived his wound, the Passionate Lord purges his unruly passions, receives the Duke's pardon, and acknowledges the Cupid as his wife – although the Duke initially takes this apparently sodomitical wedding between a man and a boy as evidence of the Lord's continuing madness. The Duke secures a more conventional comic closure by proposing that Shamont marry his sister.

In its concluding moments, *The Nice Valour* reflects on the relation between desire and gender definition explored throughout the play. A "she-Cupid" makes sense to Shamont, for "Desire is of both Genders" (5.3.175, 177). Shamont may simply mean that both men and women feel desire, yet the maxim also implies that desire itself might be gendered, expressed as either "masculine" or "feminine" passion. Where men are concerned, this distinction appears to reiterate Shamont's initial elevation of orderly or "masculine" love for manhood above disorderly or "feminine" love, which might signify any excessive passion, whether for a woman or even, paradoxically, for male honor. It is "feminine" desire that the play has represented as disruptive: the Soldier's pursuit of the Lady breaks orderly male bonds; the Passionate Lord's courtly lechery and delight in violence provokes bloody revenge; Shamont's extreme devotion to masculine honor reduces him to a sense of disgrace even lower than that felt by the effeminate, publicly sodomitical Lapet. Shamont, however, never displays "feminine" heteroerotic passion: his masculinity is not compromised by his marriage to the Duke's sister because, as she herself realizes, he never loved women "for Wealth, or lust, / After the worlds foule dotage, he nere courted / The body but the beauty of the mind" (3.2.119–21). Significantly, the one man who courted the body, the Soldier, remains unmarried at the end of the play. In Fletcher's plays, men constitute their virility not through the pursuit of heteroerotic desire and marriage but through the establishment of homosocial and homoerotic bonds. The Soldier's attack on the Passionate Lord, after all, finally allows the Duke and Shamont to make political amends through the exchanged body of the Lady.

The Humorous Lieutenant subordinates male heteroerotic desire to male homoerotic bonds even more insistently than *The Nice Valour*. Although Demetrius and Celia are established as lovers from the start of the play, Demetrius's desire for military honor quickly surpasses his desire to remain at court with his future wife. In the language of heteroerotic passion, Demetrius begs his father, King Antigonus, for the opportunity to win glory among his male peers:

> Bid me go on, no lesse fear'd, then *Antigonus*,
> And to my maiden sword, tye fast your fortune;
> I know 'twill fight it selfe then: deare sir honour me:
> Never faire virgin long'd so.   (1.1.274–77)

Demetrius not only eroticizes his longing for military honor, he banters with Celia in military terms: "when I come home againe / I'le fight with thee, at thine owne weapon *Celia*, / And conquer thee too" (1.2.6–8). As Linda Charnes has written of the similar imbrication of heterosocial and homosocial languages in *Troilus and Cressida*, "If heterosexual activity is spoken of in terms of war, war is spoken of in terms of homoeroticized sex."[33] Extending Charnes's insight into a syllogism, one could say that if heterosexual activity is spoken of in terms of war, and if war is spoken of in terms of homoeroticized sex, then heterosexual activity is spoken of in terms of homoeroticized sex. Fletcher subordinates erotic relations between men and women to erotic relations between men.

Demetrius's cross-gender identification as a "faire virgin" longing for her first sexual encounter reinforces the eroticization of male military relations. Possessed of a "male spirit," Celia desires to emulate Demetrius's role as soldier, but he already identifies with her role as virgin (1.2.16). Losing his first battle, he loses to Seleucus both his "mayden honour" and his honorable friends, "men that twin'd their loves to mine, their virtues" (2.4.56). Significantly, it is precisely the maiden quality of Demetrius that redeems his friends from captivity. As a released captive explains, Seleucus became "enamour'd on [Demetrius's] virtue" and "with an eye of mercy inform'd his judgement, / How yet unripe we were, unblowne, unhardened, / Unfitted for such fatall ends" (2.4.79, 87–89). The story of a hardened warrior softened by youthful, virginal soldiers recalls Jupiter's loving adoption of his prisoner Ganymede in Heywood's *The Golden Age*. When Seleucus himself suffers defeat by Demetrius and the prototypical warrior Leontius, he articulates a similar ideal of military love:

> LEONTIUS, you and I have serv'd together,
> And run through many a fortune with our swords,
> Brothers in wounds, and health; one meat has fed us,
> One tent a thousand times from cold night cover'd us:
> Our loves have been but one; and had we died then,
> One monument had held our names, and actions: (3.7.42–47)

The love that unites soldiers in sickness and health, love and death, transcends even the boundaries of enmity. For this reason, Demetrius redeems his virgin honor not by forcefully subduing Seleucus, but, paradoxically, by generously giving him the victory. Demetrius's love conquers not his mistress but his foe.

Demetrius's erotically charged pursuit of honor takes place in the context of the erotic and gender disorderliness of two other men: the Humorous Lieutenant and King Antigonus. Both men debase their masculinity through the dishonorable pursuit of women. The Lieutenant demonstrates reckless bravery in battle only because fighting temporarily eases the pain of a venereal disease he contracted when he "served . . . under Captain Cupid, / And crackt a pike in's youth" (1.1.354–55). The Lieutenant reveals his true effeminacy when, relieved of his disease, he excuses himself from further combat duty by claiming an impending marriage. Having threatened to geld and beat the Lieutenant, Leontius finally succeeds in returning him to the battlefield only by convincing him that his venereal illness has returned. Likewise, King Antigonus debases the ideals of masculinity when he disguises himself as a courtier in order to seduce Celia. Celia evokes images of war to shame her wooer into more appropriate behavior:

> Canst thou forget, thou wert begot in honour?
> A free companion for a King? a souldier?
> Whose noblenesse dare feele no want, but enemies?
> Canst thou forget this, and decline so wretchedly,
> To eat the bread of bawdrie, of base bawdrie?
> Feed on the scum of sin? fling thy sword from thee,
> Dishonour to the noble name that nursed thee:
> Goe, beg diseases: let them be thy Armors,
> Thy fights, the flames of lust, and their foule issues.   (4.1.134–42)

Even this sermon, which recalls the shame of the Lieutenant's "bawdrie" and "diseases," does not dampen the King's desire, but spurs him on to a more drastic method of seduction: a magic love potion.

The potion ultimately serves as the means by which both Antigonus and the Lieutenant are punished for their dishonorable sexual exploits. When he accidentally drinks the potion intended for Celia, the Lieutenant falls desperately in love with Antigonus. Ironically, the lustful soldier who once ran away from men in honorable combat must now pursue his sovereign in an absurd and futile courtship. According to the astonished courtiers who are ignorant of the potion's effect, the Lieutenant

> Is really in love with the King, most doatingly,
> And sweares *Adonis* was a devill to him:
> A sweet King, a most comely King, and such a King –
> 2. GENTLEMAN. Then down on's mary-bones: O excellent King:

> Thus he begins, Thou light and life of creatures,
> Angell-ey'd King, vouchsafe at length thy favour;
> And so proceeds to incision: what think ye of this sorrow?
> I. GENTLEMAN. Will as familiarly kisse the Kings horses
> As they passe by him: ready to ravish his footmen.   (4.4.160–68)

Clearly, what the courtiers find incredible is not homoerotic desire *per se* but the absurd language and behavior with which the Lieutenant sues for his sovereign's favor. Especially grotesque is the disjunction between the chaste Petrarchan posture the Lieutenant strikes in wooing the King and the crass enthusiasm with which he molests the King's footmen and horses. Believing him to be mad or bewitched, Leontius openly mocks the Lieutenant, while the King is humiliatingly cast in the role of a reluctantly courted mistress, the same role in which he cast Celia. Moreover, the Lieutenant's flattering hyperboles expose the old King's ridiculous status as a lover: if he were as attractive as the Lieutenant claims, he would not have needed a love potion in the first place. In a final irony, whereas Antigonus had slandered Celia as a witch, his own use of witchcraft backfires, exposing his shameful duplicity through an episode of disorderly homoerotic courtship. The presence of witchcraft and the diminution of the King's bodily and political integrity in this episode push the Lieutenant's disruptive erotic humor into the ideological realm of the sodomitical.

It should now be clear that while homoeroticism plays a dramatically marginal role in *The Nice Valour* and *The Humorous Lieutenant*, it is ideologically central to the construction of masculinity in these plays. The relatively brief comic episodes involving Lapet's sodomitical catalog of kicks or Antigonus's sodomitical love potion represent disorderly homoeroticism as the effect or symptom of a prior disorder in masculine identity and heteroerotic desire. Disorderly homoeroticism, at times approaching the extreme of sodomy, may result from a lapse of "masculine" reason: a governing psychological humor, a distorted sensory perception, a chemically induced folly. The sexual madness of the Passionate Lord, who mistakenly woos a courtier when he should have married the woman he dishonored, resembles that of the Humorous Lieutenant, who foolishly woos his king at court when he should have pursued honor on the battlefield. Unlike more familiar comic plots in which homoerotic confusion is produced by a cross-dressed character, error in these plays resides not in the disguised gender identity of the *object* of desire, but in the unruly desires of the (male) *subject* of desire.

Fletcher's depictions of "mistaken" homoerotic desire might therefore be adduced as evidence for the gradual construction of male homoeroticism as a marginalized subjectivity in seventeenth-century England.

Numerous historians and literary critics have concurred in viewing the seventeenth century as a turning point in the development of early modern homoeroticism into more modern forms of homosexuality.[34] Recently, the works of Beaumont and Fletcher have been taken as evidence for this development. Jeff Masten argues that the homoerotic friendship and collaborative writing practice between Beaumont and Fletcher, unremarkable in early seventeenth-century England, could be interpreted as "strange production" as early as mid-century.[35] Masten reads the contradictory prefatory materials in the 1647 Beaumont and Fletcher folio as symptomatic of uneven transformations in seventeenth-century notions of authorship and sexuality. As notions of singular authorship and companionate marriage emerged during this period, the argument goes, the once normative writing and living arrangements sanctioned by a residual discourse of male homoerotic friendship were rewritten as "queer."

Focusing on the actual plays of Beaumont and Fletcher, Nicholas Radel constructs a similar narrative of stigmatization. By structurally isolating homoeroticism as a temporary, conditional, or ultimately unreal desire, he argues, Fletcherian tragicomedies begin to construct the modern "closet." Whereas Shakespeare's audience knows the true sex of a cross-dressed Ganymede or Cesario, Fletcher's audience does not necessarily know that certain "boys" (Bellario in *Philaster*) are actually cross-dressed girls or that certain "girls" (Alinda in *The Loyal Subject* [1618]) are actually cross-dressed boys. Spectators therefore witness what appear to be sincere expressions of homoerotic desire (e.g., from Bellario to "his" master) only finally to discover that these desires were based in male–female gender difference all along. From this analysis, Radel concludes that Fletcher's plays ultimately marginalize the homoerotic desire central to plot and character development.[36]

While scenes of mistaken homoeroticism in Fletcher's plays may contribute to the eventual "closeting" of homoeroticism, it is important to emphasize the unevenness of the development of Renaissance "sodomy" into more modern forms of homophobia.[37] We must measure the ideological specification and stigmatization of homoeroticism during the seventeenth century against the competing understandings of homoeroticism simultaneously available. In Fletcherian tragicomedy, as I have shown, celebrations of orderly male homoeroticism, often manifested through military friendship, exist alongside stigmatizations of disorderly homoeroticism.

Moreover, scenes of "mad" or mistaken homoeroticism in Fletcher's plays do not universally stigmatize male–male desire; rather, they offer homoerotic disorder as a striking emblem for heteroerotic disorder. We can see this dynamic at work in *The Captain* (1609–12), whose title character hates women but "love[s] a Souldier."[38] Captain Jacomo insists that he thinks of women only when drunk, "and then 'tis but to cast / A cheap way how they may be all destroy'd / Like vermine" (2.2, p. 262). When Jacomo and his tavern companions do get drunk, however, women are far from their thoughts:

> HOST. Shall we bear up still? Captain how I love thee!
> Sweet Captain let me kiss thee, by this hand
> I love thee next to a Malmsey in a morning,
> Of all things transitory.
> JAC. I love thee too, as far as I can love a fat man.
> HOST. Do'st thou Captain?
> Sweetly? and heartily?
> JAC. With all my heart Boy.
> HOST. Then welcom death, come close mine eyes sweet Captain
> Thou shalt have all.   (4.2, pp. 284–85)

Upon departing, the Host blabbers like a stock lover: "Captain, adieu, adieu, sweet bully Captain, / One kiss before I dye, one kiss" (4.2, p. 285). Through this ridiculously amorous exchange, the play succinctly exposes the social disorderliness of Jacomo's excessive misogyny and exclusive interest in other men.

After punishing Jacomo for his misogyny, the play then cures him of it, allowing him to participate in a traditional comic marriage. Jacomo's characteristic misogyny functions as a defense against women; when drink lowers his inhibitions he confesses that he "could love / Any man living now, or any woman" (4.2, p. 287). Encountering Frank, Clora, and Frederick, Jacomo demands to kiss not only the two women whom he has continually disparaged, but their male companion as well. Like the Passionate Lord in *The Nice Valour*, Jacomo absurdly courts a gentleman as his mistress: "Pray be not coy sweet woman, for I'le kiss ye" (4.3, p. 290). Although the humiliation to which Jacomo is subjected for this homoerotic courtship at first exacerbates his anger against women, it finally allows him to recognize and accept the sincerity of Frank's love. Jacomo marks his entrance into marriage and civilian society through a "feminine" softening of his rough manner – "I'le have my head curl'd, and powder'd to morrow" – and a properly placed heteroerotic desire, signaled by an orderly kiss: "if you love me, I pray you kiss me" (5.4, p. 312). As in *The Humorous Lieutenant*, the disorderly male homoeroticism temporarily produced by drink becomes the catalyst for correcting a prior condition of disorderly male hetero-eroticism.

In *The Night Walker* (1611), another comedy contemporary with *The

Captain, Jack Wildbraine rakishly pursues women as eagerly as Jacomo avoids them. Jack's sexual irresponsibility approaches tragedy when the secret liaison he arranges between his cousin and her lover accidentally exposes her to public dishonor and causes her apparent death. The play symbolizes Jack's heteroerotic disorderliness in an episode of mistaken homoerotic seduction. Fooled by the complete darkness, Jack mistakes a male servant for the "mad" citizen's wife he desires because she "must needes have rare new trickes."³⁹ He drags the terrified servant into his chamber:

> WILDBRAINE.   Are you there? In, in,
>   In presently.
> TOBIE [*aside*]. I feele his talents through me,
>   Tis an old haggard devill, what will he doe with me?
> WILDBRAINE. Let me kisse thee first, quicke, quicke.
> TOBIE [*aside*].   A lecherous Devill.
> WILDBRAINE [*aside*]. What a hairie whore tis, sure she has a muffler.
> TOBIE [*aside*]. If I should have a young Satan by him, for I dare not
>   deny him,
>   In what case were I? who durst deliver me?
> WILDBRAINE [*aside*]. Tis but my fancie, she is the same, — in
>   quickly,
>   Gently, my sweete girle.
> TOBIE   Sweete Devill be good to me.   (2.3.69–77)

Jack's inability to discern any anatomical difference between a woman and a man suggests his capability to perform with his male servant the "rare new tricks" he craved. Although the play never makes clear whether or not Tobie prevented the "lecherous Devill" from having his way, both men later complain of being tricked by devils, and Tobie affectionately declares that he and Jack "have beene fellow devils together" (3.1.47).

The comic scenes I have discussed from *The Humorous Lieutenant*, *The Nice Valour*, *The Captain*, and *The Night Walker* embed disorderly homoerotic desire within a larger context of disorderly heteroerotic desire. Only *The Nice Valour* and *The Captain* conclude by reforming the erring lover and marrying him off to the "proper" woman. In *The Humorous Lieutenant*, the Lieutenant wants not a wife but money: for the love "potion" he mistakenly ingested, the King compensates him with a hefty "portion" of wealth (5.2.47–48). Although the play concludes by reuniting Demetrius and Celia, the Lieutenant returns to the wars and ultimately to the male playgoers, whose love and approval will cure him of his disruptive "passion" (Epilogue 2). As for *The Night Walker*, a series of sexual misadventures does not reform but humiliates Jack Wildbraine. His final disgrace is learning that his new mistress belongs to his friend Tom, who sarcastically suggests that they marry: "Let's ha a wedding, you will be wondrous rich; / For she is impudent, and thou art miserable" (5.1.154–55). Exhausted, Jack declines the further company of women: "No, no, I thanke you *Tom*, I can watch for / A groat a night, and be every gentlemans fellow" (5.1.159–60). Despite announcing his intention to socialize henceforth with men, Jack returns "soundly sham'd" at the play's end to his aunt's household (5.2.191). Obliquely, Jack points the way to those heroes in Fletcher's tragicomedies who remain unwed either because like him they have failed as lovers, or because they never loved women in the first place. Yet unlike Jack, who returns to a female domestic sphere, these men begin and end in male homosocial worlds, moving during the course of their plays from rivalry to reconciliation with other men.[40]

Perhaps the best example of such a hero is Memnon, the archetypal soldier and title character of *The Mad Lover*. The play opens as Memnon returns from the wars, and his glorious entrance speech sharply dramatizes the split between soldiers and lovers that characterizes the play. A "Souldier and Souldiers Mate these twenty five years," Memnon considers peace a "lazie end" and admits his ignorance of courtly language and behavior.[41] What Memnon announces with pride, Princess Calis and her ladies regard with amusement. According to Lucippe, "I doe not thinke he knowes us what we are, / Or to what end" (1.1.89–90). Lucippe means that Memnon neither recognizes noblewomen nor possesses the gentle arts by which to address them, but her words are ambiguous enough to suggest that Memnon has no sexual experience with women at all.

Memnon's shocking behavior towards Calis bears out Lucippe's assessment of his erotic incompetence. Having returned to Paphos, the island of Venus, Memnon instantly falls in love with a princess who brings the goddess's name to his lips. At his first sight of Calis he cries out "O Venus" then "*kneeles amaz'd, and forgets to speake*" (1.1.108 sd). Fletcher develops the comic and tragic potential of the venereal soldier trope, showing Memnon's pursuit of Calis, however well intentioned and sincere, to be absurd and inept. The situation rapidly approaches disaster when Memnon takes literally the Petrarchan trope of giving his heart to his mistress. Much of the subsequent action concerns the efforts of Memnon's brother Polidor and the other soldiers to prevent Memnon's suicide and to cure him of his unrequited passion for Calis.

As his perverse understanding of Petrarchan conventions suggests, Memnon refuses to idealize Calis as a distant and chaste mistress. Instead, he insists that underneath her regal title Calis is merely a biological female:

> what was she made for then?
> Is she not young and handsome, bred to breed?
> Doe not men kisse faire women? if they doe,
> If lips be not unlawfull warre, why a Princesse
> Is got the same way that we get a begger,
> Or I am cosen'd; and the selfe-same way
> Shee must be handled e're she get another:
> That's rudenesse is it not?   (1.1.199–206)

Memnon's crude view of women as reproductive vessels is reinforced by
Chilax, an old soldier who resents the obsolescence of military personnel
during "dead peace, / This bastard breeding lowzie, lazie idlenesse"
(1.1.226–27). For such career soldiers, the prevalence of women (breed-
ers) and of male desire for women (breeding) taints civilian society with
effeminacy. In order to love Calis, then, Memnon must transcend base
(hetero)sexual practices, as he explains to one of his soldiers:

> SIPHAX. Why doe we love in this World then?
> MEMNON.   To preserve it,
>   The maker lost his worke els: but marke *Siphax*:
>   What issues that love beares.
> SIPHAX.   Why Children Sir; –
>   [*Aside*] I never heard him talke thus; thus devinelie
>   And sensible before.
> MEMNON.   It does so *Siphax*,
>   Things like our selves, as sensuall, vaine; unvented
>   Bubles and breaths of ayre, got with an itching
>   As blisters are; and bred, as much corruption
>   Flowes from their lives; sorrow conceives and shapes 'em
>   And oftentimes the deaths of those we love most:
>   The breeders bring them to the World to curse 'em . . .   (2.1.155–65)

Although Memnon sounds like a Platonist, glorifying nonreproductive
love between men and women as a spiritual ideal, he actually speaks
more like a satirist, stigmatizing love between men and women as bestial
and diseased.

Moreover, by speaking so vehemently against reproductive (hetero)-
sexuality, this unmarried and erotically disorderly warrior seems to speak
for sodomitical sexual practices, those that do not lead to the "issue" of
children within marriage. Memnon's heteroerotic desire for Calis, then, is
a "mad love" akin to sodomy. Even his celebration of spiritual love can
be interpreted as a symptom of madness, since he evokes the ephemeral
and corrupt nature of (hetero)sexual breeding as justification for killing
himself in the name of love.

Suffering from mad love, Memnon significantly calls upon Orpheus to
show him the blissful state of lovers in Elizium. As I demonstrated in

chapter 2, late sixteenth-century texts represent Orpheus as a man who rejects women, lives with other disillusioned husbands in a pastoral golden world, and advocates the love of boys. In *The Mad Lover*, the homoerotic aspects of the Orpheus myth are strongly implied by the context and content of the masque presented to cure Memnon of mad love. Dressing as the animals and plants charmed by Orpheus' music, the masquers represent "bestial" or "wooden" men who died for love and were shamefully transformed in the afterlife. Playing Orpheus, the soldier Stremon warns Memnon:

> This lion was a man of Warre that died,
> As thou wouldst doe, to guild his Ladies pride:
> This Dog a foole that hung himselfe for love:
> This Ape with daily hugging of a glove,
> Forgot to eat and died. This goodly tree,
> An usher that still grew before his Ladie,
> Wither'd at roote.   (4.1.78–84)

As his reference to the ambitious usher makes especially clear, Stremon essentially produces a satiric catalog of disorderly lovers. Instead of revealing the beauties of spiritual love, the masquers reveal "the plagues of love" and urge Memnon to "love no more" (4.1.25, 88). Having felt the plagues of love, of course, Orpheus loved no more women – but he did love boys. Stremon's song anatomizes a degrading and dangerous love clearly gendered as "feminine": foolish men die for a "glove" and a "Ladies pride." It fails, however, to condemn male–male love. Even though the masque may recall Orpheus' pederastic desire, it suggests that disorder results from excessive *heteroerotic* desire. Orpheus becomes a pederast only because he loved Eurydice too much.

Perhaps because it employs the erotically ambiguous figure of Orpheus, the masque fails to dissuade Memnon from his mad love. He is cured only when he subordinates his heteroerotic desires to more orderly male kinship bonds. Discovering that Calis loves his brother, Memnon relinquishes his claim to her and celebrates Polidor's success: "'tis all love / To me, all marriage rites, the joy of issues, / To know him fruitfull, that has been so faithfull" (5.4.334–36). The old soldier returns to his old love, war: "That shall be now my Mistresse, there my Courtship" (5.4.346). As at the conclusion of *The Nice Valour*, a courtly brother marries a noblewoman while a military brother remains unwed. Memnon may not demonstrate an explicitly sexual desire for other men. Nevertheless, his degradation of reproductive (hetero)sexuality and his elevation of nonreproductive love opens the space for whatever (homo)erotic desires and practices – Platonic, Orphic, or otherwise – such a love might entail.

Making a (racial) difference: masculinity and eroticism in
The Island Princess

To the threat of disruptive heteroerotic desire commonly found in Fletcher's tragicomedies, *The Island Princess* adds the threat of racial and religious difference. According to the *dramatis personae*, the action takes place in "India," more accurately in the Moluccan islands, where Portuguese colonists have united with the King of Tidore and his sister Quisara against the wicked Governor of Ternata. The production of "racial" difference in the play, as in early modern texts generally, occurs largely through discourses of nationality (European/Indian), religion (Christian/heathen), and morality (civility/savagery), not through the "paradigms of physical and phenotypical difference that would become the basis of later discourses of racism and racial difference."[42] In the particular case of *The Island Princess*, the relative absence of a discourse of physical racial difference is perhaps also attributable to the perceived similarity between the Moluccan islanders and the English. According to the English voyager George Best, "in the Ilands Moluccae the people are not blacke, but tauney and white, with long haire uncurled as wee have."[43] A discourse of blackness does not emerge in the play even where we might reasonably expect it to: when the Governor disguises himself "like a Moore Priest," nothing indicates that he alters his skin color or physiognomy to appear black.[44] His disguise depends upon the theatrical conventions of a costume, a fake beard, and a wig, which may or may not be "curled."

The play's only allusion to skin color regards the beauty of the native women. A Portuguese soldier remarks that Quisara's white skin distinguishes her from all those natives who wear the sun's "tauny Livery" (1.1.62). Whoever these darker islanders may be, Armusia's description of Moluccan women as being "of delicate aspects, faire, clearly beauteous" implies that they are light-skinned and therefore worthy of admiration (1.3.35). Because skin color in the play mainly serves to determine female beauty, Fletcher apparently finds it unnecessary to clarify whether Moluccan men are white, tawny, or black.[45]

The play's particularly gendered encoding of race is significant because the Portuguese colonists base their religious conviction and military might on an ideology of potent masculinity. Captain Pyniero boasts that wherever the Portuguese travel, "new worlds disclose their riches, / Their beauties, and their prides to [their] embraces" (1.3.10–11). To Armusia the Moluccas are the "blessed Islands" (1.3.16):

> The treasure of the Sun dwels here, each tree
> As if it envied the old Paradice,
> Strives to bring forth immortall fruit; the spices

> Renewing nature, though not deifying,
> And when that fals by time, scorning the earth,
> The sullen earth, should taint or sucke their beauties,
> But as we dreamt, for ever so preserve us:
> Nothing we see, but breeds an admiration;
> The very rivers as we floate along,
> Throw up their pearles, and curle their heads to court us;
> The bowels of the earth swell with the births
> Of thousand unknowne gems, and thousand riches;
> Nothing that beares a life, but brings a treasure.   (1.3.19–31)

Although the colonists typically allegorize their conquest of "new worlds" as a masculine penetration of a virginal body, they paradoxically regard their pillaging of native resources as a feminine seduction of passive men.[46] Not only do the virile Portuguese "sucke adventures" from the breasts of their "hardy nurses" (1.2.87), they represent the landscape they dominate as an overburdened maternal body that will nurture and thus reproduce their masculine power.[47]

Rejected as inimical to military discipline in *The Mad Lover*, reproductive (hetero)sexuality sustains the ideology of masculine colonial domination in *The Island Princess*. Yet the powerful fantasy of a feminine island freely opening itself to male invaders is immediately contradicted by the Island Princess herself, who resists being positioned as a passive sexual object. When Quisara refuses to honor her promise to marry Armusia, his companions recommend force:

> Doe what you should doe,
> What a man would doe in this case, a wise man,
> An understanding man that knowes a woman;
> Knowes her and all her tricks, her scorns and all her trifles:
> Goe to her and take her in your armes and shake her,
> Take her and tosse her like a barre.   (3.2.19–24)

Another companion appeals to "commonsense" knowledge about coy women: "They love a man that crushes 'em to verjuice; / A woman held at hard meat is your spanniel" (3.2.40–41). The anger and frustration of these men, who can understand Quisara's sexual resistance only as a symptom of repressed desire, attest to the power of her challenge to masculine identity. The play's acknowledgment that female treasures are not always freely given – and may even be actively withheld – reveals that from the perspective of the colonized, colonizers may be constructed as hated rapists instead of welcome lovers.

Despite her resistance to Armusia, Quisara claims to "love a Souldier" and admire masculine "vallour" (1.2.81–82). Consequently, she promises her cowardly Portuguese suitor Ruy Dias that she will convert to Christianity provided that he can perform some deed "[o]f such an

unmatcht noblenesse, that I may know / You have a power beyond ours
that preserves you" (1.2.59–60). The superior power of the Christian
God, however, does not prevent Quisara from inciting a destructive
sexual rivalry between Ruy Dias and Armusia. As a result of courting
Quisara, Armusia laments that he must "court [his] sword against [his]
countriman" and goes on to observe, "'Tis me thinkes, a strange dearth
of enemies, / When we seeke foes among our selves" (4.3.2, 10–11). Their
duel hazards not only each man's life but the very basis of Portuguese
military power, for the Governor sees in this microcosm of the Moluccan
civil war an opportunity to eradicate the colonists altogether: "Let 'em
alone, let 'em kill one another: – / These are the maine postes, if they fall,
the buildings / Will tumple quickly" (4.3.26–28). Thanks to Armusia's
temperance, the duel ends harmoniously. Armusia and Ruy Dias establish a noble friendship, and Ruy Dias foregoes his claim to Quisara,
devoting himself to the pursuit of honor. Nevertheless, the incident
shows how quickly heteroerotic desire has turned the ideology of masculine honor from a unifying into a divisive force.

Aside from the duel, other disorderly consequences follow the aggressive pursuit of masculine honor in tandem with heteroerotic desire.
Armusia is motivated to redeem the King of Tidore from captivity by the
double hope of winning glory and Quisara; he fails to anticipate that the
King, impressed by his "manhood" and "mighty hand," will adopt him
as the royal favorite (5.2.5). In his homoerotic affection for a favorite, the
King of Tidore significantly resembles Marlowe's Edward II. Just as
Edward II feels unable to reward Gaveston – "Thy worth, sweet friend,
is far above my gifts" (1.1.162) – so the King of Tidore worries that he
"never can reward, nor hope / To be once worthy of the name of friend"
to Armusia (2.6.135–36). The King of Tidore also recalls Edward II when
he is mocked for lamenting the loss of his favorite. Moreover, at different
points in their respective plays, each king finds himself scandalously
imprisoned in a filthy dungeon. The dungeon keeper in *The Island
Princess* echoes the admiration of his counterpart in *Edward II*:

> I wonder the king dies not,
> Being in a vault up to the knees in water,
> To which the channels of the castle run,
> From whence a damp continually ariseth
> That were enough to poison any man,
> Much more a king, brought up so tenderly.   (*Edward II*, 5.5.1–6)

> I have kept many a man, and many a great one,
> Yet I confesse, I nere saw before
> A man of such a sufferance; he lies now
> Where I would not lay my dog, for sure 'twould kill him;

> Where neither light or comfort can come neare him;
> Nor aire, nor earth that's wholsome: it grieves me
> To see a mighty King with all his glory,
> Sunke o'th'sudden to the bottome of a dungeon.
>
> (*The Island Princess*, 2.1.1–8)

Both speeches generate sympathy for an abused king. Unlike Edward II, however, the King of Tidore suffers this wretched incarceration at the beginning of the play, only later degenerating into solicitous folly with a favorite. Significantly, in calling Armusia "[t]his sister this, this all man, this all valour, / This pious man," the passionate King reveals that he is capable of weakening his own people by replacing his sole relative and heir with a foreigner and a Christian (2.6.129–30).

Whereas Gaveston actively elicits his king's desire, Armusia resists the King of Tidore's homoerotic patronage, which threatens to break down the ideological and political distance between Christian colonizer and pagan native. Edward II's establishment of a bodily and spiritual union with Gaveston empowers the favorite: "Embrace me, Gaveston, as I do thee. / Why shouldst thou kneel? knows't thou not who I am? / Thy friend, thyself, another Gaveston!" (1.1.141–43). In contrast, when the King of Tidore similarly greets his favorite – "Thus in my armes my deare" (2.6.184) – the unwanted intimacy makes Armusia blush. Armusia's blush can be attributed to his characteristic humility: he is known to be "blushing-chaste, and temperate, / Valiant, without vaineglory, modest" (5.2.112–13). Nevertheless, his "blushing-chaste" response may also function more strategically to distance himself from the King's "sweet intreaties" (4.4.13). Refusing to acknowledge Armusia's superior status as a European and a Christian, the King of Tidore, like Edward II, insists on the metaphysical identity he shares with his favorite: "Me my selfe sir, / My better selfe" (3.2.58–59).

Subsequent events unfold the danger of Armusia's proximity to the doting King, whose essentially "barbarous" nature inevitably manifests itself in dishonorable practices. In the opening scene of the play, the Portuguese wonder how the King could stoop to rowing his own boat; Pyniero reasons that

> Base breedings love base pleasure;
> They take as much delight in a Baratto,
> A little scurvy boate, to row her tithly,
> And have the art to turne and winde her nimbly,
> Thinke it as noble too, though it be slavish,
> And a dull labour that declines a Gentleman:
> As we Portugalls, or the Spaniards do in riding.   (1.1.18–24)

Ambushed by the treacherous Governor while enjoying this base recreation, the King is blamed for his own captivity on the principle that "where no faith is, there's no trust" (1.1.28). The religion, values, and culture of Indians – whether the enemies or the allies of Europeans – are essentially antithetical to noble behavior.⁴⁸ When the King imprisons Armusia, Pyniero and his followers voice these sentiments more crassly, branding the Tidoreans "barbarous slaves," "Barbarians," and "a kind of hounds" (5.1.19, 24, 36). Most tellingly, Pyniero's Marlovian fantasy of murdering the Tidoreans through anal rape – "Take stakes and thrust into their tailes for glisters" (5.1.41) – provides a sodomitical spin on the King of Tidore's disorderly patronage of Armusia.

By the end of the play the unleashing of disorderly heteroerotic and homoerotic desires has exposed the Portuguese to formidable political dangers. They are ultimately preserved from ruin only by rechanneling masculine energies into national honor and military force. Inspired by Armusia's angry defiance of her heathen gods, Quisara rejects them too. Her religious conversion parallels Ruy Dias's transformation from a cowardly lover into a brave soldier. The exposure of the Governor's treachery delegitimizes his criticism of Portuguese colonialism. Finally, Armusia's betrothal to Quisara not only removes the threat of the King's homoerotic patronage but projects the action of the play into the future, implying a Portuguese heir to the Tidorean crown. The Governor had previously warned the King of the detrimental consequences of a Portuguese ruler over Tidore: "What reverence shall the Gods have? and what justice / The miserable people? what shall they doe?" (4.1.66–67). Although the King concedes that the Governor "points at truth directly" (4.1.68), in the comic finale he forgets this political insight as he celebrates the masculine sexual potency that secures Portuguese colonial domination. The Portuguese fantasy of the Moluccan landscape as a breeding, nurturing body is finally realized in the promise of (hetero)sexual reproductivity and female fertility that will produce a Portuguese heir.⁴⁹

The significance of reproductive (hetero)sexuality to the resolution of *The Island Princess* can be underscored by considering the very different alignment of reproduction and race that concludes *The Knight of Malta* (1616–19). *The Knight of Malta* elevates the chaste masculinity of the knighthood over (hetero)sexual reproductivity and represents disorderly heteroerotic desire through the transgressive interracial union between Montferrat, a wicked knight, and Zanthia, a Moorish servant. Conflating racial discourses of complexion, religion, sexuality, and colonialism, the naval commander Norandine derides Zanthia as Montferrat's "black gib, his *Succuba*, his devils seed, his spawn of *Phlegton*, that . . . was bred o' the spume of *Cocitus*; do ye snarl you black Jill? she looks like the Picture of *America*."⁵⁰ When Montferrat is forced to marry Zanthia,

Norandine scoffs, "Away *French* stallion, now you have a *Barbary* mare of your own, go leap her, and engender young devlings" (5.2, p. 163). Not only is Zanthia the monstrous spawn of black seed, her body will monstrously reproduce its own blackness. The idea of a union between a white man and a black woman greatly disturbed Renaissance Englishmen, argues Lynda Boose, because their child would take on its mother's skin color. The black woman's "signifying capacity as a mother threatens nothing less than the wholesale negation of white patriarchal authority."[51] In *The Knight of Malta*, Montferrat's loss of masculine authority to Zanthia provides the precise measure of his punishment and of Norandine's disgust. By contrast, in *The Island Princess* Armusia triumphs because he marries an assuredly white island princess. Whereas in *The Knight of Malta* reproductive (hetero)sexuality promotes dishonorable lust, social disorder, and racial degeneration, in *The Island Princess* it guarantees masculine colonial hegemony over threatening racial difference.[52]

Coda

By examining the homoerotics of masculinity in Fletcherian tragicomedy, I have tried to establish one model for how sexuality, gender, status, and race might be considered as intersecting categories of political and ideological meaning in early modern drama. That "homoeroticism" and "sodomy" make more tenuous appearances in my reading of tragicomedy than elsewhere in this study results from two factors: the texture of the plays themselves, and my eagerness at the end of the project to locate homoeroticism more directly within other economies of difference. In the final stages, it seemed less urgent to demonstrate that both orderly and disorderly homoerotic relations were present in early modern drama than to examine how their presence was at once revealed and occluded by related discourses of masculinity, militarism, reproductive sexuality, colonialism, or race.

Nevertheless, the dominant focus of the chapter – and of the book – undeniably remains on male eroticism: the readings have done justice neither to the complex histories of female homoeroticism and racial difference in the early modern period nor to the rapidly growing scholarship in these areas. What I take to be the inadequacy of critical practice to advance all our political and theoretical commitments simultaneously should not be lamented, I think, but acknowledged as a condition of current work and as a starting point for subsequent inquiry. With this particular project, my immediate goal was to historicize early modern homoeroticism and to make it central to scholarly discourse on both

Shakespearean and non-Shakespearean drama. To my mind, *The Homo-erotics of Early Modern Drama* will achieve this goal if it provokes reconsideration not only of the "homoerotics" of early modern culture and contemporary critical practice, but of the interests served and knowledges promoted by the ways in which we define, write about, and teach "early modern drama."

Notes

1 INTRODUCTION

1 Eve Kosofsky Sedgwick, *Between Men: English Literature and Male Homosocial Desire* (New York: Columbia University Press, 1985), pp. 1–5, 83–89.

2 On the normativity of male homoerotic relations in the earlier Renaissance, see Jonathan Goldberg, *Sodometries: Renaissance Texts, Modern Sexualities* (Stanford: Stanford University Press, 1992), especially pp. 18–19, 162–63. According to Alan Bray, a homosexual subculture and social identity (the "molly") first emerged in the late seventeenth century (*Homosexuality in Renaissance England* [London: Gay Men's Press, 1982], pp. 92, 103–4). The emergence of homophobia in the eighteenth century and its relation to the theater is the topic of Kristina Straub's *Sexual Suspects: Eighteenth-Century Players and Sexual Ideology* (Princeton: Princeton Univeristy Press, 1992).

3 David M. Halperin, "One Hundred Years of Homosexuality," in his *One Hundred Years of Homosexuality and Other Essays on Greek Love* (New York: Routledge, 1990), p. 26.

4 Ed Cohen, *Talk on the Wilde Side: Toward a Genealogy of a Discourse on Male Sexualities* (New York: Routledge, 1993), p. 102.

5 Eve Kosofsky Sedgwick, "Tales of the Avunculate: Queer Tutelage in *The Importance of Being Earnest*," in her *Tendencies* (Durham, NC: Duke University Press, 1993), pp. 58, 56.

6 Ibid., p. 58.

7 Sedgwick is rightly skeptical of rhetorical appeals to commonsense knowledge about homosexuality. She warns against "counterposing to the alterity of the past a relatively unified homosexuality that 'we' *do* 'know today'" (*Epistemology of the Closet* [Berkeley: University of California Press, 1991], p. 45).

8 Valerie Traub, *Desire and Anxiety: Circulations of Sexuality in Shakespearean Drama* (London: Routledge, 1992), p. 12.

9 Goldberg, *Sodometries*, p. 22.

10 Despite speaking of "homosexual desire," Bruce Smith acknowledges that "homosexuality" and "homosexuals" did not properly exist in Renaissance England. Building on Halperin and Foucault, Smith clearly distinguishes modern from early modern discourses of "homosexuality" (*Homosexual Desire in Shakespeare's England: a Cultural Poetics* [Chicago: University of Chicago Press, 1991], pp. 9–18). Traub more completely eschews the term "homosexuality," promoting the alternative "homoerotic":

In the absence of a historically accurate term for such desires, I will provisionally call them "homoerotic," in order to differentiate between, on the one hand, the early modern legal and medical discourses of sodomy and tribadism, and, on the other hand, the modern identificatory classifications of "lesbian," "gay," and "homosexual." Neither a category of self nor normatively male, the term "homoerotic" retains both the necessary strangeness and historical contiguity between early modern and postmodern forms of desire.

("The [In]Significance of 'Lesbian' Desire in Early Modern England," *Erotic Politics: Desire on the Renaissance Stage*, ed. Susan Zimmerman [New York: Routledge, 1992], 150–69, p. 156)

11 An implicit (basically Freudian) disagreement with social constructionism appears in Joseph Pequigney, "The Two Antonios and Same-Sex Love in *Twelfth Night* and *The Merchant of Venice*," *ELR* 22 (1992): 201–21. Labeling Shakespearean characters "bisexual" and "homosexual," Pequigney anachronistically attributes to them a modern notion of "sexual orientation" (pp. 206, 201).

12 Halperin, "One Hundred Years," p. 40.

13 Alan Sinfield, *The Wilde Century: Effeminacy, Oscar Wilde and the Queer Moment* (New York: Columbia University Press, 1994), p. 121. Sinfield traces the changing "uses of effeminacy" in the construction of gender and erotic roles from the early modern to the modern period (pp. 25–51).

14 Cf. Halperin: "'Sexuality,' for cultures not shaped by some very recent European and American bourgeois developments, is not a cause but an effect. The social body precedes the sexual body" ("One Hundred Years," pp. 37–38).

15 Thomas Laqueur, *Making Sex: Body and Gender from the Greeks to Freud* (Cambridge, MA: Harvard University Press, 1990), p. 6.

16 Judith Butler, *Bodies That Matter: on the Discursive Limits of "Sex"* (New York: Routledge, 1993), pp. 65–69.

17 Jean E. Howard, "Sex and Social Conflict: the Erotics of *The Roaring Girl*," *Erotic Politics*, ed. Zimmerman, 170–90, pp. 177–78, 188n.12. See also Stephen Orgel, "Nobody's Perfect: or Why Did the English Stage Take Boys for Women?" *Displacing Homophobia: Gay Male Perspectives in Literature and Culture*, ed. Ronald R. Butters, John M. Clum, and Michael Moon (Durham: Duke University Press, 1989), 7–29, pp. 13, 22–23. About the erotic interchangeability of boys and women, however, Howard is careful to add, "Boys and women were 'the same' in their hierarchical relationship to adult males, but they were also 'different,' if only in the crucial matter of their respective roles in reproduction" (p. 171).

18 Bray's identification of the molly houses with a homosexual subculture and a protohomosexual identity has come under scrutiny. Ed Cohen critiques Bray's "subjectifying approach" to the molly (*Talk on the Wilde Side*, p. 246); Margaret Hunt questions the appropriateness of calling the molly houses "homosexual" or a "subculture," preferring to see them as "communities that were relatively tolerant of sex outside the patriarchal nuclear family" ("Afterword," *Queering the Renaissance*, ed. Jonathan Goldberg [Durham: Duke University Press, 1994], 359–78, p. 370). Rictor Norton's interpretations of the evidence for a molly subculture are weakened by anachronistic concepts such as "gay identity," "gay lifestyle," and "gay pride" (*Mother Clap's Molly House: the Gay Subculture in England, 1700–1830* [London: Gay Men's Press,

1992], p. 10). A more rigorous sociological analysis of the molly houses appears in David F. Greenberg, *The Construction of Homosexuality* (Chicago: University of Chicago Press, 1988), pp. 328–42.

19 Bray, *Homosexuality in Renaissance England*, p. 74.

20 Goldberg, *Sodometries*, p. 205.

21 Gregory W. Bredbeck, *Sodomy and Interpretation: Marlowe to Milton* (Ithaca: Cornell University Press, 1991), p. 10.

22 Ibid., p. 3.

23 Ibid., p. 167. The speaker of Shakespeare's sonnets *may* exhibit "sodomitical" desire; however, Bredbeck's analysis is not concerned to demonstrate this. It therefore leaves unresolved the implications of the claim that "the Shake-spearean sodomite procures the poet's subjectivity at the expense of sexual meaning" (p. 169). Is the "sexual meaning" the poems disrupt and frustrate really *sodomitical* – or is it a nonsodomitical form of homoeroticism? In the context of what Bredbeck argues is the "linguistic purpose" of the sequence, does this distinction even matter? Do the *Sonnets* in fact frustrate our ability to distinguish among different forms of homoerotic meaning?

24 My separation of "sodomy" from a larger field of "homoeroticism" diverges from Bruce Smith's similar effort in several ways, the most important being a more materialist stress on the social and economic effects of homoerotic practices. I discuss Smith's methodology (as well as those of Bredbeck and Traub) in a review essay, "Reading Homoeroticism in Early Modern England: Imaginations, Interpretations, Circulations," *Textual Practice* 7 (1993): 483–97.

25 Traub, *Desire and Anxiety*, p. 106.

26 Alan Bray, "Homosexuality and the Signs of Male Friendship in Elizabethan England," *Queering the Renaissance*, ed. Goldberg, 40–61, pp. 40, 42.

27 On Bray's occasional reification and anachronistic use of "homosexual" and "homosexuality," see Sedgwick, *Between Men*, pp. 84–87; Goldberg, *Sodometries*, pp. 68–71; and Elizabeth Pittenger, "'To Serve the Queere': Nicholas Udall, Master of Revels," *Queering the Renaissance*, ed. Goldberg, 162–89, pp. 166–69.

28 Bray, "Homosexuality and the Signs of Male Friendship," p. 54.

29 Lewes Machin, *Three Eglogs* . . . (London, 1607), sig. E5v.

30 Cf. Forest Tyler Stevens, "Erasmus's 'Tigress': the Language of Friendship, Pleasure, and the Renaissance Letter," *Queering the Renaissance*, ed. Goldberg, 124–40.

31 As Guy Hocquenghem notes, psychoanalysis defines male sociality by the sublimation, as opposed to the direct expression, of homosexual desire (*Homosexual Desire*, trans. Daniella Dangoor, introduction by Michael Moon [Durham: Duke University Press, 1993]). Whereas early modern ideology incorporates homoeroticism into the definition and practice of friendship, modern ideology sees homoeroticism as an outside threat to friendship, a relation defined by the desexualization of male–male desire. An important future project would be to trace the ideological transformations of male friendship from an early modern (potentially erotic) system to a modern (nonerotic, or sublimated erotic) system.

32 A few of the exceptions appear in *Queering the Renaissance*, notably Elizabeth

Pittenger's essay on Nicholas Udall and Forest Tyler Stevens's essay on Erasmus. Nevertheless, these essays still focus on well-known individual figures.

33 Smith, *Homosexual Desire*, p. 73.
34 Leah S. Marcus, "Renaissance/Early Modern Studies," *Redrawing the Boundaries: the Transformation of English and American Literary Studies*, ed. Stephen Greenblatt and Giles Gunn (New York: MLA, 1992), 41–63, p. 47.
35 Otherwise historically minded critics may display a blindspot with regard to homoeroticism. In his introduction to *As You Like It* (New York: Bantam, 1988), editor David Bevington assures us that no "deviate sexual practice" is to be feared in Orlando's romantic courtship of Ganymede (xxii–xxiii). This formulation leaves only two options for Renaissance homoerotic desire: no sex (platonic friendship) or sex (sodomy).
36 While I deplore the use of hate-promoting media tactics for antigay agendas, I do not believe that men who engage in sadomasochism, leather fetishism, or cross-dressing should be demonized for providing "negative images"; nor do I advocate burying subcultural visibility underneath a massive proliferation of "positive images" of "normal" gay people, an agenda promoted by Marshall Kirk and Hunter Madsen, *After the Ball: How America Will Conquer Its Fear of Gays in the '90s* (New York: Doubleday, 1989). Douglas Crimp provides a withering response to the homophobia of Kirk and Madsen in "Mourning and Militancy," *Out There: Marginalization and Contemporary Cultures*, ed. Russell Ferguson, *et al.* (New York: New Museum of Contemporary Art, 1990), 233–45.
37 On the homophobic politics of the film, see Douglas Crimp, "Right On, Girlfriend!" *Fear of a Queer Planet: Queer Politics and Social Theory*, ed. Michael Warner (Minneapolis: University of Minnesota Press, 1993), 300–20.
38 Sinfield, *The Wilde Century*, p. 202.
39 Louis Crompton, "Gay Genocide: From Leviticus to Hitler," *The Gay Academic*, ed. Louie Crew (Palm Springs, CA: ETC Publications, 1978), 67–91, p. 70.
40 Ibid., p. 82.
41 Joseph Cady, "Renaissance Awareness and Language for Heterosexuality: 'Love' and 'Feminine Love,'" *Renaissance Discourses of Desire*, ed. Claude J. Summers and Ted-Larry Pebworth (Columbia: University of Missouri Press, 1993), 143–58, p. 145.
42 Joseph Cady, "'Masculine Love,' Renaissance Writing, and the 'New Invention' of Homosexuality," *Homosexuality in Renaissance and Enlightenment England: Literary Representations in Historical Context*, ed. Claude J. Summers (New York: Harrington Park, 1992). Cady's identification of "masculine love" with "homosexuality" is problematic even on the linguistic level at which he operates, since "masculine love" may or may not signify homoeroticism depending on the context. For instance, it is not clear that masculine love has erotic connotations in Richard Brome's *The Love-sick Court*: "Thou / Masculine love, known by the name of friendship / Art peaceful and morigerous: But that / Of woman is imperious and cruel" (quoted in Laurens J. Mills, *One Soul in Bodies Twain: Friendship in Tudor Literature and Stuart Drama* [Bloomington, IN: Principia Press, 1937], p. 350).

43 Cady writes in the tradition of John Boswell, who posits the rise and later decline of a "gay subculture" in the Middle Ages. Because Boswell uses "gay" to describe a supposed "minority" of people in the premodern era who were "conscious of erotic inclination toward their own gender as a distinguishing characteristic," his attempt to posit a nonsodomitical homosexual subjectivity or subculture in medieval Europe has been widely characterized as essentialist (*Christianity, Social Tolerance, and Homosexuality: Gay People in Western Europe from the Beginning of the Christian Era to the Fourteenth Century* [Chicago: University of Chicago Press, 1980], p. 44).

44 Cady, "Renaissance Awareness," p. 157.

45 Cady, " 'Masculine Love,' " p. 32.

46 E. M. Forster, *Maurice* (New York: Norton, 1971), p. 250.

47 Vito Russo, *The Celluloid Closet: Homosexuality in the Movies*, revised edn (New York: Harper and Row, 1987), p. 156.

48 Janet E. Halley, "*Bowers* v. *Hardwick* in the Renaissance," *Queering the Renaissance*, ed. Goldberg, 15–39.

49 John Fletcher, *The Honest Man's Fortune, The Works of Francis Beaumont and John Fletcher*, ed. Arnold Glover and A. R. Waller, 10 vols. (Cambridge: Cambridge University Press, 1912), X: 4.1, p. 258.

50 James I, *Basilicon Doron, King James VI and I: Political Writings*, ed. Johann P. Sommerville (Cambridge: Cambridge University Press, 1994), p. 23.

51 Quoted in *Marlowe: the Critical Heritage, 1588–1896*, ed. Millar MacLure (London: Routledge, 1979), p. 37. Jonathan Goldberg discusses the statement in "Sodomy and Society: the Case of Christopher Marlowe," *Staging the Renaissance: Reinterpretations of Elizabethan and Jacobean Drama*, ed. David Scott Kastan and Peter Stallybrass (New York: Routledge, 1991), 75–82.

52 James I, *A Counterblaste to Tobacco, Minor Prose Works of King James VI and I*, ed. James Craigie (Edinburgh: Scottish Text Society, 1982), pp. 97, 88.

53 Ibid., p. 96.

54 William Perkins, *The Foundation of Christian Religion, The Workes of that Famous and Worthy Minister of Christ in the Universitie of Cambridge, Mr. William Perkins*, 3 vols. (London, 1616–18), I: 58, sig. F2v.

55 Given the precedent of Paul de Man, it might not be inappropriate to evoke an unwitting insight from *All in the Family*'s Archie Bunker. Justifying the sexual double standard for husbands and wives, Archie appeals to the example of polygamous Old Testament patriarchs such as Abraham, David, and "Solomon and Gommorah." Despite his attempt to authorize male heterosexual promiscuity, Archie instead identifies it with the unauthorized homosexual promiscuity of Sodom. In Renaissance terms, Solomon's disorderly lust for women might be rendered as sodomy.

56 Traub, *Desire and Anxiety*, p. 106.

57 Smith, *Homosexual Desire*, p. 45. The rest of this paragraph summarizes Smith, pp. 42–53. Cf. Donald N. Mager, "John Bale and Early Tudor Sodomy Discourse," *Queering the Renaissance*, ed. Goldberg, 141–61.

58 Butler, *Bodies That Matter*, p. 107.

59 Raymond-Jean Frontain, "*Ruddy and goodly to look at withal*: Drayton, Cowley, and the Biblical Model for Renaissance Hom[m]osexuality," *Cahiers Elizabethains* 36 (October 1989): 11–24, pp. 13, 19. On the significance of

Jonathan and David in the writings of the American Puritan John Winthrop, see Michael Warner, "New English Sodom," *Queering the Renaissance*, ed. Goldberg, 330–58. Both Warner and Goldberg (*Sodometries*, pp. 223–46) point to the tension in American Puritan texts between the condemnation of sodomy and the promotion of brotherly love.

60 James M. Saslow, "The Tenderest Lover: Saint Sebastian in Renaissance Painting: a Proposed Homoerotic Iconology for North Italian Art 1450–1550," *Gai Saber* 1.1 (1977): 58–66.

61 Cynthia Lewis, " 'Wise Men, Folly-Fall'n': Characters Named Antonio in English Renaissance Drama," *Renaissance Drama* ns 20 (1989): 197–236. According to Lewis, the "identification between these saints and their sexually promiscuous wards may have been transformed, over several decades' time, into a link between sexual appetite and the saints themselves." She believes this transformation may explain "why critics of *The Merchant of Venice* and of *Twelfth Night* have sensed a homoerotic attraction between each play's Antonio and Sebastian," and she notes that "Bastiano," the Italian diminutive for "Sebastian," closely resembles "Bassanio" (pp. 206–7, 205).

Critics who have detected a homoerotic code in the names Sebastian and/or Antonio in Renaissance drama include Jan Kott ("The Gender of Rosalind," *The Gender of Rosalind*, trans. Jadwiga Kosicka [Evanston, IL: Northwestern University Press, 1992], p. 38n.6); Joseph Pequigney ("The Two Antonios," p. 205); and Jean Howard ("Sex and Social Conflict," p. 175).

62 Richard Rambuss, "Pleasure and Devotion: the Body of Jesus in Seventeenth-Century Religious Lyric," *Queering the Renaissance*, ed. Goldberg, 253–79.

63 Quoted in MacLure, *Marlowe*, p. 37.

64 Robert Wilkinson, *Lot's Wife. A Sermon Preached at Paules Crosse* (London, 1607), p. 54, sig. H3v.

65 Bredbeck, *Sodomy and Interpretation*, pp. 215–16.

66 John Marston, *The Dutch Courtesan, The Works of John Marston*, ed. A. H. Bullen, 3 vols. (London: John C. Nimmo, 1887), II: 3.1.42–47.

67 As an institution, the early modern theater was the site of intense struggle regarding social mobility, an emergent market economy, and gender definition. While I tend to discuss the ideological implications of theatrical representations rather than of theatrical practices, I have relied for the latter on the excellent materialist accounts provided by Steven Mullaney (*The Place of the Stage: License, Play, and Power in Renaissance England* [Chicago: University of Chicago Press, 1988]) and Jean E. Howard (*The Stage and Social Struggle in Early Modern England* [London: Routledge, 1994]).

68 I say "a dominant strand of modern homosexual definition" so as not to erase the competing modern definition of homosexuality in terms of gender separatism and universal sexual possibility. For the implications of these competing models, as well as a consideration of their incoherent conflation in much modern thinking about homosexuality, see Sedgwick, *Epistemology of the Closet*, pp. 82–90. Sedgwick also provides a suggestive list of erotic microvariants that may be more pertinent to certain individuals' sexual "preference" than gender of object choice, or homo/hetero definition (p. 25).

69 Ibid., p. 88.

70 Hunt, "Afterword," p. 373.
71 Philippa Berry, *Of Chastity and Power: Elizabethan Literature and the Unmarried Queen* (London: Routledge, 1989); Theodora A. Jankowski, *Women in Power in the Early Modern Drama* (Urbana: University of Illinois Press, 1992), " 'Where There Can Be No Cause of Affection': Redefining Virgins, Their Desires, and Their Pleasures in John Lyly's *Gallathea*," *Feminist Readings of Early Modern Culture: Emerging Subjects*, ed. Dympna Callaghan, M. Lindsay Kaplan, and Valerie Traub (Cambridge: Cambridge University Press, 1996).
72 Margaret Hunt advocates a criticism that will illuminate the "intersections between sodomy fears, the discourse of male friendship, and the domination of women" ("Afterword," *Queering the Renaissance*, ed. Goldberg, p. 373).
73 Francis Barker, *The Tremulous Private Body: Essays on Subjection* (London: Methuen, 1984), pp. 16–17. Susan Zimmerman argues that students of Renaissance eroticism need "to shift attention to the flatter, more formulaic terrain of much non-Shakespearean Jacobean drama, and eventually to consider Shakespeare in terms of it" ("Disruptive Desire: Artifice and Indeterminacy in Jacobean Comedy," in her *Erotic Politics*, 39–63, p. 39).

2 THE HOMOEROTICS OF MARRIAGE IN OVIDIAN COMEDY

1 Lawrence Stone, *The Family, Sex and Marriage in England 1500–1800* (New York: Harper and Row, 1977). Other historical accounts that neglect the homoerotic as a category of early modern domestic experience include Ralph A. Houlbrooke, *The English Family 1450–1700* (London: Longman, 1984) and Alice T. Friedman, *House and Household in Elizabethan England: Wollaton Hall and the Willoughby Family* (Chicago: University of Chicago Press, 1989).
2 Evidence of homoeroticism within the early modern domestic sphere has been provided by methodologically diverse studies: Alan Bray, *Homosexuality in Renaissance England* (London: Gay Men's Press, 1982), pp. 44–51; Bruce R. Smith, *Homosexual Desire in Shakespeare's England: a Cultural Poetics* (Chicago: University of Chicago Press, 1991), pp. 82–88; Gregory W. Bredbeck, *Sodomy and Interpretation: Marlowe to Milton* (Ithaca: Cornell University Press, 1991), pp. 115–34; Bredbeck, "Sodomesticity," MLA Convention, New York City, 29 December 1992; Richard Rambuss, "The Secretary's Study: the Secret Designs of *The Shepherd's Calender*," *ELH* 59 (1992): 313–35, pp. 318–21; Jonathan Goldberg, *Sodometries: Renaissance Texts, Modern Sexualities* (Stanford: Stanford University Press, 1992), pp. 123–43. See also the following essays in *Erotic Politics: Desire on the Renaissance Stage*, ed. Susan Zimmerman (New York: Routledge, 1992): Valerie Traub, "The (In)significance of 'Lesbian' Desire in Early Modern England," 150–69, pp. 158–65; Lisa Jardine, "Twins and Travesties: Gender, Dependency, and Sexual Availability in *Twelfth Night*," 27–38; and Jean E. Howard, "Sex and Social Conflict: the Erotics of *The Roaring Girl*," 170–90, pp. 174–79.
3 The early modern household, also known as a "family," was comprised not only of parents and children but also of "non-kin inmates, sojourners,

boarders or lodgers ... as well as indentured apprentices and resident servants" (Stone, *The Family*, pp. 26–27). Bray observes that the practice of sharing beds within the household could facilitate sex between servants or between masters and servants (*Homosexuality*, pp. 50–51).

Non-Shakespearean (indeed, un-Shakespearean) representations of homo-erotic master–servant relations are the subject of chapter 3 below, as well as Theodore B. Leinwand's "Redeeming Beggary/Buggery in *Michaelmas Term*," *ELH* 61 (1994): 53–70.

4 Lynda E. Boose, "The Family in Shakespeare Studies; or – Studies in the Family of Shakespeareans; or – The Politics of Politics," *Renaissance Quarterly* 40 (1987): 707–61. Boose develops the metaphor of feminism as a "liminal daughter" and new historicism as a "legitimate son" (p. 738).

5 Catherine Belsey, "Disrupting Sexual Difference: Meaning and Gender in the Comedies," *Alternative Shakespeares*, ed. John Drakakis (London: Routledge, 1988), 166–90; Mary Beth Rose, *The Expense of Spirit: Love and Sexuality in English Renaissance Drama* (Ithaca: Cornell University Press, 1988).

6 Rose, *The Expense of Spirit*, p. 14. Belsey simply says that she is "not entirely persuaded" by the argument that boy actors had a homoerotic appeal ("Disrupting Sexual Difference," p. 235n.2). She says nothing, however, about the homoerotic valence of the name Ganymede in *As You Like It*.

7 Smith, *Homosexual Desire*, pp. 33–41, 56–77. Whereas Smith believes that male homoerotic friendships were broken by marriage, Joseph Pequigney argues that Shakespeare's homoerotically inclined Antonios are incorporated into the marriages that conclude their comedies ("The Two Antonios and Same-Sex Love in *Twelfth Night* and *The Merchant of Venice*," *ELR* 22 [1992]: 201–21).

8 Stephen Orgel, "Nobody's Perfect: or Why Did the English Stage Take Boys for Women?," *Displacing Homophobia: Gay Male Perspectives in Literature and Culture*, ed. Ronald R. Butters, John M. Clum, and Michael Moon (Durham, NC: Duke University Press, 1989), 7–30, p. 26; and Howard, "Sex and Social Conflict," p. 172.

9 On Ovidianism in Shakespearean comedy, see Jonathan Bate, *Shakespeare and Ovid* (Oxford: Oxford University Press, 1993), 118–70.

10 Edmund Spenser, *The Faerie Queene*, ed. A. C. Hamilton (London: Longman, 1977), 3.12.7–8. Subsequent references (by book, canto, and stanza) will be cited parenthetically in the text.

11 Leonard Barkan, *The Gods Made Flesh: Metamorphosis and the Pursuit of Paganism* (New Haven: Yale University Press, 1986), pp. 234–35; James W. Broaddus, "Renaissance Psychology and Britomart's Adventures in *Faerie Queene* III," *ELR* 17 (1987): 186–206, p. 203; Harry Berger Jr., "Busirane and the War Between the Sexes: an Interpretation of *The Faerie Queene* III.x-i-xii," *ELR* 1 (1971): 99–121, p. 108; Simon Shepherd, *Spenser* (New York: Harvester Wheatsheaf, 1989), p. 88.

12 The question of Amoret's desires is taken up by Dorothy Stephens, who argues that her evasion of Scudamour allows her to pursue other women ("Into Other Arms: Amoret's Evasion," *Queering the Renaissance*, ed. Jonathan Goldberg [Durham: Duke University Press, 1994], 190–217).

13 William Rossky, "Imagination in the English Renaissance: Psychology and Poetic," *Studies in the Renaissance* 5 (1958): 49–73, p. 53.

14 Ben Jonson, *Cynthia's Revels, Ben Jonson*, ed. C. H. Herford and Percy Simpson, 11 vols. (Oxford: Oxford University Press–Clarendon, 1925–52), IV: 4.1.172.

15 According to Camille Paglia, "Amoret, due to her spiritual limitations, may have invoked this morbid scene of martyrdom as an imaginative projection" (*Sexual Personae: Art and Decadence from Nefertiti to Emily Dickinson* [New York: Vintage, 1991], p. 186).

16 Broaddus, "Renaissance Psychology," p. 199. This is a reading of the masque Broaddus himself denies.

17 On the association of the public theater with sodomy, see Bray, *Homosexuality*, pp. 54–55; Lisa Jardine, *Still Harping on Daughters: Women and Drama in the Age of Shakespeare*, 2nd edn (New York: Columbia University Press–Morningside, 1989), pp. 9–36; Susan Zimmerman, "Disruptive Desire: Artifice and Indeterminacy in Jacobean Comedy," in her *Erotic Politics*, 39–63, pp. 43–46; Laura Levine, *Men in Women's Clothing: Anti-theatricality and Effeminization, 1579–1642* (Cambridge: Cambridge University Press, 1994), pp. 22–23, 146–47.

18 Thomas Cooper, *Dictionarium Historicum & Poeticum . . . in Thesaurus Linguae Romanae & Brittanicae . . .* (London, 1565), sig. J4r. On Shakespeare's probable use of this dictionary, see DeWitt T. Starnes and Earnest William Talbert, *Classical Myth and Legend in Renaissance Dictionaries: a Study of Renaissance Dictionaries in Their Relation to the Classical Learning of Contemporary English Writers* (Chapel Hill: University of North Carolina Press, 1955), pp. 111–34.

19 Christopher Marlowe, *Dido, Queen of Carthage, Christopher Marlowe: the Complete Plays*, ed. J. B. Steane (Harmondsworth: Penguin, 1986), 1.1 sd, 1.1.51.

20 Whatever the anatomical similarities between the sexes posited by the Galenic one-sex model, certain bodily functions particular to women or attributed to women by Renaissance gender discourses were considered "different" enough to evoke male anxiety and disgust. The sixteenth-century physician Thomas Raynalde feared that knowledge of women's unique reproductive processes might lead men "the more to abhorre and loath the companie of women" (quoted in Gail Kern Paster, *The Body Embarrassed: Drama and the Disciplines of Shame in Early Modern England* [Ithaca: Cornell University Press, 1993], p. 187). On the Galenic one-sex model, see Thomas Laqueur, *Making Sex: Body and Gender from the Greeks to Freud* (Cambridge, MA: Harvard University Press, 1990). Laqueur has been criticized for downplaying differences, namely the competing Aristotelian model of *sexual* difference and the construction of *gender* differences in early modern texts about women. This argument is advanced by Patricia Parker, "Gender Ideology, Gender Change: the Case of Marie Germain," *Critical Inquiry* 19 (1993): 337–64, esp. pp. 339–40; and Sally Shuttleworth, review of Laqueur, *Journal of the History of Sexuality* 3 (1993): 633–34. Paster provides a convincing corrective to Laqueur regarding the physiological and ethical gender differences posited by Renaissance humoral theory (pp. 16–17 *et passim*).

21 According to Arthur Golding's 1567 translation of Ovid, Jupiter advances Ganymede "against Dame *Junos* will" (*Shakespeare's Ovid: Being Arthur Golding's Translation of the Metamorphoses*, ed. W. H. D. Rouse [Carbondale: Southern Illinois University Press, 1961], book 10, line 167).

22 James M. Saslow, *Ganymede in the Renaissance: Homosexuality in Art and Society* (New Haven: Yale University Press, 1986), p. 116.

23 John Lyly, *Gallathea*, ed. Anne Begor Lancashire, Regents Renaissance Drama (Lincoln: University of Nebraska Press, 1969), 5.2.65. John Mason, *The Turk*, ed. Fernand Lagarde (Salzburg: Institut für Anglistik und Amerikanistik, 1979), 1.2.130–48. This play was performed in 1607 by the King's Revels Children at Whitefriars. Christopher Marlowe, *Edward II*, *The Complete Plays*, 1.4.179–82. John Marston, *The Malcontent*, *The Works of John Marston*, ed. A. H. Bullen, 3 vols. (London: John C. Nimmo, 1887), I: 1.1.15–16.

24 Marston, *The Scourge of Villainy*, Bullen, ed., *The Works*, I: satire 2, lines 48–49. Thomas Heywood, *Pleasant Dialogues and Dramas*, *The Dramatic Works of Thomas Heywood*, 6 vols. (1874; New York: Russell and Russell, 1964), VI: 203, 205. Robert Greene, *Penelopes Web*, *The Complete Life and Works . . . of Robert Greene*, ed. Alexander B. Grosart, 15 vols. (London: Hazell, Watson and Viney, 1881–86), V: 165.

25 Cooper, *Dictionarium*, sig. K.

26 Scudamour's book 2 analogue in effeminate indulgence is Cymocles, a "womanish weake knight" naturally drawn to dally with "loose Ladies and lascivious boyes" (2.5.36, 28).

27 Berger, "Busirane," p. 113.

28 Ollyphant and Scudamour are further linked via Fancy. Berger suggests that *Ollyphant* is an "etymological cipher composed of the Greek *ollumni* – to die, destroy, lose something – and phant, i.e., destructive phantasy" ("Busirane," p. 113). Moreover, Ollyphant is related to Lust, who has the prodigious ears of an elephant, for which "ollyphant" was the Renaissance spelling (3.7.48n.2).

29 For a persuasive discussion of the homoerotic relation between Antonio and Sebastian, see Traub, *Desire and Anxiety*, pp. 130–44. Even the names Antonio and Sebastian had homoerotic connotations in the Renaissance (see p. 20 above). On Orsino's problematic attitude towards women, see Cristina Malcolmson, "'What You Will': Social Mobility and Gender in *Twelfth Night*," *The Matter of Difference: Materialist Feminist Criticism of Shakespeare*, ed. Valerie Wayne (Ithaca: Cornell University Press, 1991), 29–58, pp. 41–42.

30 William Shakespeare, *Twelfth Night*, ed. J. M. Lothian and T. W. Craik, Arden Shakespeare (London: Routledge, 1988), 1.1.9–15.

31 Stephen Greenblatt, "Fiction and Friction," *Shakespearean Negotiations: the Circulation of Social Energy in Renaissance England* (Berkeley: University of California Press, 1988), p. 68; Laqueur, *Making Sex*, pp. 114–15; Pequigney, "The Two Antonios," p. 208.

32 This reading becomes more plausible if we read "bias" not as an allusion to bowling, but as the characteristic tendency of a personification (here, Nature – so capitalized in the folio). Cf. *OED*, bias, B. *sb.* 3. *trans.* a. "Bias" clearly has this meaning in *Love's Labour's Lost*: "Study his bias leaves and makes

his book thine eyes" (ed. R. W. David, Arden Shakespeare [London: Methuen, 1968], 4.2.105). Reading "bias" as an allusion to bowling, however, also admits an allusion to female homoeroticism, since the "rubbing" that occurs in bowling is also the most common term used to describe the sexual activity of *tribades* or "rubsters." In *Love's Labour's Lost*, again, the rubbing of bowls is distinguished from the male pricking of archery: "*Cost*. She's too hard for you at pricks, sir: challenge her to bowl. *Boyet*. I fear too much rubbing" (4.1.139–40).

33 Joseph Pequigney, *Such is My Love: a Study of Shakespeare's Sonnets* (Chicago: University of Chicago Press, 1985), p. 39.

34 Pequigney, "The Two Antonios," p. 208.

35 Thomas Palmer, *The Emblems of Thomas Palmer: Two Hundred Poosees*, ed. John Manning (New York: AMS Press, 1988), p. 142.

36 The *OED* provides a sixteenth-century example for "to draw in" as "to contract, draw tight; to cause to shrink" (draw, *v*., B. 82. draw in. b. *trans.*).

37 Baldassare Castiglione, *The Book of the Courtier*, trans. Thomas Hoby (1561), Tudor Translations 23, ed. W. E. Henley (London: David Nutt, 1900), p. 226.

38 Ibid., p. 235.

39 Bredbeck, *Sodomy and Interpretation*, p. 179.

40 Cf. Jean E. Howard, *The Stage and Social Struggle in Early Modern England* (London: Routledge, 1994), p. 115; Traub, *Desire and Anxiety*, p. 135.

41 For more on the connection between the master–mistress of *Sonnet* 20 and the androgynous boys of *Twelfth Night*, see Stephen Orgel, *Impersonations: the Performance of Gender in Shakespeare's England* (Cambridge: Cambridge University Press, 1996), pp. 56–57.

42 Traub, *Desire and Anxiety*, p. 135.

43 My reading of this passage has been anticipated by Shepherd (*Spenser*, p. 63). However, Shepherd believes that Spenser denies the physical expression of sexual desire to these idealized male lovers.

44 *A Critical Edition of Alexander Ross's 1647 Mystagogus Poeticus, or The Muses Interpreter*, ed. John R. Glenn, Renaissance Imagination, 31 (New York: Garland, 1987), p. 335. Ross himself provides multiple and sometimes conflicting interpretations of mythological figures.

45 This accusation may represent a mischievously sexual reinscription of the medieval tradition of linking St. John, whose symbol was the eagle, with Ganymede (Barkan, *The Gods Made Flesh*, p. 115). That Christ and John could be represented as sodomites is more important to me here than the issue of the reliability of the Baines libel that supposedly records Marlowe's blasphemies.

46 Edmund Spenser, *The Shepherd's Calendar*, *The Yale Edition of the Shorter Poems of Edmund Spenser*, ed. William A. Oram *et al.* (New Haven: Yale University Press, 1989), p. 34.

47 Goldberg, *Sodometries*, pp. 63–81.

48 Thomas H. Cain, "Spenser and the Renaissance Orpheus," *University of Toronto Quarterly* 41 (1972): 24–47, p. 36.

49 *Shakespeare's Ovid*, book 10. 88–89, 91–92.

50 Lee Edelman provides a fascinating discussion of the way in which Freud constructs the sodomitical primal scene "from behind," i.e., extrapolating from effect to cause, which Edelman calls "(be)hindsight" ("Seeing Things:

Representation, the Scene of Surveillance, and the Spectacle of Gay Male Sex," *Inside/Out: Lesbian Theories, Gay Theories*, ed. Diana Fuss [New York: Routledge, 1991], 93–118). On Spenser's backwards narrative movement, see Jonathan Goldberg, *Endlesse Worke: Spenser and the Structures of Discourse* (Baltimore: Johns Hopkins University Press, 1981), pp. 63–67.

51 Peggy Muñoz Simonds attempts "to synthesize what Orpheus might have signified to the mature Shakespeare" of the tragicomedies. Although she cites many contemporary allusions to Orpheus as a figure of consolation, she bypasses entirely the homoerotic elements of the myth ("'Killing Care and Grief of Heart': Orpheus and Shakespeare," *Renaissance Papers* 1990, ed. Dale B. J. Randall and Joseph A. Porter [Durham, NC: Southeastern Renaissance Conference, 1990], 79–90).

52 In his *Epistle . . . in Laud and Praise of Matrimony*, Erasmus describes Orpheus as an eloquent advocate for marriage and an opponent of sodomy. A century later, Francis Bacon cites an Orpheus "averse from women and from marriage" to justify why single life is superior to marriage. For Erasmus, promoting the propagation of the family as the foundation of civil society, Orpheus represents orderly marriage; for Bacon, illustrating how married life can weaken male service to the commonwealth, Orpheus represents orderly bachelorhood. See Francis Bacon, *The Wisdom of the Ancients*, Sidney Warhaft, ed., *Francis Bacon: a Selection of His Works* (New York: Macmillan, 1985), p. 289.

53 Cooper, *Dictionarium*, sig. N2v.

54 Cf. Harry Berger, Jr., "Orpheus, Pan, and the Poetics of Misogyny: Spenser's Critique of Pastoral Love and Art," *ELH* 50 (1983): 27–60.

55 John Dickenson, *The Shepherd's Complaint* (London, 1596), sig. C2v.

56 R. B., *Orpheus His Journey to Hell, And his Musicke to the Ghosts, for the regaining of faire Eurydice his Love, and new spoused Wife* (London, 1595), sig. D4r.

57 *Of Loves Complaint with the Legend of Orpheus and Eurydice* (London, 1597), sig. E6v.

58 William Perkins, *Christian Economy*, trans. Thomas Pickering (1609), in *Daughters, Wives, and Widows: Writings by Men about Women and Marriage in England, 1500–1640*, ed. Joan Larsen Klein (Urbana: University of Illinois Press, 1992), 151–73, pp. 170, 158–59.

59 Francis Bacon, *New Atlantis*, in Warhaft, ed., *Francis Bacon*, p. 443. Bachelorhood was not uncommon in early modern England: Lawrence Stone claims that "about one fifth of the younger sons [of the landed elite] were obliged to remain bachelors for life" (*The Family*, p. 43).

Compare Giacomo della Marca on the problem of married sodomites in Renaissance Italy:

> Youths do not want to take wives because the dowry is not sufficient for the vain and superfluous ornaments of the wife . . . And he remains unmarried. The father keeps his daughter beyond marriageable age because there is not sufficient dowry to give a girl enough for useless clothes. . . And thus she remains unmarried. . . This is the reason that there are more sodomites in Italy than almost anywhere else in the world, because in his 20s and unmarried – just as the woman is – he and even she fall into the vice of sodomy, from which even married men aren't able to abstain.

Della Marca is quoted in Diane Owen Hughes, "Distinguishing Signs: Ear-Rings, Jews and Franciscan Rhetoric in the Italian Renaissance City," *Past and Present* 112 (1986): 3–59, p. 37n.102. James Shapiro directed me to Hughes's article.

60 William Perkins, *The Foundation of Christian Religion, The Workes of that Famous and Worthy Minister of Christ in the Universitie of Cambridge, Mr. William Perkins*, 3 vols. (London, 1616–18), I: 58, sig. F2v. Sodomy "is a sin which they commit, when God hath given them over into a reprobate sense" (p. 59, sig. F3r).

61 Joseph Cady presents the mention of "masculine love" in the *New Atlantis* as evidence for a Renaissance distinction between heterosexual and homosexual orientations. However, he fails to cite the passage above that equates heteroerotic and homoerotic lust, and then argues that the absence of such an equation in Bacon's text proves his conclusion! See "'Masculine Love,' Renaissance Writing, and the 'New Invention' of Homosexuality," *Homosexuality in Renaissance and Enlightenment England: Literary Representations in Historical Context*, ed. Claude J. Summers (New York: Harrington Park, 1992), 9–40, pp. 17–21.

62 Quoted in Bray, "Homosexuality and the Signs of Male Friendship in Elizabethan England," *Queering*, ed. Goldberg, p. 55. Bray cites the autobiography of Simonds D'Ewes, written between 1622 and 1624 (British Museum, Harleian MSS, 646/59–59v).

63 Steven Mullaney, *The Place of the Stage: License, Play, and Power in Renaissance England* (Chicago: University of Chicago Press, 1988). Bray mentions the London tavern as a likely site of homosexual prostitution (*Homosexuality*, pp. 53–54), and Goldberg remarks on the sodomitical taint of Prince Hal's male tavern companions in the *Henriad* (*Sodometries*, pp. 155–56).

64 Paul S. Seaver, *Wallington's World: a Puritan Artisan in Seventeenth-Century London* (Stanford: Stanford University Press, 1985), p. 49.

65 Orgel, *Impersonations*, p. 40.

66 On sexuality in ballads, see Joy Wiltenberg, *Disorderly Women and Female Power in the Street Literature of Early Modern England and Germany* (Charlottesville: University of Virginia Press, 1992). "The Lamentation of a new-married man," *The Roxburghe Ballads*, ed. William Chappell, 9 vols. (Hertford: Stephen Austin and Sons, 1871–99), II: 33–40, p. 34.

67 Marlowe, *Edward II*, 1.4.30, 1.4.87, 1.4.393. "Minion," according to Eric Partridge, is "a man's – especially a king's or a prince's – male favourite; not necessarily a homosexual" (*Shakespeare's Bawdy*, 3rd edn. [London: Routledge, 1968], p. 148). On the roles of "master" and "minion" in *Edward II*, see Smith, *Homosexual Desire*, pp. 209–23.

68 "Robin and Kate; or, A bad husband converted by a good wife" (1634), *The Roxburghe Ballads*, II: 413–18, pp. 415–16.

69 Simonds D'Ewes, quoted in Bray, "Homosexuality," p. 55.

70 Thomas Heywood, *A Woman Killed with Kindness*, ed. R. W. Van Fossen, Revels Plays (London: Methuen, 1961), 6.41–43.

71 Traub, *Desire and Anxiety*, p. 123.

72 Traub, "The (In)significance of 'Lesbian' Desire," p. 158.

73 William Barksted, *Mirrha the Mother of Adonis: or Lustes Prodegies* (1607), *The Poems of William Barksted*, ed. Alexander B. Grosart (Manchester: Charles E. Simms, 1876), p. 45.

74 James Holstun, "'Will You Rent Our Ancient Love Asunder?' Lesbian Elegy in Donne, Marvell, and Milton," *ELH* 54 (1987): 835–67. Significantly, Hebe was the goddess of youth (cf. Cooper, *Dictionarium*, sig. J4r). For more on the abandonment of youthful female love, see Traub's "The (In)significance of 'Lesbian' Desire," and Dorothea Kehler, "Shakespeare's Emilias and the Politics of Celibacy," *In Another Country: Feminist Perspectives on Renaissance Drama*, ed. Dorothea Kehler and Susan Baker (Metuchen, NJ: Scarecrow Press, 1991), 157–78.

75 Abraham Fraunce, *The Third Part of the Countesse of Pembrokes Yvychurch: Entituled, Amintas Dale* (London, 1592), sig. E1r. Sir Robert Staplyton, glossing a line in Juvenal's *Second Satire*, explains, "A man used to make protestation by his *Genius*, a woman by her *Juno*" (*Juvenal's Sixteen Satyrs or, A Survey of the Manners and Actions of Mankind* [London, 1647], p. 28).

76 *The Maid's Metamorphosis*, ed. John S. Farmer, Tudor Reprinted and Parallel Texts (London: Hazell, Watson and Viney, 1908), sig. C1v.

77 *Shakespeare's Ovid*, book 10, lines 157–58. Shakespeare alludes to the homoerotic dimensions of the Orpheus myth in *The Two Gentlemen of Verona*, where Proteus ironically advises his rival, Sir Thurio, to woo Silvia like Orpheus: "For Orpheus' lute was strung with poets' sinews, / Whose golden touch could soften steel and stones" (ed. Clifford Leech, Arden Shakespeare [New York: Routledge, 1989], 3.2.76–77). Proteus recalls Orpheus' homoerotic pastoral life in the image of a "golden" touch applied to male "sinews"; these dismembered sinews also prefigure Orpheus' own destruction by the Maenads. The next scene of the play assigns an Orphic role to Valentine, who, banished from Silvia and the court, agrees to lead the band of forest outlaws. The Orpheus myth helps explain why the outlaws find their new commander a "proper man" who is "beautified / With goodly shape" and gifted as a "linguist" (4.1.10, 55–56, 58). We can identify a characteristically Shakespearean associative cluster in both plays – Orpheus/golden world/ homoeroticism/outlaws – a cluster fulfilled in *As You Like It* when Duke Senior and his lords enter "like Outlaws" (2.7 sd).

78 R. B., *Orpheus His Journey to Hell*, sigs. D4r–v.

79 Holland is quoted and discussed by Bruce Smith (*Homosexual Desire*, p. 40), who shows that the translation of explicitly homoerotic Greek and Latin texts played an important role in the discursive construction of homoeroticism in Renaissance England. For Renaissance humanism as an anthropological encounter with another culture, specifically in regard to the Ganymede myth, see Leonard Barkan, *Transuming Passion: Ganymede and the Erotics of Humanism* (Stanford: Stanford University Press, 1991).

80 Cf. Orgel, *Impersonations*, pp. 57–58.

81 Jardine surveys historical accounts of the high proportion of adolescent male servants in early modern England ("Twins and Travesties," p. 29).

82 Michael Drayton (*The Moone-Calfe, The Works of Michael Drayton*, ed. W. Hebel, 5 vols. [Oxford, 1932], III: 173–74) is cited in Bray, *Homosexuality*, p. 33. Many of the studies cited in notes 1 and 2 above assert that the word

"ganymede" was used colloquially to signify a dependent boy, whether a page, prostitute, or player. Ganymedes and catamites are stock characters in the verse satires that begin to appear in the late 1590s. See Bray, *Homosexuality*, pp. 33–57; Bredbeck, *Sodomy and Interpretation*, pp. 10–18, 33–39; and Smith, *Homosexual Desire*, pp. 159–87.

83 John Marston, *Histrio-Mastix, The Plays of John Marston*, ed. H. Harvey Wood, 3 vols. (Edinburgh: Oliver and Boyd, 1939), III: 243–302, p. 271.

84 John Boswell traces the hyena lore back to its early Christian and ancient sources (*Christianity, Social Tolerance, and Homosexuality: Gay People in Western Europe from the Beginning of the Christian Era to the Fourteenth Century* [Chicago: University of Chicago Press, 1980], pp. 137–43). The commonplace belief in the hyena's sex change appears in the *Physiologus*, which Boswell characterizes as the "single most popular work of natural science of the Middle Ages, [and] one of the most widely read treatises of any sort prior to the seventeenth century" (p. 141). Ann Rosalind Jones and Peter Stallybrass call the *Physiologus* "one of the most popular books of the early Renaissance" and they cite its account of the hyena as an example of the Renaissance discourse of hermaphroditism: "At one time it becomes a male, at another a female" ("Fetishizing Gender: Constructing the Hermaphrodite in Renaissance Europe," *Body Guards: the Cultural Politics of Gender Ambiguity*, ed. Julia Epstein and Kristina Straub [New York: Routledge, 1991], 80–111, pp. 80–81).

85 *Shakespeare's Ovid*, book 15, lines 451–52.

86 Traub, *Desire and Anxiety*, pp. 125–26.

87 "Ganymede and Hebe" (*Post aquile raptus*, twelfth or thirteenth century), quoted in Boswell, *Christianity*, 392–98, p. 395. On gender and race in Renaissance discourses of beauty, see Kim F. Hall, "'I Rather Would Wish to Be a Black-Moor': Beauty, Race, and Rank in Lady Mary Wroth's *Urania*," *Women, "Race," and Writing in the Early Modern Period*, ed. Margo Hendricks and Patricia Parker (London: Routledge, 1994), 178–94.

88 Cf. Smith, *Homosexual Desire*, p. 147.

89 Traub, *Desire and Anxiety*, p. 128.

90 Michèle Barrett and Mary McIntosh, *The Anti-social Family*, 2nd edn. (New York: Verso, 1991), p. 171.

91 Jeffrey Weeks, "Pretended Family Relationships," *Marriage, Domestic Life and Social Change: Writings for Jacqueline Burgoyne (1944–88)*, ed. David Clark (London: Routledge, 1991), 214–34, p. 227. Weeks's title quotes the phrase used to delegitimize same-sex families in Britain's antigay statute Section 28.

3   THE HOMOEROTICS OF MASTERY IN SATIRIC COMEDY

1 Theodore B. Leinwand, *The City Staged: Jacobean Comedy, 1603–1613* (Madison: University of Wisconsin Press, 1986), pp. 89–90.

2 Thomas Dekker, *Satiromastix, The Dramatic Works of Thomas Dekker*, ed. Fredson Bowers, 4 vols. (Cambridge: Cambridge University Press, 1953) vol. I. "Ningle" and "enghle" are variants of *ingle*, a catamite or boy used for sexual purposes.

3 All references to Jonson come from *Ben Jonson*, ed. C. H. Herford and Percy and Evelyn Simpson, 11 vols. (Oxford: Oxford University Press–Clarendon, 1925–52).

4 Edmund Wilson attributes the scatological elements in Jonson's writing to neurotic anal impulses ("Morose Ben Jonson," *Ben Jonson: a Collection of Critical Essays*, ed. Jonas A. Barish [Englewood Cliffs, NJ: Prentice-Hall, 1963], 60–74, p. 71). On anality in Middleton, see Arthur Marotti, "The Purgations of Thomas Middleton's *The Family of Love*," *Papers on Language and Literature* 7.1 (1971): 80–84.

5 Gail Kern Paster, "Covering His Ass: the Scatological Imperatives of Comedy," in her *The Body Embarrassed: Drama and the Disciplines of Shame in Early Modern England* (Ithaca: Cornell University Press, 1993). Paster's analysis largely ignores homoeroticism in an attempt to reconstruct the psychic and social significance of purging. Nevertheless, our projects concur in finding anality a cultural rather than an authorial preoccupation: "to attach anality to Jonson as a psychological component of the author function is to deny scatological and anal discourse a wider cultural significance and to protect Shakespeare from anal contamination" (p. 143). Frank Whigham discusses the anality of Shakespearean drama in "Reading Social Conflict in the Alimentary Tract: More on the Body in Renaissance Drama," *ELH* 52 (1988): 333–50.

6 Frankie Rubinstein, *A Dictionary of Shakespeare's Sexual Puns and Their Significance*, 2nd edn. (London: Macmillan, 1989), "Ass," pp. 17–18. According to Eric Partridge, "ass" was pronounced "*ahss*" in Elizabethan English (*Shakespeare's Bawdy*, 3rd edn. [London: Routledge, 1968], "ass," p. 59). Regarding Shakespeare's Bottom, Annabel Patterson corroborates and develops Rubinstein's explication of the pun on "ass" (*Shakespeare and the Popular Voice* [Cambridge, MA: Basil Blackwell, 1989], pp. 66–67).

7 Mark Thornton Burnett has analyzed an emblem from the early 1580s that depicts a servant with the head of an ass ("The 'Trusty Servant': a Sixteenth-Century English Emblem," *Emblematica* 6.2 [1992]: 1–17). The emblem is accompanied by a Latin verse which describes the servant's attributes thusly: "Patient, the ass, his master's rage will hear." I am grateful to Professor Burnett for sharing with me his research on servants and his thoughts on the present chapter.

8 Transformations in the social and economic relations of service are described by Alan Bray, "Homosexuality and the Signs of Male Friendship in Elizabethan England," *Queering the Renaissance*, ed. Jonathan Goldberg (Durham, NC: Duke University Press, 1994), 40–61, pp. 50–53; Felicity Heal, *Hospitality in Early Modern England* (Oxford: Clarendon, 1990), pp. 164–67; A. L. Beier, *Masterless Men: the Vagrancy Problem in England 1560–1640* (London: Methuen, 1985), pp. 22–25; and Lawrence Stone, *The Crisis of the Aristocracy 1558–1641*, abridged edn (London: Oxford University Press, 1967), pp. 103–4.

9 Gregory W. Bredbeck shows that in Renaissance dictionaries definitions of homoerotic terms become increasingly specific throughout the seventeenth century (*Sodomy and Interpretation: Marlowe to Milton* [Ithaca: Cornell University Press, 1991], pp. 10–21).

10 Bruce R. Smith, *Homosexual Desire in Shakespeare's England: a Cultural Poetics* (Chicago: University of Chicago Press, 1991), pp. 165–68, 174–85.

11 Bredbeck, *Sodomy and Interpretation*, p. 35.

12 Steve Brown, "The Boyhood of Shakespeare's Heroines: Notes on Gender Ambiguity in the Sixteenth Century," *SEL* 30 (1990): 243–63, p. 251.

13 Alan Bray, *Homosexuality in Renaissance England* (London: Gay Men's Press, 1988), pp. 33–37, 49–55; and Smith, *Homosexual Desire*, pp. 161–67.

14 My use of the term *homosocial* to describe the bonds between Jonson's male characters is not meant to deny the potential *homoeroticism* of those bonds. A more psychoanalytic or author-centered account than my own might pursue the implications for his plays of Jonson's own eroticism, which seems to have been heavily mediated through his relations with other men. According to his recorded conversations with William Drummond, for instance, he thought only married women worth his sexual advances.

15 In early modern usage, *effeminacy* refers primarily to *gender*, not sexual, deviance: it signifies the absence of "masculine" reason and self-control. Those most prone to effeminacy are the lover who dotes excessively on women, and the "gallant and courtier [who] have imitated women in giving themselves up to pleasures of all sorts" (Smith, *Homosexual Desire*, p. 180). See also Alan Sinfield, *The Wilde Century: Effeminacy, Oscar Wilde and the Queer Moment* (New York: Columbia University Press, 1994), pp. 25–33.

16 John Aubrey, *Aubrey's Brief Lives*, ed. Oliver Lawson Dick (Harmondsworth: Penguin, 1987), p. 253.

17 Everard Guilpin, *Skialetheia Or A Shadow of Truth, in Certain Epigrams and Satyres*, ed. D. Allen Carroll (Chapel Hill: University of North Carolina Press, 1974), p. 49.

18 John Marston, *The Scourge of Villainy, The Works of John Marston*, ed. A. H. Bullen, 3 vols. (London: John C. Nimmo, 1887), III: satire 3, line 53; Marston, *Satires*, Bullen, ed., *The Works*, III: satire 3, lines 33–35.

19 John Florio, *A Worlde of Wordes* (London, 1598). Allan H. Gilbert uses Florio to gloss all the names in the play *except* Cinedo, of which he says nothing ("The Italian Names in *Every Man out of his Humour*," *Studies in Philology* 44 [1947]: 195–208).

20 Marston, *The Scourge of Villainy*, satire 1, line 59; satire 3, line 49.

21 *Marlowe: the Critical Heritage*, ed. Millar MacLure (London: Routledge, 1979), p. 37, my emphasis. Bruce Smith notes that in early modern English usage "boy" did not necessarily refer to minority age; the label also designated a difference in social status, as when used by a master to his servant (*Homosexual Desire*, pp. 195–96).

22 In the pseudo-Lucianic *Erotes*, a pederast evokes Orestes and Pylades as proof that "physical affection [is] the natural end of friendship between equals." Quoted in Smith (*Homosexual Desire*, p. 40), who notes that the *Erotes* was available to Renaissance readers in a Latin translation of 1563.

23 On the significance of names and renaming in the play see Anne Barton, *Ben Jonson, Dramatist* (Cambridge: Cambridge University Press, 1984), p. 179.

24 Ronald Huebert, "'A Shrew Yet Honest': Manliness in Jonson," *Renaissance Drama* ns 20 (1984): 31–68, p. 44.

25 W. I., *The Whipping of the Satyre* (London, 1601), sig. F8v.

26 James Shapiro, *Rival Playwrights: Marlowe, Jonson, Shakespeare* (New York: Columbia University Press, 1991), p. 14.

27 George E. Rowe, *Distinguishing Jonson: Imitation, Rivalry, and the Direction of a Dramatic Career* (Lincoln: University of Nebraska Press, 1988), pp. 111, 122.

28 Jonathan Goldberg, *Sodometries: Renaissance Texts, Modern Sexualities* (Stanford: Stanford University Press, 1992), pp. 18–19; on the multiplicity of acts signified by "sodomy" see also Bredbeck, *Sodomy and Interpretation*, pp. xi–xii.

29 Goldberg, *Sodometries*, pp. 196–98.

30 Quoted in Bray, "Homosexuality," pp. 54–55.

31 Goldberg, *Sodometries*, p. 19.

32 Likewise in *Bartholomew Fair*, Jonson's achievement of authorial mastery over antitheatrical polemicists, represented by Busy, hinges on distinguishing the homoeroticism of his source material, Marlowe's *Hero and Leander*, from the sodomy of stage playing. The puppeteer Leatherhead even reveals that he has chosen to stage the story of Hero and Leander instead of "*Sodom and Gommorah*" (5.1.9–10). For a related analysis, see Laura Levine, *Men in Women's Clothing: Anti-theatricality and Effeminization, 1579–1642* (Cambridge: Cambridge University Press, 1994), pp. 89–107.

33 Frances Dolan, "The Subordinate('s) Plot: Petty Treason and the Forms of Domestic Rebellion," *Shakespeare Quarterly* 43 (1992): 317–40, p. 323; Thomas Moisan, "'Knock Me Here Soundly': Comic Misprision and Class Consciousness in Shakespeare," *Shakespeare Quarterly* 42 (1991): 276–90, pp. 279–80. For another analysis of service in *The Taming of the Shrew*, see David Evett, "'Surprising Confrontations': Ideologies of Service in Shakespeare's England," *Renaissance Papers* 1990, ed. Dale B. J. Randall and Joseph A. Porter (Durham, NC: Southeastern Renaissance Conference, 1990), 67–78.

34 Ann Kussmaul, *Servants in Husbandry in Early Modern England* (Cambridge: Cambridge University Press, 1981); Keith Wrightson, *English Society 1580–1680* (New Brunswick: Rutgers University Press, 1982); Beier, *Masterless Men*, pp. 22–25, 44.

35 Beier, *Masterless Men*, p. 24. For accounts of servants in conduct and pamphlet literature, see Mark Thornton Burnett, "Masters and Servants in Moral and Religious Treatises, *c.* 1580–*c.* 1642," *The Arts, Literature and Society*, ed. Arthur Marwick (London: Routledge, 1990), 48–75; and Linda Anderson, "Shakespeare's Servants," *Shakespeare Yearbook* 2 (1991): 149–61.

36 Dolan, "The Subordinate('s) Plot," p. 324.

37 Using an anachronistic analogy to the supposedly heterosexual "manliness" of contemporary professional athletes, Ronald Huebert argues that the relationship between Volpone and Mosca may look erotic, "but that's precisely what it's not" ("'A Shrew Yet Honest,'" p. 47).

38 In reference to Antonio's love for Sebastian, Valerie Traub suggests that male homoeroticism became especially threatening to early modern social order when it altogether replaced heterosexual reproductivity (*Desire and Anxiety: Circulations of Sexuality in Shakespearean Drama* [London: Routledge, 1992], p. 139).

39 Bray, *Homosexuality*, pp. 21–23.
40 According to Sir Edward Coke, a certain woman conceived from intercourse with a baboon (*The Third Part of the Institutes of the Laws of England*, 3rd edn. [London: J. Flesher, 1660], p. 59). The relevance of this point and the one recorded in the above note were suggested to me by Bruce Smith. On prodigious births, see also Katherine Park and Lorraine J. Daston, "Unnatural Conceptions: the Study of Monsters in Sixteenth- and Seventeenth-Century France and England," *Past and Present* 92 (1981): 20–54.
41 *The Policy of the Turkish Empire* (London, 1597), sig. N2r.
42 Jonson may also be alluding to the Antinous who is Penelope's suitor in the *Odyssey* (Tay Fizdale, "Jonson's *Volpone* and the 'Real' Antinous," *Renaissance Quarterly* 26 [1973]: 454–59). The Antinous passage is perceptively discussed by Richmond Barbour, "'When I Acted Young Antinous': Boy Actors and the Erotics of Jonsonian Theater," *PMLA* 110 (October 1995): 1006–22, pp. 1009–11. With its focus on the attractiveness of submissive boys, Barbour's analysis of *Volpone* and *Epicoene* overlaps in important ways with my analysis of the homoerotics of mastery. Published only a few months after my own essay on *Volpone* and *Epicoene* appeared in *ELR*, Barbour's essay appeared too late for me to consider it more fully here.
43 David C. McPherson, *Shakespeare, Jonson, and the Myth of Venice* (Newark, DE: University of Delaware Press, 1990), pp. 95, 104.
44 Guido Ruggiero, *The Boundaries of Eros: Sex Crime and Sexuality in Renaissance Venice* (New York: Oxford University Press, 1985), p. 119.
45 Marjorie Garber, *Vested Interests: Cross-Dressing and Cultural Anxiety* (New York: Routledge, 1992), pp. 86–87.
46 Dolan, "The Subordinate('s) Plot," p. 337.
47 A homoerotic dimension to early modern prisons is suggested by Geffray Minshull's *Essays and Characters of a Prison and Prisoners* (London, 1618). Of the three types of companions in prison – a "parasite," a "John indifferent," and a "true harted Titus" – Minshull describes the latter, the true friend, in very tender terms:

> The last of these thou maist call the masculine sweet heart, which may be resembled to truth, whose bosome is alwayes bare, and hath a breast of Chrystall, that thou maist looke through his body to his heart; hee is one that will love thee in adversitie, he will respect thee in the Kitchin as well as in the parlour, hee will reverence thee in the Hole as well as in the Masters side, hee will looke on thee in rags as well as in a feather-bed: come stormes, come calmes, come tempests, come Sun-shine, come what can come, he will be thine and sticke to thee. (p. 20, sig. D2v)

48 George Chapman, *The Gentleman Usher*, ed. John Hazel Smith, Regents Renaissance Drama (Lincoln: University of Nebraska Press, 1970), pp. 135–37. Further citations to Chapman's play are from this edition, and will appear parenthetically in the text.
49 As an upper servant in a noble household, Bassiolo has a very different administrative role and social status from Mosca. John Hazel Smith notes that some gentlemen servants were of equal status with their employers. Furthermore, the office of gentleman usher automatically conferred gentle status on the servant.
50 Cf. Bray, "Homosexuality," pp. 52–53.

51 Beier, *Masterless Men*, p. 23.

52 John Marston, *Histrio-Mastix, The Plays of John Marston*, ed. E. Harvey Wood, 3 vols. (Edinburgh and London: Oliver and Boyd, 1939), III: 271.

53 Braithwaite is quoted in Bredbeck, *Sodomy and Interpretation*, p. 14.

54 John Mason, *The Turk*, ed. Fernand Lagarde (Salzburg: Institut für Anglistik und Amerikanistik, 1979), 2.3.56–59.

55 Jeremy Taylor, *The Measures and Offices of Friendship* (London, 1662). A friend can never pardon "a treacherous blow, and the revealing of a secret, because these are against the nature of friendship; they are the adulteries of it, and dissolve the Union; and in the matters of friendship, which is the marriage of souls, these are the proper causes of divorce." Hence, the publication of a secret "is a prostitution and direct debauchery" (p. 101, sig. E3r).

56 Richard Rambuss, "The Secretary's Study: the Secret Designs of *The Shepherds Calender*," *ELH* 59 (1992): 313–35. The "friendlie knot of love" is Angel Day's expression.

57 Cf. Goldberg, *Sodometries*, especially pp. 48–52, on homoerotic service in the court of Henry VIII.

58 Thomas Middleton, *A Mad World, My Masters, The Selected Plays of Thomas Middleton*, ed. David L. Frost (Cambridge: Cambridge University Press, 1978), 2.1.145–47, 158–61.

59 On homoerotic allusions to boy players in Renaissance plays, see Steve Brown, "The Boyhood of Shakespeare's Heroines," especially pp. 251–52.

60 Andrew Gurr, *Playgoing in Shakespeare's London* (Cambridge: Cambridge University Press, 1987), pp. 153–59.

61 Christopher Marlowe, *Edward II, Christopher Marlowe: the Complete Plays*, ed. J. B. Steane (Harmondsworth: Penguin, 1986), 1.1.65.

62 Thomas Middleton, *Black Book, Thomas Middleton: Works*, ed. A. H. Bullen, 8 vols. (London: John Nimmo, 1886), VIII: 21.

63 Patricia Parker, "Preposterous Events," *Shakespeare Quarterly* 43 (1992): 186–213. Parker discusses the sodomitical as well as scatological connotations of the preposterous in ways that complement the opening concerns of this chapter.

64 In the jest-book *Pasquils Jestes* (London, 1609), a group of men ponder what might be the rarest thing in the world. Ignoring his companions' answers – a phoenix, a diamond, a true friend, etc. – "one plaine asse-heated foole" concludes that the rarest thing must be "a sweet arse hole" (sig. A4v).

65 In *Sodometries*, Goldberg insists on the acknowledgment that anal intercourse and "sodomy" occur in male–female as well as same-sex relations. He observes that the anus is a sexual organ common to male and female anatomy (p. 51), and he finds allusions to anal intercourse in Henry V's negotiations for Katherine in Shakespeare's *Henry V* (pp. 156–59).

66 Thomas Middleton, *Michaelmas Term*, ed. Richard Levin, Regents Renaissance Drama (Lincoln: University of Nebraska Press, 1966), 3.1.17–18.

67 Jean E. Howard, "Sex and Social Conflict: the Erotics of *The Roaring Girl*," *Erotic Politics: Desire on the Renaissance Stage*, ed. Susan Zimmerman (New York: Routledge, 1992), 170–90. It is possible that heterosexual anal intercourse was practiced as a form of birth control in early modern England. In

his study of early modern Venice, Guido Ruggiero comments that anal intercourse "was presumably an effective form of birth control; the question arises, however, whether it was primarily a form of birth control or merely another form of sexual activity that was formally believed to be especially deviant" (*The Boundaries of Eros*, p. 118). Discussing fertility control in England, Angus McLaren observes that it is "unlikely that onanism employed in marriage would ever be reported or investigated"; the same could be true for anal intercourse (*A History of Contraception: From Antiquity to the Present Day* [Oxford: Basil Blackwell, 1990], p. 155). Lawrence Stone believes that anal, oral, and manual sex, as well as coitus interruptus, were the main forms of contraception in early modern England (*The Family, Sex and Marriage in England 1500–1800* [New York: Harper and Row, 1977], p. 422).

68 Lucian, *Affairs of the Heart*, *Lucian*, trans. M. D. Macleod, Loeb Library, 8 vols. (Cambridge, MA: Harvard University Press, 1967), VIII: 193–94. David M. Halperin argues that the *Erotes* "approaches the question of male sexual object-choice not as a matter of sexual orientation but rather as a matter of taste" ("Historicizing the Sexual Body: Sexual Preferences and Erotic Identities in the Pseudo-Lucianic *Erotes*," *Discourses of Sexuality: From Aristotle to AIDS*, ed. Domna C. Stanton [Ann Arbor: University of Michigan Press, 1992], 236–61, p. 255).

69 "In Rosum Periuratam," *A Description of Love. With Certain Epigrams, Elegies, and Sonnets* . . . (London, 1620), sig. C2r.

70 For a similar analysis of this scene, see Whigham, "Reading Social Conflict in the Alimentary Tract," p. 335.

71 Although he does not mention the usher, Simon Shepherd provides a compelling discussion of what he calls Renaissance homosexual types ("What's So Funny About Ladies' Tailors? A Survey of Some Male [Homo]-sexual Types in the Renaissance," *Textual Practice* 6 [1992]: 17–30).

72 George Chapman, *The Widow's Tears*, ed. Akihiro Yamada, Revels Plays (London: Methuen, 1975), 5.5.275, 277–78.

73 John Webster, *The Duchess of Malfi*, *Drama of the English Renaissance II: the Stuart Period*, ed. Russell A. Fraser and Norman Rabkin (New York: Macmillan, 1976), 2.3.43, 45–46.

74 Leonard Barkan, *Transuming Passion: Ganymede and the Erotics of Humanism* (Stanford: Stanford University Press, 1991). Pedants were a common subject of humor, as in Jonson's "Conversations": "Owen is a pure Pedantique Schoolmaster sweeping his living from the Posteriors of litle children" (*Ben Jonson*, 1:38, lines 223–24).

75 Thomas Cooper, *Dictionarium Historicum & Poeticum* . . . in *Thesaurus Linguae Romanae & Brittanicae* . . . (London, 1565), sig. I1v. Barnabe Googe's definition of Ganymede is at once more elaborate and more coy: "the son of Tros, king of Phrygia, a boy of passing beauty and feminine countenance, taken up into the skies by an eagle at Jupiter's commandment, and made his butler" (quoted in *Barnabe Googe: Eclogues, Epitaphs, and Sonnets*, ed. Judith M. Kennedy [Toronto: University of Toronto Press, 1989], p. 144).

76 Thomas Middleton and Thomas Dekker, *The Roaring Girl*, ed. Paul Mulholland, Revels Plays (Manchester: Manchester University Press, 1987), p. 72n.8.

77 According to one Renaissance theorist of friendship, "flatterie is an utter enemie to Friendship," (Walter Dorke, *A Type or Figure of Friendship* [London, 1589], sig. A4v).

78 Charlotte Spivak, *George Chapman*, Twayne's English Authors (New York: Twayne, 1967), p. 14.; Hazel Smith, ed., *The Gentleman Usher*, p. xv.

79 George Chapman, *All Fools*, ed. Frank Manley, Regents Renaissance Drama (Lincoln: University of Nebraska Press, 1968), 2.1.79–83.

80 Bray, *Homosexuality*, pp. 68–69.

81 Giovanni Della Casa, *Galateo of Maister John Della Casa . . .* (London, 1576), sig. Dir, p. 17. I am indebted to Heidi Brayman for this reference.

82 *Ben Jonson*, VIII: 69, lines 19–21.

83 See Smith, *Homosexual Desire*, pp. 180–81.

84 Sylvanus appears in Thomas Cooper's entry for *Cyperissus*: "The sonne of Telephus, which bewayling the death of a tame hynde, slayne by his lover, Sylvanus, was tourned into a Cipres tree" (*Dictionarium*, sig. G4r). See also *The Faerie Queene*, 1.6.17.

85 The sodomitical economy of the play has recently been analyzed by Theodore B. Leinwand, "Redeeming Beggary/Buggery in *Michaelmas Term*," *ELH* 61 (1994): 53–70.

86 In a verse letter to John Donne, Thomas Woodward calls female–female sex "chaste and mistique tribadree" and an "adultery [that] no fruit did leave" (George Klaiwitter, "Verse Letters to T. W. from John Donne: 'By You My Love Is Sent,'" *Homosexuality in Renaissance and Enlightenment England: Literary Representations in Historical Context*, ed. Claude J. Summers [New York: Harrington Park, 1992], 85–102, p. 91). Cf. Traub, *Desire and Anxiety*, pp. 108–10.

87 Theodora Jankowski discusses virginity as a form of female sexual transgression in several plays: "'The Scorne of Savage People': Virginity as 'Forbidden Sexuality' in John Lyly's *Love's Metamorphosis*," *Renaissance Drama* 24 (1993), 123–53; "'Where There Can Be No Cause of Affection': Redefining Virgins, Their Desires, and Their Pleasures in John Lyly's *Gallathea*," *Feminist Readings of Early Modern Culture: Emerging Subjects*, ed. Dympna Callaghan, M. Lindsay Kaplan, and Valerie Traub (Cambridge: Cambridge University Press), 1996; "Pure Resistance: Queer(y)ing Virginity in William Shakespeare's *Measure for Measure* and Margaret Cavendish's *The Convent of Pleasure*," *Shakespeare Studies* 26 (forthcoming, 1998). Although the subtle nun of Marvell's "Appleton House" represents female homoeroticism as "chaste," her interference in the heterosexual reproduction of the Fairfax line is clearly sodomitical. The nuns are therefore associated with Amazons, witches, and gypsies. The title of *Love's Labour's Lost* alludes to a discourse of abortion clearly articulated in the play. Berowne calls the men's oath an "abortive birth" (1.1.104); the Princess believes that the company will enjoy the abortive play of the Nine Worthies: "Their form confounded makes most form in mirth / When great things labouring perish in their birth" (5.2.515–16).

88 Valerie Traub, "The (In)significance of 'Lesbian' Desire in Early Modern England," *Erotic Politics*, ed. Susan Zimmerman (New York: Routledge, 1992), 150–69, p. 164. For a similar explanation of the invisibility and

infrequent punishment of female–female sex in early modern Europe, see Judith C. Brown, "Lesbian Sexuality in Medieval and Early Modern Europe," *Hidden From History: Reclaiming the Gay and Lesbian Past*, ed. Martin Duberman, Martha Vicinus, and George Chauncey, Jr. (New York: Meridian, 1990), pp. 67–75.

89 Thomas Middleton, *No Wit, No Help Like a Woman's*, ed. Lowell E. Johnson, Regents Renaissance Drama (Lincoln: University of Nebraska Press, 1976), 1.2.14–15.

90 Paster, *The Body Embarrassed*, pp. 23–63.

91 Nicholas de Nicholay, *The Navigations into Turkey* (1585), *The English Experience* 48 (New York: Da Capo, 1968), p. 60; my emphasis.

92 Traub, "The (In)significance of 'Lesbian' Desire," p. 163.

93 George Chapman, *Monsieur D'Olive*, Allan Holaday, ed., *The Plays of George Chapman: the Comedies* (Urbana: University of Illinois Press, 1970), 2.1.101, 103, 117–18.

94 William Goddard, *A Satirical Dialogue . . .* (Low Countries, 1615), sig. C1v.

95 For a reading of the homoerotics of service in *Twelfth Night* that focuses on the interchangeability between women and boys, see Lisa Jardine, "Twins and Travesties: Gender, Dependency, and Sexual Availability in *Twelfth Night*," Zimmerman, ed., *Erotic Politics*, 27–38.

4   THE HOMOEROTICS OF FAVORITISM IN TRAGEDY

1 Mark Thornton Burnett makes this point in "The Noble Household." I am grateful to Professor Burnett for making his unpublished work available to me.

2 Cf. Pam Wright, "A Change in Direction: the Ramifications of a Female Household, 1558–1603," *The English Court: From the Wars of the Roses to the Civil War*, ed. David Starkey (London: Longman, 1987), 147–72.

3 Cf. Louis A. Montrose, "*A Midsummer Night's Dream* and the Shaping Fantasies of Elizabethan Culture: Gender, Power, Form," *Rewriting the Renaissance: the Discourses of Sexual Difference in Early Modern Europe*, ed. Margaret W. Ferguson, Maureen Quilligan, and Nancy J. Vickers (Chicago: University of Chicago Press, 1986), 65–87.

4 Simon Shepherd, "What's So Funny About Ladies' Tailors? A Survey of Some Male (Homo)sexual Types in the Renaissance," *Textual Practice* 6 (1992): 17–30, p. 24.

5 John Marston, *Parasitaster, or The Fawn*, ed. David A. Blostein, Revels Plays (Baltimore: Johns Hopkins University Press, 1978), 1.2.46–47. Blostein's gloss to these lines cites Montaigne: "Princes, who to dispatch their weightiest affaires make often their closestoole, their regall Throne or Councel-chamber" (n.47). On the creation of the Gentleman of the Stool during the reign of Henry VIII, see David Starkey, "Intimacy and Innovation: the Rise of the Privy Chamber, 1485–1547," *The English Court*, 71–118.

6 John Marston, *The Malcontent*, *The Works of John Marston*, ed. A. H. Bullen, 3 vols. (London: John C. Nimmo, 1887), I: 1.1.326–39.

7 Francis Bacon, "Of Wisdom for a Man's Self," *The Essayes or Counsels,*

Civill and Morall, 1625, *Francis Bacon: a Selection of His Works,* ed. Sidney Warhaft (New York: Macmillan, 1985), p. 107.

8 For recent assessments and overviews of James's relationships, see David M. Bergeron, *Royal Family, Royal Lovers: King James of England and Scotland* (Columbia: University of Missouri Press, 1991); Jonathan Goldberg, *James I and the Politics of Literature: Jonson, Shakespeare, Donne, and Their Contemporaries* (1983; Stanford: Stanford University Press, 1989); and Caroline Bingham, *James I of England* (London: Weidenfeld and Nicolson, 1981). Alan Bray, however, cautions against taking such accusations of sodomy as evidence for "the existence of the sexual relation which they appear to point to" ("Homosexuality and the Signs of Male Friendship in Elizabethan England," *Queering the Renaissance,* ed. Jonathan Goldberg [Durham, NC: Duke University Press, 1994], 40–61, p. 54).

9 Cf. Neil Cuddy, "The Revival of the Entourage: the Bedchamber of James I, 1603–1625," *The English Court,* ed. Starkey, 173–225.

10 For James as Tiberius see Goldberg, *James I,* pp. 164, 176–77; for Buckingham as Sejanus see James Holstun, "'God Bless Thee, Little David!': John Felton and his Allies," *ELH* 59 (1992): 513–52, p. 520. In his edition of Degoraeus Wheare's *Method and Order of Reading Both Civil and Ecclesiastical Histories . . .* (London, 1685), Edmund Bohun explains that the denunciation of royal favorites in E. F.'s 1627 *History of Edward II* (now attributed to Elizabeth Cary, Lady Falkland) was intended as a reproach to Buckingham (pp. 172–73).

11 On the sexualized discourse of political intimacy in Elizabethan history plays see Daryl W. Palmer, "Edward IV's Secret Familiarities and the Politics of Proximity in Elizabethan History Plays," *ELH* 61 (1994): 279–316.

12 For a useful analysis of Jacobean tragedy as topical political critique, see J. W. Lever, *The Tragedy of State: a Study of Jacobean Drama* (1971; London: Methuen, 1987), pp. 1–17. More recently, see Jonathan Dollimore, *Radical Tragedy: Religion, Ideology and Power in the Drama of Shakespeare and His Contemporaries* (Chicago: University of Chicago Press, 1984), especially pp. 3–28.

13 Several emblematists, including the influential Alciatus, "translated Ganymede's abduction by Zeus as the *sursum corda* or elevation of heart, mind, or soul, or joy and rapture in God or the love of God" (Lorrayne Y. Baird-Lange, "Victim Criminalized: Iconographic Traditions and Peacham's Ganymede," *Traditions and Innovations: Essays on British Literature of the Middle Ages and Renaissance,* ed. David G. Allen and Robert A. White [Newark: University of Delaware Press, 1990], 231–50, p. 241).

14 Henry Peacham, *Minerva Britanna* (1612; Leeds: Scolar Press, 1966), no. 48.

15 Jonathan Goldberg, "Sodomy and Society: the Case of Christopher Marlowe," *Staging the Renaissance: Reinterpretations of Elizabethan and Jacobean Drama,* ed. David Scott Kastan and Peter Stallybrass (New York: Routledge, 1991), 75–82, p. 80; and Goldberg, *James I,* pp. 141–47.

16 Rebecca W. Bushnell, *Tragedies of Tyrants: Political Thought and Theater in the English Renaissance* (Ithaca: Cornell University Press, 1990), p. 150.

17 Quoted in Bergeron, *Royal Family,* p. 183.

18 William Browne, from *Brittania's Pastorals Book Two. The Penguin Book of*

Renaissance Verse 1509–1659, ed. H. R. Woudhuysen (Harmondsworth: Penguin, 1993), p. 147.

19 Quoted in Bergeron, *Royal Family*, p. 183. On contemporary criticism of James see Goldberg, *James I*, p. 143, and Bruce R. Smith, *Homosexual Desire in Shakespeare's England: a Cultural Poetics* (Chicago: University of Chicago Press, 1991), pp. 176–78, 202–3.

20 Quoted in Bergeron, *Royal Family*, pp. 183–84.

21 On *Edward II*, see Jonathan Goldberg, *Sodometries: Renaissance Texts, Modern Sexualities* (Stanford: Stanford University Press, 1992), pp. 117–26.

22 Quoted in Bergeron, *Royal Family*, p. 184.

23 Francis Bacon, "Of Followers and Friends," *The Essayes or Counsels*, p. 172.

24 Bray, *Homosexuality*, pp. 37, 121 n.14.

25 Bushnell, *Tragedies of Tyrants*, p. 74.

26 Bingham, *James I*, pp. 165–66. Cf. Bray, "Homosexuality," pp. 53–56, and his *Homosexuality in Renaissance England* (London: Gay Men's Press, 1982), pp. 12–32.

27 Quoted in Holstun, "'God Bless Thee, Little David!,'" p. 540.

28 Quoted in ibid., p. 530.

29 According to the mythographer Alexander Ross, "Sin is a Circe, chiefly drunkennesse and whoredom which poyson men, and turn them into swine; Circe hath both a cup and a rod, with which she poysoned men; so in sin there is a cup of pleasure, and the rod of vengeance" (*A Critical Edition of Alexander Ross's 1647 Mystagogus Poeticus, or The Muses Interpreter*, ed. John R. Glenn, The Renaissance Imagination 31 [New York: Garland, 1987], pp. 295–96).

30 M. Claudius Paradin, *The Heroical Devises of M. Claudius Paradin*, introduced by John Doebler (1591; Delmar, NY: Scholar's Facsimiles and Reprints, 1984), pp. 119–20.

31 On the poisoned cup as a symbol of flattery, see Meredith Anne Skura, *Shakespeare the Actor and the Purposes of Playing* (Chicago: University of Chicago Press, 1993), p. 174.

32 On the elasticity and emptiness of the category "sodomy," see Goldberg, *Sodometries*, pp. 1–26.

33 These English translations of Tibullus and Ciprian are those of Baird-Lange, "Victim Criminalized," p. 246.

34 On Somerset's rise and fall, see G. P. V. Akrigg, *Jacobean Pageant, or The Court of King James I* (Cambridge, MA: Harvard University Press, 1962), pp. 177–204.

35 My reading of the play has been informed by the work of John Michael Archer, *Sovereignty and Intelligence: Spying and Court Culture in the English Renaissance* (Stanford: Stanford University Press, 1993), pp. 88–91.

36 Bray, "Homosexuality," pp. 9–10; Smith, *Homosexual Desire*, pp. 209–23; Gregory W. Bredbeck, *Sodomy and Interpretation: Marlowe to Milton* (Ithaca: Cornell University Press, 1991), pp. 56–77; Goldberg, *Sodometries*, pp. 117–26; Archer, *Sovereignty and Intelligence*, pp. 76–88.

37 Christopher Marlowe, *Edward II*, *Christopher Marlowe: the Complete Plays*, ed. J. B. Steane (Harmondsworth: Penguin, 1986), 1.1.2.

38 Bacon, "Of Friendship," *The Essayes or Counsels*, pp. 113–14.

39 Compare the weighty significance of "inconvenience" in the title of George Eglisham's *The Fore-Runner of Revenge, Being two Petitions . . . Wherein is expressed divers actions of the late Earle of Buckingham; especially concerning the death of King James, and the Marquess Hamilton, supposed by poyson. Also may be observed the inconveniences befalling a State where the Noble disposition of the Prince is mis-led by a Favourite* (London, 1642).

40 Ben Jonson, *Discoveries, Ben Jonson*, ed. C. H. Herford and Percy and Evelyn Simpson, 11 vols. (Oxford: Oxford University Press–Clarendon, 1925–51), VIII: 601.

41 Bacon, "Of Friendship," p. 114.

42 Simon Shepherd, "Shakespeare's Private Drawer: Shakespeare and Homosexuality," *The Shakespeare Myth*, ed. Graham Holderness (Manchester: Manchester University Press, 1988), 96–111, p. 102.

43 Bacon, "Of Followers and Friends," p. 172.

44 On the Renaissance ideal of the bountiful prince and the mutual obligations of patronage, see Linda Levy Peck, *Court Patronage and Corruption in Early Stuart England* (Boston: Unwin Hyman, 1990), pp. 12–29.

45 Alan Sinfield, "*Macbeth*: History, Ideology, and Intellectuals," *Faultlines: Cultural Materialism and the Politics of Dissident Reading* (Berkeley: University of California Press, 1992), p. 98; Bushnell, *Tragedies of Tyrants*, pp. 42–49.

46 Robert Aylette, *Joseph; or, Pharoh's Favourite* (London, 1623), p. 61, sig. E6.

47 Ibid., p. 58, sig. E5v.

48 Ibid., p. 61, sig. E6.

49 Emily C. Bartels, *Spectacles of Strangeness: Imperialism, Alienation, and Marlowe* (Philadelphia: University of Pennsylvania Press, 1993), p. 163. Bartels's assessment of the play resembles my own inasmuch as it concludes that Marlowe "legitimates" Edward's homoerotic desire and delegitimates the peers' accusations (p. 171). However, Bartels sometimes speaks of anal sex and homoerotic desire as "sodomy," which she considers a private matter distinct from "the political" (p. 159). While male–male sex might not always have political implications, I consider "sodomy" a "political" category in the sense that it names forms of physical intimacy socially defined as disorderly. In other words, "sodomy" is not a neutral description of a sexual act such as anal intercourse.

50 Whereas most critics, including those sensitive to the homoerotic and "homophobic" elements of the play, accept Mortimer at his word, Archer rightly perceives Mortimer's discomfort at Gaveston's erotic comportment (*Sovereignty and Intelligence*, p. 81). Viviana Comensoli describes Mortimer's obsession with the "pathologized body" of Gaveston and discusses his engineering of scatological torments for Edward much as I do below. However, she anachronistically attributes Mortimer's behavior to a homophobia generated by his own "repressed homosexuality" and "anal-erotic impulses." This approach has an unfortunate and ironic result: while creating sympathy for Edward and Gaveston as victims of a brutal homophobia, it locates the source of this homophobia in Mortimer's pathological *homosexuality* ("Homophobia and the Regulation of Desire: a Psychoanalytic Reading of Marlowe's *Edward II*," *Journal of the History of Sexuality* 4 [1993]: 175–200, pp. 190, 196–97).

51 Cf. Bredbeck, *Sodomy and Interpretation*, pp. 71–77. I find unconvincing Bredbeck's argument that Edward's replacement of Gaveston with Spenser represents a "change from personal passion to politic power," since I believe that both passion and power are involved in Edward's love for each favorite (p. 73).

52 See Peggy Muñoz Simonds, "The Marriage Topos in *Cymbeline*: Shakespeare's Variations on a Classical Theme," *ELR* 19 (1989): 94–117.

53 On the sadism of the peers, see Thomas Cartelli, *Marlowe, Shakespeare, and the Economy of Theatrical Experience* (Philadelphia: University of Pennsylvania Press, 1991), p. 131.

54 Anthony Weldon, *The Court and Character of King James* (1651; London, 1817), quoted in Goldberg, *James I*, p. 55.

55 Since the spit is not mentioned in the actual murder scene, Stephen Orgel has recently questioned the usual assumption that Lightborn kills Edward through anal rape (*Impersonations: the Performance of Gender in Shakespeare's England* [Cambridge: Cambridge University Press, 1996], pp. 47–48). Charles Forker offers several persuasive reasons why the spit might well have been brought onstage as the murder weapon, not least because "the sensational method of Edward's death was notorious, and Elizabethan audiences . . . would have expected to see it represented" (Charles R. Forker, ed., *Edward the Second*, by Christopher Marlowe, Revels Plays [Manchester: Manchester University Press, 1994], 5.5.30n.). Nevertheless, Orgel's point – that a "sodomitical" death for Edward is not based on the authority of the murder scene as actually published – is irrefutable.

56 Archer, *Sovereignty and Intelligence*, p. 85. Gregory Woods provides a detailed consideration of Lightborn's role in the sodomitical and scatological murder of Edward. While his intentions are antihomophobic, Woods problematically considers Lightborn "the last lover to penetrate the king," who "clearly wants him to be an angel, lover, and liberator" and "is expected to consent to his own death as if to the loving intercourse he craves." How does Woods know that Edward's lovers "penetrate" him, or that Edward "craves" such intercourse? More disturbingly, to whom is Woods attributing the *expectation* that Edward would consent to such a horrific death? ("Body, Costume, and Desire in Christopher Marlowe," *Homosexuality in Renaissance and Enlightenment England: Literary Representations in Historical Context*, ed. Claude J. Summers [New York: Harrington Park, 1992], 69–84, pp. 74, 79.)

57 Goldberg, *Sodometries*, p. 124.

58 William Shakespeare, *King Richard II*, ed. Peter Ure, Arden Shakespeare (London: Methuen, 1966), 2.1.17–28.

59 Although she discusses the homoerotic manipulations of royal flatterers and parasites in *Richard II*, Meredith Skura focuses mainly on the connection between flattery and acting (*Shakespeare the Actor*, pp. 166–202).

60 On the theory of the king's two bodies see Ernst H. Kantorowicz, *The King's Two Bodies: a Study in Medieval Political Theology* (Princeton: Princeton University Press, 1957).

61 W. G. Boswell-Stone, *Shakespeare's Holinshed: the Chronicle and the Historical Plays Compared* (1896; New York: Benjamin Blom, 1966), p. 129.

62 *The Tragedy of Tiberius*, ed. W. W. Greg, Malone Society Reprints (1607; Oxford: Oxford University Press, 1914), sig. H4v.

63 Ben Jonson, *Sejanus His Fall*, ed. Philip Ayres, Revels Plays (Manchester: Manchester University Press, 1990), 1.7–10. Further parenthetical citations from this edition will refer to act and line number.

64 On the relation between surveillance and male pleasure in *Sejanus*, see Archer, *Sovereignty and Intelligence*, especially pp. 103–11. My reading of the play is indebted to Archer's on several counts.

65 For a similar analysis, see Goldberg's discussion of the bodies of Tiberius and Sejanus in *James I*, pp. 183–84. On imagery of dismemberment see Christopher Ricks, "*Sejanus* and Dismemberment," *MLN* 76 (1961): 301–8.

66 Some recent psychoanalytic theories of gay male sexuality presume that the man penetrated in intercourse occupies an inherently "feminine," "powerless," or "masochistic" position. Especially where two people of the same sex are concerned, it is reductive and naive to attribute essential relations of power to the unfortunately named "active" and "passive" sexual positions.

67 Archer, *Sovereignty and Intelligence*, pp. 113, 108.

68 Bushnell, *Tragedies of Tyrants*, pp. 136, 153.

69 Cf. Bray, "Homosexuality," pp. 48–49.

70 I will cite from the following editions of Chapman's plays: *The Conspiracy and Tragedy of Charles Duke of Byron*, ed. John Margeson, Revels Plays (Manchester: Manchester University Press, 1988); *Bussy D'Ambois*, ed. N. S. Brooke, Revels Plays (Manchester: Manchester University Press, 1964); *The Revenge of Bussy D'Ambois*, *The Plays of George Chapman: the Tragedies*, ed. Thomas Marc Parrott (1910; New York: Russell and Russell, 1961).

71 On Chapman's own independent attitude towards patronage, see Goldberg, *James I*, p. 134.

72 Semele "being mortall was too weake and feeble to withstande / Such troublous tumultes of the Heavens: and therefore out of hande / Was burned in hir Lovers armes" (*Shakespeare's Ovid: Being Arthur Golding's Translation of the Metamorphoses*, ed. W. H. D. Rouse [Carbondale: Southern Illinois University Press, 1961], book 3, lines 387–89).

73 Lever, *The Tragedy of State*, p. 38. Millar MacLure notes the consistency of Chapman's own self-presentation as a beleaguered singular man (*George Chapman: a Critical Study* [Toronto: University of Toronto Press, 1966], p. 110).

74 Thomas Palmer, *The Emblems of Thomas Palmer: Two Hundred Poosees*, ed. John Manning (New York: AMS Press, 1988), p. 112. On the logical, social, and erotic manifestations of the preposterous, see Patricia Parker, "Preposterous Events," *Shakespeare Quarterly* 43 (1992): 186–213.

75 Richard S. Ide notes Bussy's seeming lack of sexual desire for Tamyra. While he provides a useful assessment of the "heroic spirits" of Bussy and Byron, Ide does not consider the possibility of homoerotic relations in Chapman's plays. He therefore misses the homoerotics of favoritism in *Bussy D'Ambois* and determines that "[l]ove is not an issue" in the *Byron* plays (*Possessed With Greatness: the Heroic Tragedies of Shakespeare and Chapman* [Chapel Hill: University of North Carolina Press, 1980], pp. 87, 132).

5 THE HOMOEROTICS OF MASCULINITY IN TRAGICOMEDY

1 Barnabe Riche, *His Farewell to Military Profession*, ed. Donald Beecher (1581; Ottawa, Canada: Dovehouse, 1992), p. 121. Further citations to Riche will appear parenthetically in the text. On early modern discourses that associated war with masculinity, peace with femininity, see Linda Woodbridge, *Women and the English Renaissance: Literature and the Nature of Womankind, 1540–1620* (Urbana: University of Illinois Press, 1984), pp. 152–71.

2 Gary Spear, "Shakespeare's 'Manly Parts': Masculinity and Effeminacy in *Troilus and Cressida*," *Shakespeare Quarterly* 44 (1993): 409–22.

3 *Haec Vir; or, The Womanish Man, Half Humankind: Contexts and Texts of the Controversy about Women in England, 1540–1640*, ed. Katherine Usher Henderson and Barbara F. McManus (Urbana: University of Illinois Press, 1985), p. 286.

4 Christopher Marlowe, *Edward II*, *Christopher Marlowe: the Complete Plays*, ed. J. B. Steane (Harmondsworth: Penguin, 1986), 1.4.394.

5 John Lyly, *Campaspe*, ed. G. K. Hunter, Revels Plays (Manchester: Manchester University Press, 1991), 2.2.67–70.

6 Ibid., 5.4.172–74.

7 Quoted in Bruce R. Smith, "Making a Difference: Male-Male 'Desire' in Tragedy, Comedy, and Tragi-comedy," *Erotic Politics: Desire on the Renaissance Stage*, ed. Susan Zimmerman (New York: Routledge, 1992), p. 145.

8 William Warner, *Albions England* (London, 1592), sig. A4v.

9 Walter Dorke, *A Tipe or Figure of Friendship* (London, 1589), sig. B1v.

10 Gregory W. Bredbeck, *Sodomy and Interpretation: Marlowe to Milton* (Ithaca: Cornell University Press, 1991), pp. 33–48; Valerie Traub, *Desire and Anxiety: Circulations of Sexuality in Shakespearean Drama* (London: Routledge, 1992), pp. 71–87; Bruce R. Smith, *Homosexual Desire in Shakespeare's England: a Cultural Poetics* (Chicago: University of Chicago Press, 1991), pp. 59–61; Spear, "Shakespeare's 'Manly Parts,'" *passim*.

11 I will use "Fletcher" throughout to designate plays written by Fletcher in collaboration with Middleton, Massinger, or Field. This rhetorical shorthand does not imply my disagreement with Jeffrey Masten's insistence on the collaborative authorship of Renaissance drama ("Beaumont and/or Fletcher: Collaboration and the Interpretation of Renaissance Drama," *ELH* 59 [1992]: 337–56). For my purposes here, it is not necessary to engage the current debate about the precise roles Beaumont, Fletcher, and others took in composing the plays of the "Beaumont and Fletcher" canon. Moreover, whatever the usefulness of the distinction Philip J. Finkelpearl draws between the dramatic sensibilities of Beaumont and of Fletcher, I am mostly concerned with plays Fletcher authored or coauthored after Beaumont's death in 1616 ("Beaumont, Fletcher, and 'Beaumont and Fletcher': Some Distinctions," *ELR* 1 [1971]: 144–64).

12 The definition of Shakespearean and Fletcherian "tragicomedy" is a knotty problem explored by several of the contributors to *Renaissance Tragicomedy: Explorations in Genre and Politics*, ed. Nancy Klein Maguire (New York: AMS Press, 1987). See also the editors' introduction to *The Politics of Tragicomedy: Shakespeare and After*, ed. Gordon McMullan and Jonathan

Hope (London: Routledge, 1992). The classic attempt to define Fletcherian tragicomedy is Eugene M. Waith, *The Pattern of Tragicomedy in Beaumont and Fletcher* (New Haven: Yale University Press, 1952).

13 Denzell S. Smith, "Francis Beaumont and John Fletcher," *The Later Jacobean and Caroline Dramatists*, ed. Terence P. Logan and Denzell S. Smith (Lincoln: University of Nebraska Press, 1978), 3–89, p. 51.

14 Nancy Cotton Pearse, *John Fletcher's Chastity Plays*: Mirrors of Modesty (Lewisburg, PA: Bucknell University Press, 1973), pp. 17, 24.

15 Recent studies include: R. A. Foakes, "Tragicomedy and Comic Form," *Comedy From Shakespeare to Sheridan: Change and Continuity in the English and European Dramatic Tradition*, ed. A. R. Braunmuller and J. C. Bulman (Newark: University of Delaware Press, 1986), 74–88; Kathleen McLuskie, *Renaissance Dramatists* (Atlantic Highlands, NJ: Humanities Press International, 1989), pp. 193–223; Verna A. Foster, "Sex Averted or Converted: Sexuality and Tragicomic Genre in the Plays of Fletcher," *SEL* 23 (1992): 311–22; Walter Cohen, "Prerevolutionary Drama," *The Politics of Tragicomedy*, 122–50; Smith, "Making a Difference"; Gordon McMullan, *The Politics of Unease in the Plays of John Fletcher* (Amherst: University of Massachusetts Press, 1994); Jeff Masten, "My Two Dads: Collaboration and the Reproduction of Beaumont and Fletcher," *Queering the Renaissance*, ed. Jonathan Goldberg (Durham, NC: Duke University Press, 1994), 280–309; Nicholas F. Radel, "Homoeroticism, Discursive Change, and Politics: Reading 'Revolution' in Seventeenth-Century English Tragicomedy," *Medieval and Renaissance Drama in England* 9 (1997).

16 Cohen, "Prerevolutionary Drama," p. 132, my emphasis. To be fair, Cohen recognizes the pitfalls of pluralistic methodologies that lose "conceptual clarity" by encompassing class, gender, sexuality, race, subjectivity, and so on (p. 146). Nevertheless, it is odd that such a self-aware criticism fails to acknowledge that "sexuality" might designate something other than erotic relations between men and women.

17 I am thinking here of Jonathan Goldberg's objection to accounts that locate Renaissance homoeroticism exclusively in cross-dressing scenarios (*Sodometries: Renaissance Texts, Modern Sexualities* [Stanford: Stanford University Press, 1993], pp. 105–43).

18 Jonathan Dollimore, *Sexual Dissidence: Augustine to Wilde, Freud to Foucault* (Oxford: Oxford University Press–Clarendon, 1991), pp. 287–29; Woodbridge, *Women and the English Renaissance*, p. 249; Jean E. Howard, *The Stage and Social Struggle in Early Modern England* (London: Routledge, 1994), especially pp. 102–6.

19 Dollimore, *Sexual Dissidence*, p. 289.

20 Roy Strong, *Henry, Prince of Wales and England's Lost Renaissance* (London: Thames and Hudson, 1986), pp. 66–67.

21 Lawrence Stone, *The Crisis of the Aristocracy 1558–1641*, abridged edn. (London: Oxford University Press, 1967), p. 116. On the contrast between Henry's militarism and James's pacifism, see also David M. Bergeron, *Royal Family, Royal Lovers: King James of England and Scotland* (Columbia: University of Missouri Press, 1991), pp. 93–102.

22 Stone, *The Crisis of the Aristocracy*, pp. 43, 51.

23 Karen Newman, *Fashioning Femininity and English Renaissance Drama* (Chicago: University of Chicago Press, 1991), pp. 111–43.

24 Philip J. Finkelpearl, *Court and Country Politics in the Plays of Beaumont and Fletcher* (Princeton: Princeton University Press, 1990), pp. 127, 29.

25 McLuskie, *Renaissance Dramatists*, pp. 212, 218. Woodbridge argues that positive images of women in drama between 1610 and 1620 were intended to attract female playgoers (*Women and the English Renaissance*, pp. 244–64).

26 *The Humorous Lieutenant* (1619, Fletcher), ed. Cyrus Hoy, *Dramatic Works*, V: epilogue 5–7.

A word on the citation of texts. In the notes, play titles are followed by date of first performance and authorial ascription, as established in Alfred Harbage, *Annals of English Drama, 975–1700*, 3rd edn, revised by Sylvia Stoler Wagonheim (New York: Routledge, 1989). I cite from the current, as yet incomplete, standard edition (*The Dramatic Works in the Beaumont and Fletcher Canon*, general editor Fredson Bowers, 8 vols. [Cambridge: Cambridge University Press, 1966–96]), abbreviated *Dramatic Works*. For plays not yet published in the Bowers edition or for those published in volumes unavailable to me at the time of writing, I cite from the former standard edition (*The Works of Francis Beaumont and John Fletcher*, ed. Arnold Glover and A. R. Waller, 10 vols. [Cambridge: Cambridge University Press, 1905–12]), abbreviated *Works*.

27 Spear, "Shakespeare's 'Manly Parts,' " p. 417.

28 *The Nice Valour, or the Passionate Madman* (1615–16; the most recent edition of the *Annals* ascribes the play to Middleton, "possibly with Fletcher"), ed. George Walton Williams, *Dramatic Works*, VII: 1.1.14, 24, 29. Waith generically classifies *The Nice Valour* (along with *The Captain* and *The Night Walker*, both discussed below) as a "mixed comedy," in which "gaiety . . . is mixed with a more serious mood" (*The Pattern of Tragicomedy*, p. 107).

29 Jonathan Dollimore detects a similar contradiction in Beaumont and Fletcher's *Love's Cure* (1606), in which Lucio's effeminacy is judged unnatural yet "actually embodies positive civilized virtues" (*Sexual Dissidence*, p. 301).

30 Although Lapet's pamphlet is a joke, King James and Francis Bacon published official condemnations of dueling in 1614.

31 Michael Moon, "A Small Boy and Others: Sexual Disorientation in Henry James, Kenneth Anger, and David Lynch," *Comparative American Identities: Race, Sex, and Nationality in the Modern Text*, ed. Hortense J. Spillers (New York: Routledge, 1991), 141–56, pp. 141–42.

32 Mervyn James, *English Politics and the Concept of Honour 1485–1642*, Past and Present Supplement 3 (1978): p. 1; Stone, *The Crisis of the Aristocracy*, p. 120.

33 Linda Charnes, " 'So Unsecret to Ourselves': Notorious Identity and the Material Subject in Shakespeare's *Troilus and Cressida*," *Shakespeare Quarterly* 40 (1989): 413–40, p. 436. Because she is interested here in the homosocial (and homoerotic) triangulation of male desire through female bodies, Charnes does not distinguish aggressive homoerotic rivalry from the homoerotic desire uniting Achilles and Patroclus.

34 Alan Sinfield provides a concise survey of the historical and literary findings in *The Wilde Century: Effeminacy, Oscar Wilde and the Queer Moment* (New

York: Columbia University Press, 1994), pp. 25–51. To Sinfield's account I would add Bredbeck's analysis of the specification of sodomy discourse during the seventeenth century (*Sodomy and Interpretation*, pp. 10–21).

35 Masten, "My Two Dads," p. 282.

36 Nicholas F. Radel, "Clothes, Closure, Closets: Constr(i)(u)cting Homoerotic Desire in Two Plays from the Beaumont and Fletcher Folio," unpublished manuscript.

37 Alan Sinfield makes a related point about the uneven development of same-sex roles in the seventeenth century. Tracing the changing meanings of "effeminacy" from the early modern to the modern period, Sinfield argues that despite the "development of a same-sex subculture" around the molly houses in late seventeenth-century England, it is a mistake to conclude "that same-sex passion became at this point identified with effeminacy. We should not suppose that the molly house model was the only one in circulation, or that it was widely known about. It is entirely likely that an elaborate social structure should entertain diverse sexual schema" (*The Wilde Century*, p. 38).

38 *The Captain* (1609–12; Fletcher, w/Beaumont?), ed. A. R. Waller, *Works*, V: 2.1, p. 249. Since this edition of the play does not include line numbers, I will provide page numbers in subsequent citations.

39 *The Night Walker* (1611, Fletcher; revised Shirley 1633), ed. Cyrus Hoy, *Dramatic Works*, VII: 2.3.61, 62.

40 Unmarried young soldiers are reconciled to their fathers at the conclusion of *The Loyal Subject* (1618, Fletcher) and *The Laws of Candy* (1619–23; the most recent edition of the *Annals* controversially ascribes the play to Ford). In *A Very Woman* (1619–22; Fletcher w/Massinger; revised Massinger), Don Martino is nearly killed fighting a duel over his mistress Almira. He regrets his unmanly behavior, undergoes a cure for melancholy, and finally resolves never to love women again. Before his cure, Martino obsessively worries about his violation of masculine honor: "Why did I wrong this man, unmanly wrong him, / Unmannerly? . . . / . . . I had forgot both man and manhood" (ed. Hans Walter Gabler, *Dramatic Works*, VII: 3.3.14–15,17). When Martino concludes that loving women is antithetical to being a "perfect man," Almira rather scornfully addresses her ex-suitor as "this new *Hippolitus*" (5.4.66, 86).

41 *The Mad Lover* (1617, Fletcher), ed. Robert Kean Turner, *Dramatic Works*, V: 1.1.52, 56.

42 Margo Hendricks and Patricia Parker, introduction to *Women, "Race," and Writing in the Early Modern Period*, ed. Margo Hendricks and Patricia Parker (London: Routledge, 1994), 1–16, p. 2.

43 George Best, *Discourse* (1578), quoted in Lynda E. Boose, "'The Getting of a Lawful Race': Racial Discourse in Early Modern England and the Unrepresentable Black Woman," *Women, "Race," and Writing*, ed. Hendricks and Parker, 35–54, p. 43.

44 *The Island Princess* (1619–21, Fletcher), ed. George Walton Williams, *Dramatic Works*, V: 4.1 sd.

45 In an analysis of the gendered binaries fair/dark and white/black in Renaissance texts, Kim F. Hall demonstrates that the "language of aesthetics is constitutive of the language of race in early modern England" ("'I Rather Would Wish to Be a Black-Moor': Beauty, Race, and Rank in Lady Mary

Wroth's *Urania*," *Women, "Race," and Writing*, ed. Hendricks and Parker, 178–94, p. 179).

46 On the rhetorical construction of the New World as a female body, see Patricia Parker, "Rhetorics of Property: Exploration, Inventory, Blazon," *Literary Fat Ladies: Rhetoric, Gender, Property* (London: Methuen, 1987), 126–54; and Louis Montrose, "The Work of Gender in the Discourse of Discovery," *Representations* 33 (1991): 1–41.

47 Gordon McMullan discusses this passage in an analysis devoted to showing how *The Island Princess* exposes the contradictions of colonialist discourse. While informative, his discussion of the play's sexual discourse omits any consideration of homoeroticism (*The Politics of Unease*, pp. 197–256).

48 According to Homi K. Bhabha, the "objective of colonial discourse is to construe the colonized as a population of degenerate types on the basis of racial origin, in order to justify conquest and to establish systems of administration and instruction" ("The Other Question: Difference, Discrimination and the Discourse of Colonialism," *Literature, Politics, and Theory: Papers from the Essex Conference 1976–84*, ed. Francis Barker *et al.* [London: Methuen, 1986], 148–72, p. 154).

49 Historically, Portuguese power in the East had been in decline since the late sixteenth century. When Philip II of Spain became King of Portugal in 1580, the "trade and possessions of Portugal in the East . . . became the legitimate prey of the sea-faring enemies of Spain," namely the English and the Dutch. The Dutch secured a monopoly on the Moluccan spice trade during the seventeenth century (J. H. Parry, *The Establishment of the European Hegemony: 1415–1715: Trade and Exploration in the Age of the Renaissance*, 3rd edn. [New York: Harper, 1966], pp. 80, 135–36). Samuel Purchas's travel book includes an account of the Moluccan situation dated 1617, a few years before the first recorded performance of *The Island Princess* in 1621: "Lastly, the Hollanders have dispossessed the Portugalls: and the Spaniards or Castilians, by meanes of the Tidorians have there fortified" (Samuel Purchas, *Hakluytus Posthumus or Purchas His Pilgrimes*, 20 vols. [1625; New York: AMS Press, 1965], II: 227). Clearly, Fletcher's play represents a fantasy on more than one level.

50 *The Knight of Malta* (1616–19, Fletcher w/Massinger and Field), ed. A. R. Waller, *Works*, VII: 5.2, p. 160.

51 Boose, "'The Getting of a Lawful Race,'" p. 46.

52 Fletcher's representation of the subjection of an "effeminized" native population by masculine conquerors represents only one possible ideological strategy for managing the anxieties of the colonial project. As Ann Rosalind Jones and Peter Stallybrass show, in late sixteenth-century English texts "the wild Irish were imagined in terms of a supposedly resolute virility," whereas "the fantasy of a degenerate masculinity was displaced from the barbarian to the Catholic Anglo-Irish, or the Old English." The English responded to this dual threat by "imposing a violent hierarchy through military subjugation" ("Dismantling Irena: the Sexualizing of Ireland in Early Modern England," *Nationalisms and Sexualities*, ed. Andrew Parker *et al.* [New York: Routledge, 1992], 157–71, pp. 163, 169).

Bibliography

Akrigg, G. P. V. *Jacobean Pageant, or The Court of King James I.* Cambridge, MA: Harvard University Press, 1962.

Anderson, Linda. "Shakespeare's Servants." *Shakespeare Yearbook* 2 (1991).

Archer, John Michael. *Sovereignty and Intelligence: Spying and Court Culture in the English Renaissance.* Stanford: Stanford University Press, 1993.

Aubrey, John. *Aubrey's Brief Lives.* Ed. Oliver Lawson Dick. Harmondsworth: Penguin, 1987.

Aylette, Robert. *Joseph, or, Pharoh's Favourite.* London, 1623.

B., R. *Orpheus His Journey to Hell, And his Musicke to the Ghosts, for the regaining of faire Eurydice his Love, and new spoused Wife.* London, 1595.

Bacon, Francis. *Francis Bacon: a Selection of His Works.* Ed. Sidney Warhaft. New York: Macmillan, 1985.

Baird-Lange, Lorrayne Y. "Victim Criminalized: Iconographic Traditions and Peacham's Ganymede." *Traditions and Innovations: Essays on British Literature of the Middle Ages and Renaissance.* Ed. David G. Allen and Robert A. White. Newark: University of Delaware Press, 1990.

Barbour, Richmond. "'When I Acted Young Antinous': Boy Actors and the Erotics of Jonsonian Theater." *PMLA* 110 (October 1995).

Barkan, Leonard. *The Gods Made Flesh: Metamorphosis and the Pursuit of Paganism.* New Haven: Yale University Press, 1986.

Transuming Passion: Ganymede and the Erotics of Humanism. Stanford: Stanford University Press, 1991.

Barker, Francis. *The Tremulous Private Body: Essays on Subjection.* London: Methuen, 1984.

Barksted, William. *Mirrha the Mother of Adonis: or Lustes Prodegies.* 1607. *The Poems of William Barksted.* Ed. Alexander B. Grosart. Manchester: Charles E. Simms, 1876.

Barrett, Michèle, and Mary McIntosh. *The Anti-social Family.* 2nd edn. London: Verso, 1991.

Bartels, Emily C. *Spectacles of Strangeness: Imperialism, Alienation, and Marlowe.* Philadelphia: University of Pennsylvania Press, 1993.

Barton, Anne. *Ben Jonson, Dramatist.* Cambridge: Cambridge University Press, 1984.

Bate, Jonathan. *Shakespeare and Ovid.* Oxford: Oxford University Press, 1993.

Beier, A. L. *Masterless Men: the Vagrancy Problem in England 1560–1640.* London: Methuen, 1985.

Belsey, Catherine. "Disrupting Sexual Difference: Meaning and Gender in the Comedies." *Alternative Shakespeares*. Ed. John Drakakis. London: Routledge, 1988.

Berger, Harry, Jr. "Busirane and the War Between the Sexes: an Interpretation of *The Faerie Queene* III.xi–xii." *ELR* 1 (1971).

"Orpheus, Pan, and the Poetics of Misogyny: Spenser's Critique of Pastoral Love and Art." *ELH* 50 (1983).

Bergeron, David M. *Royal Family, Royal Lovers: King James of England and Scotland*. Columbia: University of Missouri Press, 1991.

Berry, Philippa. *Of Chastity and Power: Elizabethan Literature and the Unmarried Queen*. London: Routledge, 1989.

Best, George. *Discourse*. London, 1578.

Bevington, David, ed. *As You Like It*. By William Shakespeare. New York: Bantam, 1988.

Bhabha, Homi K. "The Other Question: Difference, Discrimination and the Discourse of Colonialism." *Literature, Politics, and Theory: Papers from the Essex Conference 1976–84*. Ed. Francis Barker, Peter Hulme, Margaret Iverson, and Diana Loxley. London: Methuen, 1986.

Bingham, Caroline. *James I of England*. London: Weidenfeld and Nicolson, 1981.

Boose, Lynda E. "The Family in Shakespeare Studies; or – Studies in the Family of Shakespeareans; or – The Politics of Politics." *Renaissance Quarterly* 40 (1987).

" 'The Getting of a Lawful Race': Racial Discourse in Early Modern England and the Unrepresentable Black Woman." Hendricks and Parker, ed., *Women, "Race," and Writing*.

Booth, Stephen, ed. *Shakespeare's Sonnets*. New Haven: Yale University Press, 1977.

Boswell, John. *Christianity, Social Tolerance, and Homosexuality: Gay People in Western Europe from the Beginning of the Christian Era to the Fourteenth Century*. Chicago: University of Chicago Press, 1980.

Boswell-Stone, W. G. *Shakespeare's Holinshed: the Chronicle and the Historical Plays Compared*. 1896. New York: Benjamin Blom, 1966.

Brathwayte, Richard. *A Strappado for the Devil*. London, 1615.

Bray, Alan. *Homosexuality in Renaissance England*. London: Gay Men's Press, 1982.

"Homosexuality and the Signs of Male Friendship in Elizabethan England." Goldberg, ed., *Queering*.

Bredbeck, Gregory W. *Sodomy and Interpretation: Marlowe to Milton*. Ithaca: Cornell University Press, 1991.

"Sodomesticity." MLA Convention. New York City, 29 December 1992.

Broaddus, James W. "Renaissance Psychology and Britomart's Adventures in *Faerie Queene* III." *ELR* 17 (1987).

Brown, Judith C. "Lesbian Sexuality in Medieval and Early Modern Europe." *Hidden From History: Reclaiming the Gay and Lesbian Past*. Ed. Martin Duberman, Martha Vicinus, and George Chauncey, Jr. New York: Meridian, 1990.

Brown, Steve. "The Boyhood of Shakespeare's Heroines: Notes on Gender Ambiguity in the Sixteenth Century." *SEL* 30 (1990).

Browne, William. *Brittania's Pastorals Book Two. The Penguin Book of Renaissance Verse 1509–1659*. Ed. H. R. Woudhuysen. Harmondsworth: Penguin, 1993.

Burnett, Mark Thornton. "Masters and Servants in Moral and Religious Treatises, *c.* 1580–*c.* 1642." *The Arts, Literature and Society*. Ed. Arthur Marwick. London: Routledge, 1990.

"The 'Trusty Servant': a Sixteenth-Century English Emblem." *Emblematica* 6.2 (1992).

Bushnell, Rebecca W. *Tragedies of Tyrants: Political Thought and Theater in the English Renaissance*. Ithaca: Cornell University Press, 1990.

Butler, Judith. *Bodies That Matter: on the Discursive Limits of "Sex."* New York: Routledge, 1993.

Cady, Joseph. "'Masculine Love,' Renaissance Writing, and the 'New Invention' of Homosexuality." Summers, ed., *Homosexuality in Renaissance and Enlightenment England*.

"Renaissance Awareness and Language for Heterosexuality: 'Love' and 'Feminine Love.'" Summers and Pebworth, ed. *Renaissance Discourses of Desire*.

Cain, Thomas H. "Spenser and the Renaissance Orpheus." *University of Toronto Quarterly* 41 (1972).

Cartelli, Thomas. *Marlowe, Shakespeare, and the Economy of Theatrical Experience*. Philadelphia: University of Pennsylvania Press, 1991.

Castiglione, Baldassare. *The Book of the Courtier*. Trans. Thomas Hoby. 1561. *Tudor Translations* 23. Ed. W. E. Henley. London: David Nutt, 1900.

Chapman, George. *All Fools*. Ed. Frank Manley. Regents Renaissance Drama. Lincoln: University of Nebraska Press, 1968.

Bussy D'Ambois. Ed. N. S. Brooke. Revels Plays. Manchester: Manchester University Press, 1964.

The Conspiracy and Tragedy of Charles Duke of Byron. Ed. John Margeson. Revels Plays. Manchester: Manchester University Press, 1988.

The Gentleman Usher. Ed. John Hazel Smith. Regents Renaissance Drama. Lincoln: University of Nebraska Press, 1970.

The Plays of George Chapman: the Comedies. Ed. Allan Holaday. Urbana: University of Illinois Press, 1970.

The Plays of George Chapman: the Tragedies. Ed. Thomas Marc Parrott. 1910. New York: Russell and Russell, 1961.

The Widow's Tears. Ed. Akihiro Yamada. Revels Plays. London: Methuen, 1975.

Chappell, William, ed. *The Roxburghe Ballads*. 9 vols. Hertford: Stephen Austin and Sons, 1871–99.

Charnes, Linda. "'So Unsecret to Ourselves': Notorious Identity and the Material Subject in Shakespeare's *Troilus and Cressida*." *Shakespeare Quarterly* 40 (1989).

Cohen, Ed. *Talk on the Wilde Side: Toward a Genealogy of a Discourse on Male Sexualities*. New York: Routledge, 1993.

Cohen, Walter. "Prerevolutionary Drama." McMullan and Hope, ed., *The Politics of Tragicomedy*.

Coke, Sir Edward. *The Third Part of the Institutes of the Laws of England*. 3rd edn. London: J. Flesher, 1660.

Comensoli, Viviana. "Homophobia and the Regulation of Desire: a Psycho-analytic Reading of Marlowe's *Edward II*." *Journal of the History of Sexuality* 4 (1993).

Cooper, Thomas. *Dictionarium Historicum & Poeticum . . . in Thesaurus Linguae Romanae & Brittanicae . . . .* London, 1565.

Crimp, Douglas. "Mourning and Militancy." *Out There: Marginalization and Contemporary Cultures.* Ed. Russell Ferguson, Martha Gever, Trinh T. Minh-Ha, and Cornel West. New York: New Museum of Contemporary Art, 1990.

"Right On, Girlfriend!" *Fear of a Queer Planet: Queer Politics and Social Theory.* Ed. Michael Warner. Minneapolis: University of Minnesota Press, 1993.

Crompton, Louis. "Gay Genocide: From Leviticus to Hitler." *The Gay Academic.* Ed. Louie Crew. Palm Springs, CA: ETC Publications, 1978.

Cuddy, Neil. "The Revival of the Entourage: the Bedchamber of James I, 1603–1625." Starkey, ed., *The English Court.*

Dekker, Thomas. *Satiromastix.* Vol. I. *The Dramatic Works of Thomas Dekker.* Ed. Fredson Bowers. 4 vols. Cambridge: Cambridge University Press, 1953.

Della Casa, Giovanni. *Galateo of Maister John della Casa . . .* Trans. Robert Peterson. London, 1576.

A Description of Love. With Certain Epigrams, Elegies, and Sonnets . . . . London, 1620.

Dickenson, John. *The Shepheardes Complaint.* London, 1596.

DiGangi, Mario. "Reading Homoeroticism in Early Modern England: Imaginations, Interpretations, Circulations." *Textual Practice* 7 (1993).

Dolan, Frances. "The Subordinate('s) Plot: Petty Treason and the Forms of Domestic Rebellion." *Shakespeare Quarterly* 43 (1992).

Dollimore, Jonathan. *Radical Tragedy: Religion, Ideology and Power in the Drama of Shakespeare and His Contemporaries.* Chicago: University of Chicago Press, 1984.

Sexual Dissidence: Augustine to Wilde, Freud to Foucault. Oxford: Oxford University Press–Clarendon, 1991.

Dollimore, Jonathan, and Alan Sinfield, eds. *Political Shakespeare: New Essays in Cultural Materialism.* Ithaca: Cornell University Press, 1985.

Dorke, Walter. *A Tipe or Figure of Friendship.* London, 1589.

Drayton, Michael. *The Moone-Calfe.* Vol III. *The Works of Michael Drayton.* Ed. W. Hebel. 5 vols. Oxford: Oxford University Press, 1932.

Edelman, Lee. "Seeing Things: Representation, the Scene of Surveillance, and the Spectacle of Gay Male Sex." *Inside/Out: Lesbian Theories, Gay Theories.* Ed. Diana Fuss. New York: Routledge, 1991.

Eglisham, George. *The Fore-Runner of Revenge . . . .* London, 1642.

Evett, David. " 'Surprising Confrontations': Ideologies of Service in Shakespeare's England." *Renaissance Papers* 1990. Ed. Dale B. J. Randall and Joseph A. Porter. Durham, NC: Southeastern Renaissance Conference, 1990.

Finkelpearl, Philip J. *Court and Country Politics in the Plays of Beaumont and Fletcher.* Princeton: Princeton University Press, 1990.

"Beaumont, Fletcher, and 'Beaumont and Fletcher': Some Distinctions." *ELR* 1 (1971).

Fizdale, Tay. "Jonson's *Volpone* and the 'Real' Antinous." *Renaissance Quarterly* 26 (1973).

Fletcher, John, and Francis Beaumont. *The Dramatic Works in the Beaumont and Fletcher Canon*. General editor Fredson Bowers, 9 vols. Cambridge: Cambridge University Press, 1966–96.

The Works of Francis Beaumont and John Fletcher. Ed. Arnold Glover and A. R. Waller. 10 vols. Cambridge: Cambridge University Press, 1905–12:

Florio, John. *A Worlde of Wordes*. London, 1598.

Foakes, R. A. "Tragicomedy and Comic Form." *Comedy From Shakespeare to Sheridan: Change and Continuity in the English and European Dramatic Tradition*. Ed. A. R. Braunmuller and J. C. Bulman. Newark: University of Delaware Press, 1986.

Forker, Charles R., ed. *Edward the Second*. By Christopher Marlowe. Revels Plays. Manchester: Manchester University Press, 1994.

Forster, E. M. *Maurice*. New York: Norton, 1971.

Foster, Verna A. "Sex Averted or Converted: Sexuality and Tragicomic Genre in the Plays of Fletcher." *SEL* 23 (1992).

Fraunce, Abraham. *The Third Part of the Countesse of Pembrokes Yvychurch, Entituled, Amintas Dale*. London, 1592.

Friedman, Alice T. *House and Household in Elizabethan England: Wollaton Hall and the Willoughby Family*. Chicago: University of Chicago Press, 1989.

Frontain, Raymond-Jean. "*Ruddy and Goodly to Look at Withal*: Drayton, Cowley, and the Biblical Model for Renaissance Hom[m]osexuality." *Cahiers Elizabethains* 36 (October 1989).

Garber, Marjorie. *Vested Interests: Cross-Dressing and Cultural Anxiety*. New York: Routledge, 1992.

Gilbert, Allan H. "The Italian Names in *Every Man Out of His Humour*." *Studies in Philology* 44 (1947).

Goddard, William. *A Satirical Dialogue . . . .* Low Countries, 1615.

Goldberg, Jonathan. *Endlesse Worke: Spenser and the Structures of Discourse*. Baltimore: Johns Hopkins University Press, 1981.

James I and the Politics of Literature: Jonson, Shakespeare, Donne, and Their Contemporaries. 1983. Stanford: Stanford University Press, 1989.

Sodometries: Renaissance Texts, Modern Sexualities. Stanford: Stanford University Press, 1992.

"Sodomy and Society: the Case of Christopher Marlowe." *Staging the Renaissance: Reinterpretations of Elizabethan and Jacobean Drama*. Ed. David Scott Kastan and Peter Stallybrass. New York: Routledge, 1991.

Goldberg, Jonathan, ed. *Queering the Renaissance*. Durham, NC: Duke University Press, 1994.

Googe, Barnabe. *Barnabe Googe: Eclogues, Epitaphs, and Sonnets*. Ed. Judith M. Kennedy. Toronto: University of Toronto Press, 1989.

Greenberg, David F. *The Construction of Homosexuality*. Chicago: University of Chicago Press, 1988.

Greenblatt, Stephen. *Shakespearean Negotiations: the Circulation of Social Energy in Renaissance England*. Berkeley: University of California Press, 1988.

Greene, Robert. *Penelopes Web*. Vol. V. *The Complete Life and Works . . . of*

Robert Greene. Ed. Alexander B. Grosart. 15 vols. Huth Library. London: Hazell, Watson and Viney, 1881–86.

Guilpin, Everard. *Skialetheia Or A Shadow of Truth, in Certain Epigrams and Satyres*. Ed. D. Allen Carroll. Chapel Hill: University of North Carolina Press, 1974.

Gurr, Andrew. *Playgoing in Shakespeare's London*. Cambridge: Cambridge University Press, 1987.

Haec Vir; or, The Womanish Man. 1620. *Half Humankind: Contexts and Texts of the Controversy about Women in England, 1540–1640*. Ed. Katherine Usher Henderson and Barbara F. McManus. Urbana: University of Illinois Press, 1985.

Hall, Kim F. "'I Rather Would Wish to Be a Black-Moor': Beauty, Race, and Rank in Lady Mary Wroth's *Urania*." Hendricks and Parker, eds., *Women, "Race," and Writing*.

Halley, Janet E. "*Bowers* v. *Hardwick* in the Renaissance." Goldberg, ed., *Queering*.

Halperin, David M. *One Hundred Years of Homosexuality and Other Essays on Greek Love*. New York: Routledge, 1990.

"Historicizing the Sexual Body: Sexual Preferences and Erotic Identities in the Pseudo-Lucianic *Erotes*." *Discourses of Sexuality: From Aristotle to AIDS*. Ed. Domna C. Stanton. Ann Arbor: University of Michigan Press, 1992.

Harbage, Alfred. *Annals of English Drama, 975–1700*. 3rd edn. Revised Sylvia Stoler Wagonheim. New York: Routledge, 1989.

Heal, Felicity. *Hospitality in Early Modern England*. Oxford: Clarendon, 1990.

Hendricks, Margo, and Patricia Parker, eds. *Women, "Race," and Writing in the Early Modern Period*. London: Routledge, 1994.

Hennessy, Rosemary. *Materialist Feminism and the Politics of Discourse*. New York: Routledge, 1993.

Heywood, Thomas. *Pleasant Dialogues and Dramma's*. Vol. VI. *The Dramatic Works of Thomas Heywood*. 6 vols. 1874. New York: Russell and Russell, 1964.

A Woman Killed with Kindness. Ed. R. W. Van Fossen. Revels Plays. London: Methuen, 1961.

Hocquenghem, Guy. *Homosexual Desire*. Trans. Daniella Dangoor, 1978. Introduction by Michael Moon. Durham, NC: Duke University Press, 1993.

Holstun, James. "'God Bless Thee, Little David!': John Felton and his Allies." *ELH* 59 (1992).

"'Will You Rent Our Ancient Love Asunder?' Lesbian Elegy in Donne, Marvell, and Milton." *ELH* 54 (1987).

Houlbrooke, Ralph A. *The English Family 1450–1700*. London: Longman, 1984.

Howard, Jean E. *The Stage and Social Struggle in Early Modern England*. London: Routledge, 1994.

"Sex and Social Conflict: the Erotics of *The Roaring Girl*," Zimmerman, ed., *Erotic Politics*.

Huebert, Ronald. "'A Shrew Yet Honest': Manliness in Jonson." *Renaissance Drama* ns 20 (1984).

Hughes, Diane Owen. "Distinguishing Signs: Ear-Rings, Jews and Franciscan Rhetoric in the Italian Renaissance City." *Past and Present* 112 (1986).

Hunt, Margaret. "Afterword." Goldberg, ed., *Queering*.

I., W. *The Whipping of the Satyre*. London, 1601.

Ide, Richard S. *Possessed With Greatness: the Heroic Tragedies of Shakespeare and Chapman*. Chapel Hill: University of North Carolina Press, 1980.

James I. *Basilicon Doron. King James VI and I: Political Writings*. Ed. Johann P. Sommerville. Cambridge: Cambridge University Press, 1994.

A Counterblaste To Tobacco. Minor Prose Works of King James VI and I. Ed. James Craigie. Edinburgh: Scottish Text Society, 1982.

James, Mervyn. *English Politics and the Concept of Honour 1485–1642. Past and Present* Supplement 3 (1978).

Jankowski, Theodora A. *Women in Power in the Early Modern Drama*. Urbana: University of Illinois Press, 1992.

"Pure Resistance: Queer(y)ing Virginity in William Shakespeare's *Measure for Measure* and Margaret Cavendish's *The Convent of Pleasure*." *Shakespeare Studies* 26 (forthcoming, 1998).

"'The Scorne of Savage People': Virginity as 'Forbidden Sexuality' in John Lyly's *Love's Metamorphosis*." *Renaissance Drama* 24 (1993).

"'Where There Can Be No Cause of Affection': Redefining Virgins, Their Desires, and Their Pleasures in John Lyly's *Gallathea*." *Feminist Readings of Early Modern Culture: Emerging Subjects*. Ed. Dympna Callaghan, M. Lindsay Kaplan, and Valerie Traub. Cambridge: Cambridge University Press, 1996.

Jardine, Lisa. *Still Harping on Daughters: Women and Drama in the Age of Shakespeare*. 2nd edn. New York: Columbia University Press–Morningside, 1989.

"Twins and Travesties: Gender, Dependency, and Sexual Availability in *Twelfth Night*." Zimmerman, ed., *Erotic Politics*.

Jones, Ann Rosalind, and Peter Stallybrass. "Dismantling Irena: the Sexualizing of Ireland in Early Modern England." *Nationalisms and Sexualities*. Ed. Andrew Parker, Mary Russo, Doris Sommer, and Patricia Yaeger. New York: Routledge, 1992.

"Fetishizing Gender: Constructing the Hermaphrodite in Renaissance Europe." *Body Guards: the Cultural Politics of Gender Ambiguity*. Ed. Julia Epstein and Kristina Straub. New York: Routledge, 1991.

Jonson, Ben. *Ben Jonson*. Ed. C. H. Herford and Percy and Evelyn Simpson. 11 vols. Oxford: Oxford University Press–Clarendon, 1925–51.

Sejanus His Fall. Ed. Philip Ayres. Revels Plays. Manchester: Manchester University Press, 1990.

Kantorowicz, Ernst H. *The King's Two Bodies: a Study in Medieval Political Theology*. Princeton: Princeton University Press, 1957.

Kehler, Dorothea. "Shakespeare's Emilias and the Politics of Celibacy." *In Another Country: Feminist Perspectives on Renaissance Drama*. Ed. Dorothea Kehler and Susan Baker. Metuchen, NJ: Scarecrow Press, 1991.

Kirk, Marshall, and Hunter Madsen. *After the Ball: How America Will Conquer its Fear of Gays in the '90s*. New York: Doubleday, 1989.

Klaiwitter, George. "Verse Letters to T. W. from John Donne: 'By You My Love Is Sent.'" Summers, ed., *Homosexuality in Renaissance and Enlightenment England*.

Kott, Jan. "The Gender of Rosalind." Trans. Jadwiga Kosicka. *The Gender of Rosalind: Interpretations: Shakespeare, Buchner, Gautier.* Evanston, IL: Northwestern University Press, 1992.

Kussmaul, Ann. *Servants in Husbandry in Early Modern England.* Cambridge: Cambridge University Press, 1981.

Laqueur, Thomas. *Making Sex: Body and Gender from the Greeks to Freud.* Cambridge, MA: Harvard University Press, 1990.

Leinwand, Theodore B. *The City Staged: Jacobean Comedy, 1603–1613.* Madison: University of Wisconsin Press, 1986.

"Redeeming Beggary/Buggery in *Michaelmas Term.*" *ELH* 61 (1994).

Lever, J. W. *The Tragedy of State: a Study of Jacobean Drama.* 1971. Introduction by Jonathan Dollimore. London: Methuen, 1987.

Levine, Laura. *Men in Women's Clothing: Anti-theatricality and Effeminization, 1579–1642.* Cambridge: Cambridge University Press, 1994.

Lewis, Cynthia. "'Wise Men, Folly Fall'n': Characters Named Antonio in English Renaissance Drama." *Renaissance Drama* ns 20 (1989).

Of Loves Complaint with the Legend of Orpheus and Eurydice. London, 1597.

Lucian. *Affairs of the Heart.* Vol. VIII. *Lucian.* Trans. M. D. Macleod. Loeb Library. 8 vols. Cambridge, MA: Harvard University Press, 1967.

Lyly, John. *Campaspe.* Ed. G. K. Hunter. Revels Plays. Manchester: Manchester University Press, 1991.

Gallathea. Ed. Anne Begor Lancashire. Regents Renaissance Drama. Lincoln: University of Nebraska Press, 1969.

Machin, Lewes. *Three Eglogs. The First is of Menalcas and Daphnis: the Other Two is of Apollo and Hiacinth.* London, 1607.

MacLure, Millar. *George Chapman: a Critical Study.* Toronto: University of Toronto Press, 1966.

MacLure, Millar, ed. *Marlowe: the Critical Heritage, 1588–1896.* London: Routledge, 1979.

Mager, Donald N. "John Bale and Early Tudor Sodomy Discourse." Goldberg, ed., *Queering.*

Maguire, Nancy Klien, ed. *Renaissance Tragicomedy: Explorations in Genre and Politics.* New York: AMS Press, 1987.

The Maid's Metamorphosis. 1600. Ed. John S. Farmer. Tudor Reprinted and Parallel Texts. London: Hazell, Watson and Viney, 1908.

Malcolmson, Cristina. "'What You Will': Social Mobility and Gender in *Twelfth Night.*" Wayne, ed., *The Matter of Difference.*

Marcus, Leah S. "Renaissance/Early Modern Studies." *Redrawing the Boundaries: the Transformation of English and American Literary Studies.* Ed. Stephen Greenblatt and Giles Gunn. New York: MLA, 1992.

Marlowe, Christopher. *Christopher Marlowe: the Complete Plays.* Ed. J. B. Steane. Harmondsworth: Penguin, 1986.

Marotti, Arthur. "The Purgations of Thomas Middleton's *The Family of Love.*" *Papers on Language and Literature* 7.1 (1971).

Marston, John. *Parasitaster, or The Fawn.* Ed. David A. Blostein. Revels Plays. Baltimore: Johns Hopkins University Press, 1978.

The Plays of John Marston. Ed. E. Harvey Wood. 3 vols. Edinburgh: Oliver and Boyd, 1939.

The Works of John Marston. Ed. A. H. Bullen. 3 vols. London: John C. Nimmo, 1887.

Mason, John. *The Turk.* Ed. Fernand Lagarde. Salzburg: Institut für Anglistik und Amerikanistik, 1979.

Masten, Jeff. "Beaumont and/or Fletcher: Collaboration and the Interpretation of Renaissance Drama." *ELH* 59 (1992).

———. "My Two Dads: Collaboration and the Reproduction of Beaumont and Fletcher." Goldberg, ed., *Queering.*

McLaren, Angus. *A History of Contraception: From Antiquity to the Present Day.* Oxford: Basil Blackwell, 1990.

McLuskie, Kathleen. *Renaissance Dramatists.* Atlantic Highlands, NJ: Humanities Press International, 1989.

McMullan, Gordon. *The Politics of Unease in the Plays of John Fletcher.* Amherst: University of Massachusetts Press, 1994.

McMullan, Gordon, and Jonathan Hope, eds. *The Politics of Tragicomedy: Shakespeare and After.* London: Routledge, 1992.

McPherson, David C. *Shakespeare, Jonson, and the Myth of Venice.* Newark, DE: University of Delaware Press, 1990.

Middleton, Thomas. *Black Book.* Vol. VIII. *The Works of Thomas Middleton.* Ed. A. H. Bullen. 8 vols. London: John C. Nimmo, 1886.

———. *A Mad World, My Masters. The Selected Plays of Thomas Middleton.* Ed. David L. Frost. Cambridge: Cambridge University Press, 1978.

———. *Michaelmas Term.* Ed. Richard Levin. Regents Renaissance Drama. Lincoln: University of Nebraska Press, 1966.

———. *No Wit, No Help Like a Woman's.* Ed. Lowell E. Johnson. Regents Renaissance Drama. Lincoln: University of Nebraska Press, 1976.

Middleton, Thomas, and Thomas Dekker. *The Roaring Girl.* Ed. Paul Mulholland. Revels Plays. Manchester: Manchester University Press, 1987.

Mills, Laurens J. *One Soul in Bodies Twain: Friendship in Tudor Literature and Stuart Drama.* Bloomington, IN: Principia Press, 1937.

Minshull, Geffray. *Essays and Characters of a Prison and Prisoners.* London, 1618.

Moisan, Thomas. "'Knock Me Here Soundly': Comic Misprision and Class Consciousness in Shakespeare." *Shakespeare Quarterly* 42 (1991).

Montrose, Louis. "*A Midsummer Night's Dream* and the Shaping Fantasies of Elizabethan Culture: Gender, Power, Form." *Rewriting the Renaissance: the Discourses of Sexual Difference in Early Modern Europe.* Ed. Margaret W. Ferguson, Maureen Quilligan, and Nancy J. Vickers. Chicago: University of Chicago Press, 1986.

———. "The Work of Gender in the Discourse of Discovery." *Representations* 33 (1991).

Moon, Michael. "A Small Boy and Others: Sexual Disorientation in Henry James, Kenneth Anger, and David Lynch." *Comparative American Identities: Race, Sex, and Nationality in the Modern Text.* Ed. Hortense J. Spillers. New York: Routledge, 1991.

Mullaney, Steven. *The Place of the Stage: License, Play, and Power in Renaissance England.* Chicago: University of Chicago Press, 1988.

Newman, Karen. *Fashioning Femininity and English Renaissance Drama.* Chicago: University of Chicago Press, 1991.

Newton, Judith, and Deborah Rosenfelt, eds. *Feminist Criticism and Social Change: Sex, Class and Race in Literature and Culture*. New York: Methuen, 1985.

Nicholay, Nicholas de. *The Navigations into Turkey*. 1585. *The English Experience* 48. New York: Da Capo, 1968.

Norton, Rictor. *Mother Clap's Molly House: the Gay Subculture in England, 1700–1830*. London: Gay Men's Press, 1992.

Orgel, Stephen. *Impersonations: the Performance of Gender in Shakespeare's England*. Cambridge: Cambridge University Press, 1996.

"Nobody's Perfect: or Why Did the English Stage Take Boys for Women?" *Displacing Homophobia: Gay Male Perspectives in Literature and Culture*. Ed. Ronald R. Butters, John M. Clum, and Michael Moon. Durham, NC: Duke University Press, 1989.

Paglia, Camille. *Sexual Personae: Art and Decadence from Nefertiti to Emily Dickinson*. New York: Vintage, 1991.

Palmer, Daryl W. "Edward IV's Secret Familiarities and the Politics of Proximity in Elizabethan History Plays." *ELH* 61 (1994).

Palmer, Thomas. *The Emblems of Thomas Palmer:* Two Hundred Poosees. Ed. John Manning. New York: AMS Press, 1988.

Paradin, Claude. *The Heroical Devises of M. Claudius Paradin*. 1591. Introduction by John Doebler. Delmar, NY: Scholar's Facsimiles and Reprints, 1984.

Park, Katherine, and Lorraine J. Daston. "Unnatural Conceptions: the Study of Monsters in Sixteenth- and Seventeenth-Century France and England." *Past and Present* 92 (1981).

Parker, Patricia. *Literary Fat Ladies: Rhetoric, Gender, Property*. London: Methuen, 1987.

"Gender Ideology, Gender Change: the Case of Marie Germain." *Critical Inquiry* 19 (1993).

"Preposterous Events." *Shakespeare Quarterly* 43 (1992).

Parry, J. H. *The Establishment of the European Hegemony: 1415–1715: Trade and Exploration in the Age of the Renaissance*. 3rd edn. New York: Harper, 1966.

Partridge, Eric. *Shakespeare's Bawdy*. 3rd edn. London: Routledge, 1968.

Pasquils Jestes. London, 1609.

Paster, Gail Kern. *The Body Embarrassed: Drama and the Disciplines of Shame in Early Modern England*. Ithaca: Cornell University Press, 1993.

Patterson, Annabel. *Shakespeare and the Popular Voice*. Cambridge, MA: Basil Blackwell, 1989.

Peacham, Henry. *Minerva Britanna*. 1612. Leeds: Scolar, 1966.

Pearse, Nancy Cotton. *John Fletcher's Chastity Plays:* Mirrors of Modesty. Lewisburg, PA: Bucknell University Press, 1973.

Peck, Linda Levy. *Court Patronage and Corruption in Early Stuart England*. Boston: Unwin Hyman, 1990.

Pequigney, Joseph. *Such Is My Love: a Study of Shakespeare's Sonnets*. Chicago: University of Chicago Press, 1985.

"The Two Antonios and Same-Sex Love in *Twelfth Night* and *The Merchant of Venice*." *ELR* 22 (1992).

Perkins, William. *Christian Economy*. 1609. Trans. Thomas Pickering. *Daughters, Wives, and Widows: Writings by Men about Women and Marriage in*

England, 1500–1640. Ed. Joan Larsen Klein. Urbana: University of Illinois Press, 1992.

The Foundation of Christian Religion. Vol. I. *The Workes of that Famous and Worthy Minister of Christ in the Universitie of Cambridge, Mr. William Perkins.* 3 vols. London, 1616–18.

Pittenger, Elizabeth. " 'To Serve the Queere': Nicholas Udall, Master of Revels." Goldberg, ed., *Queering.*

The Policy of the Turkish Empire. London, 1597.

Purchas, Samuel. *Hakluytus Posthumus or Purchas His Pilgrimes.* 1625. Vol. II. 20 vols. New York: AMS Press, 1965.

Radel, Nicholas F. "Clothes, Closure, Closets: Constr(i)(u)cting Homoerotic Desire in Two Plays from the Beaumont and Fletcher Folio." Unpublished manuscript.

"Homoeroticism, Discursive Change, and Politics: Reading 'Revolution' in Seventeenth-Century English Tragicomedy." *Medieval and Renaissance Drama in England* 9 (1997).

Rambuss, Richard. "Pleasure and Devotion: the Body of Jesus in Seventeenth-Century Religious Lyric." Goldberg, ed., *Queering.*

"The Secretary's Study: the Secret Designs of *The Shepherd's Calender.*" *ELH* 59 (1992).

Riche, Barnabe. *His Farewell to Military Profession.* 1581. Ed. Donald Beecher. Ottawa: Dovehouse, 1992.

Ricks, Christopher. "*Sejanus* and Dismemberment." *MLN* 76 (1961).

Rose, Mary Beth. *The Expense of Spirit: Love and Sexuality in English Renaissance Drama.* Ithaca: Cornell University Press, 1988.

Ross, Alexander. *A Critical Edition of Alexander Ross's 1647 Mystagogus Poeticus, or The Muses Interpreter.* Ed. John R. Glenn. Renaissance Imagination 31. New York: Garland, 1987.

Rossky, William. "Imagination in the English Renaissance: Psychology and Poetic." *Studies in the Renaissance* 5 (1958).

Rowe, George E. *Distinguishing Jonson: Imitation, Rivalry, and the Direction of a Dramatic Career.* Lincoln: University of Nebraska Press, 1988.

Rubinstein, Frankie. *A Dictionary of Shakespeare's Sexual Puns and Their Significance.* 2nd edn. London: Macmillan, 1989.

Ruggiero, Guido. *The Boundaries of Eros: Sex Crime and Sexuality in Renaissance Venice.* New York: Oxford University Press, 1985.

Russo, Vito. *The Celluloid Closet: Homosexuality in the Movies.* Revised edn. New York: Harper and Row, 1987.

Saslow, James M. *Ganymede in the Renaissance: Homosexuality in Art and Society.* New Haven: Yale University Press, 1986.

"The Tenderest Lover: Saint Sebastian in Renaissance Painting: a Proposed Homoerotic Iconology for North Italian Art, 1450–1550." *Gai Saber* 1.1 (1977).

Seaver, Paul S. *Wallington's World: a Puritan Artisan in Seventeenth-Century London.* Stanford: Stanford University Press, 1985.

Sedgwick, Eve Kosofsky. *Between Men: English Literature and Male Homosocial Desire.* New York: Columbia University Press, 1985.

Epistemology of the Closet. Berkeley: University of California Press, 1991.

Tendencies. Durham, NC: Duke University Press, 1993.

Shakespeare, William. *As You Like It*. Ed. Agnes Latham. Arden Shakespeare. London: Routledge, 1989.

King Richard II. Ed. Peter Ure. Arden Shakespeare. London: Methuen, 1966.

Love's Labour's Lost. Ed. R. W. David. Arden Shakespeare. London: Methuen, 1968.

Twelfth Night. Ed. J. M. Lothian and T. W. Craik. Arden Shakespeare. London: Routledge, 1988.

The Two Gentlemen of Verona. Ed. Clifford Leech. Arden Shakespeare. London: Routledge, 1989.

Shakespeare's Ovid: Being Arthur Golding's Translation of the Metamorphoses. Ed. W. H. D. Rouse. Carbondale: Southern Illinois University Press, 1961.

Shapiro, James. *Rival Playwrights: Marlowe, Jonson, Shakespeare*. New York: Columbia University Press, 1991.

Shepherd, Simon. *Spenser*. New York: Harvester Wheatsheaf, 1989.

"Shakespeare's Private Drawer: Shakespeare and Homosexuality." *The Shakespeare Myth*. Ed. Graham Holderness. Manchester: Manchester University Press, 1988.

"What's So Funny About Ladies' Tailors? A Survey of Some Male (Homo)sexual Types in the Renaissance." *Textual Practice* 6 (1992).

Shuttleworth, Sally. Review of *Making Sex: Body and Gender from the Greeks to Freud*, by Thomas Laqueur. *Journal of the History of Sexuality* 3 (1993).

Simonds, Peggy Muñoz. "'Killing Care and Grief of Heart': Orpheus and Shakespeare." *Renaissance Papers* 1990. Ed. Dale B. J. Randall and Joseph A. Porter. Durham, NC: Southeastern Renaissance Conference, 1990.

"The Marriage Topos in *Cymbeline*: Shakespeare's Variations on a Classical Theme." *ELR* 19 (1989).

Sinfield, Alan. *Faultlines: Cultural Materialism and the Politics of Dissident Reading*. Berkeley: University of California Press, 1992.

The Wilde Century: Effeminacy, Oscar Wilde and the Queer Moment. New York: Columbia University Press, 1994.

Skura, Meredith Anne. *Shakespeare the Actor and the Purposes of Playing*. Chicago: University of Chicago Press, 1993.

Smith, Bruce R. *Homosexual Desire in Shakespeare's England: a Cultural Poetics*. Chicago: University of Chicago Press, 1991.

"Making a Difference: Male-Male 'Desire' in Tragedy, Comedy, and Tragicomedy." Zimmerman, ed., *Erotic Politics*.

Smith, Denzell S. "Francis Beaumont and John Fletcher." *The Later Jacobean and Caroline Dramatists*. Ed. Terence P. Logan and Denzell S. Smith. Lincoln: University of Nebraska Press, 1978.

Spear, Gary. "Shakespeare's 'Manly Parts': Masculinity and Effeminacy in *Troilus and Cressida*." *Shakespeare Quarterly* 44 (1993).

Spenser, Edmund. *The Faerie Queene*. Ed. A. C. Hamilton. London: Longman, 1977.

The Shepherd's Calender. The Yale Edition of the Shorter Poems of Edmund Spenser. Ed. William A. Oram, Einar Bjorvand, Ronald Bond, Thomas H. Cain, Alexander Dunlop, and Richard Schell. New Haven: Yale University Press, 1989.

Spivak, Charlotte. *George Chapman*. Twayne's English Authors. New York: Twayne, 1967.

Staplyton, Robert. *Juvenal's Sixteen Satyrs or, A Survey of the Manners and Actions of Mankind*. London, 1647.

Starkey, David, ed. *The English Court: from the Wars of the Roses to the Civil War*. London: Longman, 1987.

"Intimacy and Innovation: The Rise of the Privy Chamber, 1485–1547." Starkey, ed., *The English Court*.

Starnes, DeWitt T., and Earnest William Talbert. *Classical Myth and Legend in Renaissance Dictionaries: a Study of Renaissance Dictionaries in Their Relation to the Classical Learning of Contemporary English Writers*. Chapel Hill: University of North Carolina Press, 1955.

Stephens, Dorothy. "Into Other Arms: Amoret's Evasion." Goldberg, ed., *Queering*.

Stevens, Forest Tyler. "Erasmus's 'Tigress': the Language of Friendship, Pleasure, and the Renaissance Letter." Goldberg, ed., *Queering*.

Stone, Lawrence. *The Crisis of the Aristocracy 1558–1641*. Abridged edn. London: Oxford University Press, 1967.

The Family, Sex and Marriage in England 1500–1800. New York: Harper and Row, 1977.

Straub, Kristina. *Sexual Suspects: Eighteenth-Century Players and Sexual Ideology*. Princeton: Princeton University Press, 1992.

Strong, Roy. *Henry, Prince of Wales and England's Lost Renaissance*. London: Thames and Hudson, 1986.

Summers, Claude J., ed. *Homosexuality in Renaissance and Enlightenment England: Literary Representations in Historical Context*. New York: Harrington Park, 1992.

Summers, Claude J., and Ted-Larry Pebworth, eds. *Renaissance Discourses of Desire*. Columbia: University of Missouri Press, 1993.

Taylor, Jeremy. *The Measures and Offices of Friendship*. London, 1662.

The Tragedy of Tiberius. 1607. Ed. W. W. Greg. Malone Society Reprints. Oxford: Oxford University Press, 1914.

Traub, Valerie. *Desire and Anxiety: Circulations of Sexuality in Shakespearan Drama*. London: Routledge, 1992.

"The (In)Significance of 'Lesbian' Desire in Early Modern England." Zimmerman, ed., *Erotic Politics*.

Waith, Eugene M. *The Pattern of Tragicomedy in Beaumont and Fletcher*. New Haven: Yale University Press, 1952.

Warner, Michael. "New English Sodom." Goldberg, ed., *Queering*.

Warner, William. *Albions England*. London, 1592.

Wayne, Valerie, ed. *The Matter of Difference: Materialist Feminist Criticism of Shakespeare*. Ithaca: Cornell University Press, 1991.

Webster, John. *The Duchess of Malfi*. *Drama of the English Renaissance II: the Stuart Period*. Ed. Russell A. Fraser and Norman Rabkin. New York: Macmillan, 1976.

Weeks, Jeffrey. "Pretended Family Relationships." *Marriage, Domestic Life and Social Change: Writings for Jacqueline Burgoyne (1944–88)*. Ed. David Clark. London: Routledge, 1991.

Weldon, Anthony. *The Court and Character of King James*. 1651. London, 1817.

Wheare, Degoraeus. *Method and Order of Reading Both Civil and Ecclesiastical Histories* . . . . 1625. Translated and enlarged by Edmund Bohun. London, 1685.

Whigham, Frank. "Reading Social Conflict in the Alimentary Tract: More on the Body in Renaissance Drama." *ELH* 52 (1988).

Wilkinson, Robert. *Lot's Wife. A Sermon Preached at Paules Crosse*. London, 1607.

Wilson, Edmund. "Morose Ben Jonson." *Ben Jonson: a Collection of Critical Essays*. Ed. Jonas A. Barish. Englewood Cliffs, NJ: Prentice-Hall, 1963.

Wiltenburg, Joy. *Disorderly Women and Female Power in the Street Literature of Early Modern England and Germany*. Charlottesville: University of Virginia Press, 1992.

Woodbridge, Linda. *Women and the English Renaissance: Literature and the Nature of Womankind, 1540–1620*. Urbana: University of Illinois Press, 1984.

Woods, Gregory. "Body, Costume, and Desire in Christopher Marlowe." Summers, ed., *Homosexuality in Renaissance and Enlightenment England*.

Woodstock: A Moral History. Ed. A. P. Rossiter. London: Chatto and Windus, 1946.

Wright, Pam. "A Change in Direction: the Ramifications of a Female Household, 1558–1603." Starkey, ed., *The English Court*.

Wrightson, Keith. *English Society 1580–1680*. New Brunswick: Rutgers University Press, 1982.

Zimmerman, Susan. "Disruptive Desire: Artifice and Indeterminacy in Jacobean Comedy." Zimmerman, *Erotic Politics* 39–63.

Zimmerman, Susan, ed. *Erotic Politics: Desire on the Renaissance Stage*. New York: Routledge, 1992.

Index

Cambridge Studies in Renaissance Literature and Culture

General editor
STEPHEN ORGEL
Jackson Eli Reynolds Professor of Humanities, Stanford
University